THE STORY OF THE
MALAKAND FIELD FORCE

Winston S. Churchill

The Story of the
Malakand Field Force

An Episode of Frontier
War

BIBLIOBAZAAR

THE STORY OF THE
MALAKAND FIELD FORCE

"They (Frontier Wars) are but the surf that marks the edge and the advance of the wave of civilisation."

LORD SALISBURY, Guildhall, 1892

CONTENTS

THIS BOOK
IS INSCRIBED TO
MAJOR-GENERAL SIR BINDON BLOOD, K.C.B.
UNDER WHOSE COMMAND THE OPERATIONS THEREIN
RECORDED WERE CARRIED OUT; BY WHOSE
GENERALSHIP
THEY WERE BROUGHT TO A SUCCESSFUL CONCLUSION;
AND TO WHOSE KINDNESS THE AUTHOR IS INDEBTED
FOR THE MOST VALUABLE AND FASCINATING
EXPERIENCE OF HIS LIFE.

PREFACE

"According to the fair play of the world,
Let me have an audience."

"King John," Act v., Sc. 2.

On general grounds I deprecate prefaces. I have always thought that if an author cannot make friends with the reader, and explain his objects, in two or three hundred pages, he is not likely to do so in fifty lines. And yet the temptation of speaking a few words behind the scenes, as it were, is so strong that few writers are able to resist it. I shall not try.

While I was attached to the Malakand Field Force I wrote a series of letters for the London Daily Telegraph. The favourable manner in which these letters were received, encouraged me to attempt a more substantial work. This volume is the result.

The original letters have been broken up, and I have freely availed myself of all passages, phrases, and facts, that seemed appropriate. The views they contained have not been altered, though several opinions and expressions, which seemed mild in the invigorating atmosphere of a camp, have been modified, to suit the more temperate climate of peace.

I have to thank many gallant officers for the assistance they have given me in the collection of material. They have all asked me not to mention their names, but to accede to this request would be to rob the story of the Malakand Field Force of all its bravest deeds and finest characters.

The book does not pretend to deal with the complications of the frontier question, nor to present a complete summary of its phases and features. In the opening chapter I have tried to describe the general character of the numerous and powerful tribes of the

Indian Frontier. In the last chapter I have attempted to apply the intelligence of a plain man to the vast mass of expert evidence, which on this subject is so great that it baffles memory and exhausts patience. The rest is narrative, and in it I have only desired to show the reader what it looked like.

As I have not been able to describe in the text all the instances of conduct and courage which occurred, I have included in an appendix the official despatches.

The impartial critic will at least admit that I have not insulted the British public by writing a party pamphlet on a great Imperial question. I have recorded the facts as they occurred, and the impressions as they arose, without attempting to make a case against any person or any policy. Indeed, I fear that assailing none, I may have offended all. Neutrality may degenerate into an ignominious isolation. An honest and unprejudiced attempt to discern the truth is my sole defence, as the good opinion of the reader has been throughout my chief aspiration, and can be in the end my only support.

Winston S. Churchill

Cavalry Barracks,
Bangalore, 30th December, 1897

CHAPTER I:

THE THEATRE OF WAR

The Ghilzaie chief wrote answer: "Our paths are narrow
    and steep.
The sun burns fierce in the valleys, and the snow-fed
    streams run deep;

* * * * *

So a stranger needs safe escort, and the oath of a valiant
    friend."

"The Amir's Message," SIR A. LYALL.

All along the north and north-west frontiers of India lie the
Himalayas, the greatest disturbance of the earth's surface that
the convulsions of chaotic periods have produced. Nearly four
hundred miles in breadth and more than sixteen hundred in length,
this mountainous region divides the great plains of the south from
those of Central Asia, and parts as a channel separates opposing
shores, the Eastern Empire of Great Britain from that of Russia.
The western end of this tumult of ground is formed by the peaks
of the Hindu Kush, to the south of which is the scene of the
story these pages contain. The Himalayas are not a line, but a great
country of mountains. By one who stands on some lofty pass or
commanding point in Dir, Swat or Bajaur, range after range is seen
as the long surges of an Atlantic swell, and in the distance some
glittering snow peak suggests a white-crested roller, higher than
the rest. The drenching rains which fall each year have washed the
soil from the sides of the hills until they have become strangely

grooved by numberless water-courses, and the black primeval rock is everywhere exposed. The silt and sediment have filled the valleys which lie between, and made their surface sandy, level and broad. Again the rain has cut wide, deep and constantly-changing channels through this soft deposit; great gutters, which are sometimes seventy feet deep and two or three hundred yards across. These are the nullahs. Usually the smaller ones are dry, and the larger occupied only by streams; but in the season of the rains, abundant water pours down all, and in a few hours the brook has become an impassable torrent, and the river swelled into a rolling flood which caves the banks round which it swirls, and cuts the channel deeper year by year.

From the level plain of the valleys the hills rise abruptly. Their steep and rugged slopes are thickly strewn with great rocks, and covered with coarse, rank grass. Scattered pines grow on the higher ridges. In the water-courses the chenar, the beautiful eastern variety of the plane tree of the London squares and Paris boulevards, is occasionally found, and when found, is, for its pleasant shade, regarded with grateful respect. Reaching far up the sides of the hills are tiers of narrow terraces, chiefly the work of long-forgotten peoples, which catch the soil that the rain brings down, and support crops of barley and maize. The rice fields along both banks of the stream display a broad, winding strip of vivid green, which gives the eye its only relief from the sombre colours of the mountains.

In the spring, indeed, the valleys are brightened by many flowers—wild tulips, peonies, crocuses and several kinds of polyanthus; and among the fruits the water melon, some small grapes and mulberries are excellent, although in their production, nature is unaided by culture. But during the campaign, which these pages describe, the hot sun of the summer had burnt up all the flowers, and only a few splendid butterflies, whose wings of blue and green change colour in the light, like shot silk, contrasted with the sternness of the landscape.

The valleys are nevertheless by no means barren. The soil is fertile, the rains plentiful, and a considerable proportion of ground is occupied by cultivation, and amply supplies the wants of the inhabitants.

The streams are full of fish, both trout and mahseer. By the banks teal, widgeon and wild duck, and in some places, snipe, are plentiful. Chikor, a variety of partridge, and several sorts of pheasants, are to be obtained on the hills.

Among the wild animals of the region the hunter may pursue the black or brown mountain bear, an occasional leopard, markhor, and several varieties of wild goat, sheep and antelope. The smaller quadrupeds include hares and red foxes, not unlike the British breed, only with much brighter coats, and several kinds of rats, some of which are very curious and rare. Destitute of beauty but not without use, the scaly ant-eater is frequently seen; but the most common of all the beasts is an odious species of large lizard, nearly three feet long, which resembles a flabby-skinned crocodile and feeds on carrion. Domestic fowls, goats, sheep and oxen, with the inevitable vulture, and an occasional eagle, complete the fauna.

Over all is a bright blue sky and powerful sun. Such is the scenery of the theatre of war.

The inhabitants of these wild but wealthy valleys are of many tribes, but of similar character and condition. The abundant crops which a warm sun and copious rains raise from a fertile soil, support a numerous population in a state of warlike leisure. Except at the times of sowing and of harvest, a continual state of feud and strife prevails throughout the land. Tribe wars with tribe. The people of one valley fight with those of the next. To the quarrels of communities are added the combats of individuals. Khan assails khan, each supported by his retainers. Every tribesman has a blood feud with his neighbor. Every man's hand is against the other, and all against the stranger.

Nor are these struggles conducted with the weapons which usually belong to the races of such development. To the ferocity of the Zulu are added the craft of the Redskin and the marksmanship of the Boer. The world is presented with that grim spectacle, "the strength of civilisation without its mercy." At a thousand yards the traveller falls wounded by the well-aimed bullet of a breech-loading rifle. His assailant, approaching, hacks him to death with the ferocity of a South-Sea Islander. The weapons of the nineteenth century are in the hands of the savages of the Stone Age.

Every influence, every motive, that provokes the spirit of murder among men, impels these mountaineers to deeds of treachery and violence. The strong aboriginal propensity to kill, inherit in all human beings, has in these valleys been preserved in unexampled strength and vigour. That religion, which above all others was founded and propagated by the sword—the tenets and principles of which are instinct with incentives to slaughter and which in three continents has produced fighting breeds of men—stimulates a wild and merciless fanaticism. The love of plunder, always a characteristic of hill tribes, is fostered by the spectacle of opulence and luxury which, to their eyes, the cities and plains of the south display. A code of honour not less punctilious than that of old Spain, is supported by vendettas as implacable as those of Corsica.

In such a state of society, all property is held directly by main force. Every man is a soldier. Either he is the retainer of some khan—the man-at-arms of some feudal baron as it were—or he is a unit in the armed force of his village—the burgher of mediaeval history. In such surroundings we may without difficulty trace the rise and fall of an ambitious Pathan. At first he toils with zeal and thrift as an agriculturist on that plot of ground which his family have held since they expelled some former owner. He accumulates in secret a sum of money. With this he buys a rifle from some daring thief, who has risked his life to snatch it from a frontier guard-house. He becomes a man to be feared. Then he builds a tower to his house and overawes those around him in the village. Gradually they submit to his authority. He might now rule the village; but he aspires still higher. He persuades or compels his neighbors to join him in an attack on the castle of a local khan. The attack succeeds. The khan flies or is killed; the castle captured. The retainers make terms with the conqueror. The land tenure is feudal. In return for their acres they follow their new chief to war. Were he to treat them worse than the other khans treated their servants, they would sell their strong arms elsewhere. He treats them well. Others resort to him. He buys more rifles. He conquers two or three neighboring khans. He has now become a power.

Many, perhaps all, states have been founded in a similar way, and it is by such steps that civilisation painfully stumbles through her earlier stages. But in these valleys the warlike nature of the people and their hatred of control, arrest the further progress of development. We have watched a man, able, thrifty, brave, fighting his way to power, absorbing, amalgamating, laying the foundations of a more complex and interdependent state of society. He has so far succeeded. But his success is now his ruin. A combination is formed against him. The surrounding chiefs and their adherents are assisted by the village populations. The ambitious Pathan, oppressed by numbers, is destroyed. The victors quarrel over the spoil, and the story closes, as it began, in bloodshed and strife.

The conditions of existence, that have been thus indicated, have naturally led to the dwelling-places of these tribes being fortified. If they are in the valley, they are protected by towers and walls loopholed for musketry. If in the hollows of the hills, they are strong by their natural position. In either case they are guarded by a hardy and martial people, well armed, brave, and trained by constant war.

This state of continual tumult has produced a habit of mind which recks little of injuries, holds life cheap and embarks on war with careless levity, and the tribesmen of the Afghan border afford the spectacle of a people, who fight without passion, and kill one another without loss of temper. Such a disposition, combined with an absolute lack of reverence for all forms of law and authority, and a complete assurance of equality, is the cause of their frequent quarrels with the British power. A trifle rouses their animosity. They make a sudden attack on some frontier post. They are repulsed. From their point of view the incident is closed. There has been a fair fight in which they have had the worst fortune. What puzzles them is that "the Sirkar" should regard so small an affair in a serious light. Thus the Mohmands cross the frontier and the action of Shabkadr is fought. They are surprised and aggrieved that the Government are not content with the victory, but must needs invade their territories, and impose punishment. Or again, the Mamunds, because a village has been burnt, assail the camp of the Second Brigade by night. It is a drawn game. They are astounded that the troops do not take it in good part.

They, when they fight among themselves, bear little malice, and the combatants not infrequently make friends over the corpses of their comrades or suspend operations for a festival or a horse race. At the end of the contest cordial relations are at once re-established. And yet so full of contradictions is their character, that all this is without prejudice to what has been written of their family vendettas and private blood feuds. Their system of ethics, which regards treachery and violence as virtues rather than vices, has produced a code of honour so strange and inconsistent, that it is incomprehensible to a logical mind. I have been told that if a white man could grasp it fully, and were to understand their mental impulses—if he knew, when it was their honour to stand by him, and when it was their honour to betray him; when they were bound to protect and when to kill him—he might, by judging his times and opportunities, pass safely from one end of the mountains to the other. But a civilised European is as little able to accomplish this, as to appreciate the feelings of those strange creatures, which, when a drop of water is examined under a microscope, are revealed amiably gobbling each other up, and being themselves complacently devoured.

I remark with pleasure, as an agreeable trait in the character of the Pathans, the immunity, dictated by a rude spirit of chivalry, which in their ceaseless brawling, their women enjoy. Many forts are built at some distance from any pool or spring. When these are besieged, the women are allowed by the assailants to carry water to the foot of the walls by night. In the morning the defenders come out and fetch it—of course under fire—and are enabled to continue their resistance. But passing from the military to the social aspect of their lives, the picture assumes an even darker shade, and is unrelieved by any redeeming virtue. We see them in their squalid, loopholed hovels, amid dirt and ignorance, as degraded a race as any on the fringe of humanity: fierce as the tiger, but less cleanly; as dangerous, not so graceful. Those simple family virtues, which idealists usually ascribe to primitive peoples, are conspicuously absent. Their wives and their womenkind generally, have no position but that of animals. They are freely bought and sold, and are not infrequently bartered for rifles. Truth is unknown among them. A single typical incident displays the standpoint from which they regard an oath. In any dispute about a field boundary, it is customary for both claimants to walk round the boundary he claims, with a Koran in his hand, swearing that all the time he is walking on his own land. To meet the difficulty of a false oath, while he is walking over his neighbor's land, he puts a little dust from his own field into his shoes. As both sides are acquainted with the trick, the dismal farce of swearing is usually soon abandoned, in favor of an appeal to force.

All are held in the grip of miserable superstition. The power of the ziarat, or sacred tomb, is wonderful. Sick children are carried on the backs of buffaloes, sometimes sixty or seventy miles, to be deposited in front of such a shrine, after which they are carried back—if they survive the journey—in the same way. It is painful even to think of what the wretched child suffers in being thus jolted over the cattle tracks. But the tribesmen consider the treatment much more efficacious than any infidel prescription. To go to a ziarat and put a stick in the ground is sufficient to ensure the fulfillment of a wish. To sit swinging a stone or coloured glass ball, suspended by a string from a tree, and tied there by some fakir, is a sure method of securing a fine male heir. To make a cow give good milk, a little should be plastered on some favorite stone near the tomb of a holy man. These are but a few instances; but they may suffice to reveal a state of mental development at which civilisation hardly knows whether to laugh or weep.

Their superstition exposes them to the rapacity and tyranny of a numerous priesthood—"Mullahs," "Sahibzadas," "Akhundzadas," "Fakirs,"—and a host of wandering Talib-ul-ilms, who correspond with the theological students in Turkey, and live free at the expense of the people. More than this, they enjoy a sort of "droit du seigneur," and no man's wife or daughter is safe from them. Of some of their manners and morals it is impossible to write. As Macaulay has said of Wycherley's plays, "they are protected against the critics as a skunk is protected against the hunters." They are "safe, because they are too filthy to handle, and too noisome even to approach."

Yet the life even of these barbarous people is not without moments when the lover of the picturesque might sympathise with their hopes and fears. In the cool of the evening, when the sun has sunk behind the mountains of Afghanistan, and the valleys are filled with a delicious twilight, the elders of the village lead the way to the chenar trees by the water's side, and there, while the men are cleaning their rifles, or smoking their hookas, and the women are making rude ornaments from beads, and cloves, and nuts, the Mullah drones the evening prayer. Few white men have seen, and returned to tell the tale. But we may imagine the conversation passing from the prices of arms and cattle, the prospects of the harvest, or the village gossip, to the great Power, that lies to the southward, and comes nearer year by year. Perhaps some former Sepoy, of Beluchis or Pathans, will recount his adventures in the bazaars of Peshawar, or tell of the white officers he has followed and fought for in the past. He will speak of their careless bravery and their strange sports; of the far-reaching power of the Government, that never forgets to send his pension regularly as the months pass by; and he may even predict to the listening circle the day when their valleys will be involved in the comprehensive grasp of that great machine, and judges, collectors and commissioners shall ride to sessions at Ambeyla, or value the land tax on the soil of Nawagai. Then the Mullah will raise his voice and remind them of other days when the sons of the prophet drove the infidel from the plains of India, and ruled at Delhi, as wide an Empire as the Kafir holds to-day: when the true religion strode proudly through the earth and scorned to lie hidden and neglected among the hills: when mighty princes ruled in Bagdad, and all men knew that there was one God, and Mahomet was His prophet. And the young men hearing these things will grip their Martinis, and pray to Allah, that one day He will bring some Sahib—best prize of all—across their line of sight at seven hundred yards so that, at least, they may strike a blow for insulted and threatened Islam.

The general aspect of the country and character of its inhabitants have thus been briefly described. At this stage it is not necessary or desirable to descend to detail. As the account proceeds the reader may derive a more lively impression of the sombre mountains, and of the peoples who dwell beneath their shadow.

The tale that I have to tell is one of frontier war. Neither the importance of the issues, nor the numbers of the combatants, are on an European scale. The fate of empires does not hang on the result. Yet the narrative may not be without interest, or material for reflection. In the quarrels of civilised nations, great armies, many thousands strong, collide. Brigades and battalions are hurried forward, and come perhaps within some fire zone, swept by concentrated batteries, or massed musketry. Hundreds or thousands fall killed and wounded. The survivors struggle on blindly, dazed and dumfoundered, to the nearest cover. Fresh troops are continuously poured on from behind. At length one side or the other gives way. In all this tumult, this wholesale slaughter, the individual and his feelings are utterly lost. Only the army has a tale to tell. With events on such a scale, the hopes and fears, the strength and weakness, of man are alike indistinguishable. Amid the din and dust little but destruction can be discerned. But on the frontier, in the clear light of morning, when the mountain side is dotted with smoke puffs, and every ridge sparkles with bright sword blades, the spectator may observe and accurately appreciate all grades of human courage—the wild fanaticism of the Ghazi, the composed fatalism of the Sikh, the stubbornness of the British soldier, and the jaunty daring of his officers. He may remark occasions of devotion and self-sacrifice, of cool cynicism and stern resolve. He may participate in moments of wild enthusiasm, or of savage anger and dismay. The skill of the general, the quality of the troops, the eternal principles of the art of war, will be as clearly displayed as on historic fields. Only the scale of the statistics is reduced.

A single glass of champagne imparts a feeling of exhilaration. The nerves are braced, the imagination is agreeably stirred, the wits become more nimble. A bottle produces a contrary effect. Excess causes a comatose insensibility. So it is with war, and the quality of both is best discovered by sipping.

I propose to chronicle the military operations of the Malakand Field Force, to trace their political results, and to give, if possible, some picture of the scenery and people of the Indian Highlands. These pages may serve to record the actions of brave and skilful men. They may throw a sidelight on the great drama of frontier war. They may describe an episode in that ceaseless struggle for Empire which seems to be the perpetual inheritance of our race. They may amuse an idle hour. But the ambition I shall associate with them is, that in some measure, however small, they may stimulate that growing interest which the Imperial Democracy of England is beginning to take, in their great estates that lie beyond the seas.

CHAPTER II:

THE MALAKAND CAMPS

Ibam forte via sacra.—HORACE.

The town and cantonment of Nowshera was the base from which all the operations of the Malakand Field Force were conducted. It is situated on the India side of the Cabul River and is six hours by rail from Rawal Pindi. In times of peace its garrison consists of one native cavalry regiment, one British, and one native infantry battalion. During the war these troops were employed at the front. The barracks became great hospitals. The whole place was crowded with transport and military stores; and only a slender force remained under the orders of Colonel Schalch, the Base Commandant.

The road from Nowshera to the Malakand Pass and camps is forty-seven miles long, and divided into four stages. Usually there is an excellent tonga service, and the distance is covered in about six hours; but while the Field Force was mobilised so much traffic and so many officers passed up and down the line, that the tonga ponies were soon reduced to a terrible condition of sores and emaciation, and could hardly drag the journey out in nine, ten, or even twelve hours. After leaving Nowshera, and crossing the Cabul River, a stage of fifteen miles brings the traveller to Mardan. This place—pronounced "Merdane"—is the permanent station of the Corps of Guides. It is shady and agreeable, though terribly hot in the summer months. It boasts an excellent polo ground and a comfortable rest-house. The passer-by should pause to see the Guides' cemetery, perhaps the only regimental cemetery in the world. To this last resting-place under the palm trees, close to the fields where they have played, and the barracks in which they lived, have been borne the bodies of successive generations of these wardens of the marches, killed in action across the frontier line. It is a green and pleasant spot. Nor is there any place in the world where a soldier might lie in braver company.

After Mardan the road becomes more dusty, and the surrounding country barren and arid. [This description applies to the autumn season. In the winter and spring the country for a time is green and the air cold.] The mountains are approached, and as the tonga advances their shapes and colours are more distinctly seen. A few knolls and ridges rising from the level plain, mark the outposts of that great array of hills. Crossing a shallow stream—a tributary of the Cabul River, Jalala, the second stage is reached. In peace time a small mud fort is the only indication, but this is expanded by the proximity of war to a considerable camp, with an entrenchment around it. Stopping only to change ponies, for it is a forsaken spot, the journey is resumed. The avenue of trees on either side has ceased. The road is seen simply as a white streak stretching towards the mountains. It is traversed in a sweltering heat and choking dust. All around the country is red, sterile and burnt up. In front the great wall of hills rises dark and ominous. At length Dargai at the foot of the pass is reached. It is another mud fort, swelled during the operations into an entrenched camp, and surrounded by a network of barbed wire entanglement. The Malakand Pass can now be seen—a great cleft in the line of mountains—and far up the gorge, the outline of the fort that guards it, is distinguishable.

The graded road winds up, with many a turn, the long ascent from Dargai to the top of the pass. The driver flogs the wretched, sore-backed ponies tirelessly. At length the summit is neared. The view is one worth stopping to look at. Behind and below, under the haze of the heat, is the wide expanse of open country—smooth, level, stretching away to the dim horizon. The tonga turns the corner and enters a new world. A cooler breeze is blowing. A single step has led from peace to war; from civilisation to savagery; from India to the mountains. On all sides the landscape is wild and rugged. Ridge succeeds ridge. Valley opens into valley. As far as the eye can reach in every direction are ragged peaks and spurs. The country of the plains is left, and we have entered a strange land, as tangled as the maze at Hampton Court, with mountains instead of hedges. So broken and so confused is the ground, that I despair of conveying a clear impression of it.

The Malakand is like a great cup, of which the rim is broken into numerous clefts and jagged points. At the bottom of this cup is the "crater" camp. The deepest cleft is the Malakand Pass. The highest of the jagged points is Guides Hill, on a spur of which the fort stands. It needs no technical knowledge to see, that to defend such a place, the rim of the cup must be held. But in the Malakand, the bottom of the cup is too small to contain the necessary garrison. The whole position is therefore, from the military point of view, bad and indefensible. In the revised and improved scheme of defence, arrangements have been made, to command the available approaches, and to block such as cannot be commanded with barbed wire entanglements and other obstructions; and by a judicious system of works much of the rim is now held. But even now I am told by competent judges that the place is a bad one for defence; that the pass could be held by the fort alone, and that the brigade stationed there would be safer and equally useful, if withdrawn to Dargai. At the time this story opens the Malakand South Camp was an impossible place to put troops in. It was easy of access. It was cramped and commanded by neighbouring heights. [Under the arrangements which have been made since the war, the Malakand position and the works at Chakdara and Dargai will be held by two battalions and some details. These will be supported by a flying column, the exact location and composition of which are as yet undetermined.]

The small area of the camp on the Kotal necessitated the formation of a second encampment in the plain of Khar. This was close under the north outer edge of the cup. It was called for political reasons North Malakand. As a military position it, also, was radically bad. It was everywhere commanded, and surrounded by ravines and nullahs, which made it easy for an enemy to get in, and difficult for troops to get out. It was, of course, of no strategic value, and was merely used as a habitation for the troops intended to hold Malakand, for whom there was no room in the crater and fort. The north camp has now been definitely abandoned.

Nobody, however—least of all those who selected the site—would seem to have contemplated the possibility of an attack. Indeed the whole situation was regarded as purely temporary. The vacillation, caused by the change of parties and policies in England, led to the Malakand garrison remaining for two years in a position which could not be well defended either on paper or in reality. At first, after the Chitral campaign of 1895, it was thought that the retention of the brigade in this advanced post, was only a matter of a few weeks. But as the months passed by the camp began, in spite of the uncertainty, to assume an appearance of permanency. The officers built themselves huts and mess rooms. A good polo ground was discovered near Khar, and under careful management rapidly improved. A race-course was projected. Many officers who were married brought their wives and families to the camp among the mountains, and the whole place was rapidly becoming a regular cantonment. No cases of Ghazi outrage broke the tranquillity. The revolvers, which all persons leaving camp were by regulations obliged to take, were either unloaded or carried by a native groom. Shooting parties were organised to the hills. A well-contested polo tournament was held in Christmas week. Distinguished travellers— even a member of Parliament—visited this outpost of empire, and observed with interest the swiftness and ease with which the Anglo-Saxon adapts every situation to his sports and habits.

At the same time the station of the Malakand Brigade was far from being a comfortable one. For two years they lived under canvas or in rude huts. They were exposed to extremes of climate. They were without punkahs or ice in the hot weather. They were nearly fifty miles from the railway, and in respect of companionship and amusements were thrown entirely on their own resources. When the British cavalry officer succeeds, in spite of official opposition, expense and discouragement, in getting on service across the frontier, he is apt to look with envious eyes at the officers of the Frontier Force, who are taken as a matter of course and compelled to do by command, what he would solicit as a favour. But he must remember that this is their compensation for long months of discomfort and monotony in lonely and out-of-the-way stations, and for undergoing hardships which, though honourable and welcome in the face of the enemy, become obnoxious in times of peace.

After crossing the Malakand Pass the first turning to the right leads to the Swat Valley. The traveller is now within the mountains. In every direction the view is restricted or terminated by walls of rock. The valley itself is broad, level and fertile. The river flows swiftly through the middle. On either side of it, is a broad strip of rice fields. Other crops occupy the drier ground. Numerous villages, some of which contain large populations, are scattered about. It is a beautiful scene. The cool breezes of the mountains temper the heat of the sun. The abundant rains preserve the verdure of the earth.

In ancient times this region was the seat of a Buddhistic kingdom, and was known as Woo-Chang or "Udyana," which means "the Park," and proclaims the appreciation which its former possessors had of their pleasant valley. "The people," says the Chinese pilgrim Fa-hien, who visited the country in the fifth century, "all use the language of Central India, 'Central India' being what we should call the 'Middle Kingdom.' The food and clothes of the common people are the same as in that Central Kingdom. The law of Buddha is very flourishing in Woo-Chang." "The Park," which includes all the country on both banks of the Swat River—then called the Subhavastu—but which perhaps applies more particularly to the upper end of the valley, was famous for its forests, flowers and fruit. But though the valley retains much of its beauty, its forests have been destroyed by the improvidence, and its flowers and fruit have declined through the ignorance, of the fierce conquerors into whose hands it fell.

The reputation which its present inhabitants enjoy is evil. Their treacherous character has distinguished them even among peoples notoriously faithless and cruel. Among Pathans it is a common saying: "Swat is heaven, but the Swatis are hell-fiends." For many years they had lain under the stigma of cowardice, and were despised as well as distrusted by the tribes of the border; but their conduct in the recent fighting has cleared them at least from this imputation.

Several minor chieftains now divide authority in the Swat Valley, but till 1870 it was governed by a single ruler. The Ahkund of Swat was by origin a cowherd, an office considered most honourable in India. The cow is a sacred beast. His service is acceptable to the Gods and men. Princes glory in the name—though they do not usually carry their enthusiasm further. "Guicowar" translated literally means "cowherd." From such employment the future Ahkund received his inspiration. He sat for many years by the banks of the Indus, and meditated. Thus he became a saint. The longer his riparian reflections were continued, the greater his sanctity became. The fame of his holiness spread throughout all the region. The Swatis besought him to come and live in their valley. After dignified and diplomatic reluctance, he consented to exchange the banks of the Indus for those of the Swat. For some years, he lived in the green valley, and enjoyed the reverence of its people. At the time of the great mutiny, Said Akbar, the King of Swat, died, and the saint succeeded to the temporal as well as the spiritual authority. In 1863 he preached the Jehad against the British, and headed the Swatis and Bunerwals in the Ambeyla campaign. The power which the Sirkar so extravagantly displayed to bring the war to an end, evidently impressed the old man, for at its close he made friends with the Government and received from them many tokens of respect.

Before he died in 1870, he summoned his people around him and declared to them that one day their valley would be the scene of a struggle between the Russians and the British. When that came to pass he charged them to fight on our side. The saying is firmly fixed in the hearts of the tribesmen, and is associated with the memory of their famous priest, known to English minds chiefly through the medium of the "Bab Ballads."

His two sons are dead, but his two grandsons, [the Mianguls of Swat] both quite young, live on in the valley, and are the owners of the Ahkund's freeholds, which are in every section of the Swat country. They have very little political influence; but their persons and property are respected by the people and by the British for the sake of their grandfather, who sleeps in an odour of sanctity at Saidu, near Mingaora.

From the Malakand the signal tower of Chakdara can be seen eight miles away to the eastward. Thither the broad graded road runs like a ribbon across the plain. Seven miles from the Kotal Camp, it crosses the Amandara Pass, a gap in a considerable underfeature, which juts from the southern mountains. After this it turns more to the north and leads to the fortified bridge across the river. I invite the reader to remark this road, for it is historic. It is not only the route by which the Malakand Field Force was able to advance, but it is the very reason of their existence. Without this road there would have been no Malakand Camps, no fighting, no Malakand Field Force, no story. It is the road to Chitral.

Here then, at once, the whole vast question of frontier policy is raised. We hold the Malakand Pass to keep the Chitral road open. We keep the Chitral road open because we have retained Chitral. We retain Chitral in accordance with the "Forward Policy." I am thus confronted at the very outset of this book, which was intended to be devoted chiefly to the narration of military events and small incidents, with that wide political question, on which the keenest intellects in England are in doubt, and the most valuable expert evidence in India is divided. The reader must not think me pusillanimous or weak if I postpone the discussion of so great and controversial a matter till a later chapter, when I may perhaps enjoy a larger measure of his sympathy and agreement. After the story has been told, it may not be inappropriate to point the moral.

Prudence encourages procrastination. But while the consideration of the advisability of the retention of Chitral may be deferred, a description of the means is convenient, if not necessary, to the present chapter.

Nowshera is the railway base of the road. Thence we have followed it to Mardan and across the frontier. Here the new and disputed portion begins. Passing at first through the Lower Ranizai country, it climbs the Malakand Pass, descends into the valley beyond and runs thence through Upper Ranizai territory and Lower Swat to Chakdara. Here it crosses the Swat River by the fine suspension bridge which the fort guards. The three spans of this bridge are together nearly 1500 feet long. It was constructed in 1895, during the operations, in about six weeks, and is a very remarkable piece of military engineering. Beyond the Swat the road runs through the territories of the Khan of Dir, north and east to Sadu, an obscure village thirty-five miles from Malakand. This marks the end of the first section, and further than this wheeled traffic cannot go. The road, now become a camel track, winds along the left bank of the Panjkora River to within five miles of Dir, where it crosses to the right bank by another suspension bridge. Thence it continues to the junction of the Dir stream, along which it finds its way to Dir itself, some fifty miles from Sadu. Beyond Dir camels cannot proceed, and here begins the third section—a path practicable only for mules, and about sixty miles long. From Dir the road is a triumph of engineering. In many places it is carried on wooden galleries perched on the faces of steep and tremendous cliffs, and at others it works round spurs by astounding zig-zags, or is scarped from the mountain side. At the end of the road is Fort Chitral with a garrison of two battalions, one company of sappers, and two mountain guns.

The road is maintained and protected by the tribes through whose territories it passes; but the two principal points where it might be closed are held by Imperial garrisons. The Malakand Fort guards the passage of the mountains. Chakdara holds the bridge across the river. The rest is left to the tribal levies. The Ranizai tribe receive an annual subsidy from the Indian Government of 30,000 rupees, out of which they maintain 200 irregulars armed with Sniders, and irreverently called by the British officers, "Catch-'em-alive-Os." These drive away marauders and discourage outrage and murder. The Khan of Dir, through whose territory the road runs for seventy-three miles, also receives a subsidy from Government of 60,000 rupees, in consideration of which he provides 400 irregulars for its service.

Until the great rising these arrangements worked admirably. The tribesmen interested in the maintenance of the route, were most reluctant to engage in hostilities against the Government. The Lower Ranizais, south of Malakand, abstained altogether. The elders of the tribe collected all the arms of their hot-headed youths, and forbade them to attack the troops. The Upper Ranizais were nearer the scene of the disturbance, and were induced by superstition and fear to join the Mullah; but very half-heartedly. The Swatis were carried away by fanaticism. The Khan of Dir throughout behaved loyally, as he is entirely dependent on British support, and his people realise the advantages of the subsidy.

If the road is interesting its story is more so, and a summary of the events and causes which have led to its construction, may also throw some light on the political history and methods of the border tribes.

The uncertainty and insecurity of their power, has always led petty chiefs to seek the support of some powerful suzerain. In 1876 the Mehtar of Chitral, Aman-ul-Mulk, was encouraged to seek the protection, and become the vassal of our vassal, the Maharaja of Cashmere. In accordance with the general scheme of advance, then already adopted by the Indian Government, a British agency was at once established at Gilgit on the Chitral-Cashmere frontier.

Aman-ul-Mulk was presented with a certain supply of arms and ammunition, and an annual subsidy of 6000 rupees, afterwards raised to 12,000 rupees. The British thus obtained an interest in Chitral, and a point of observation on its borders. In 1881 the agency was withdrawn, but the influence remained, and in 1889 it was re-established with a much larger garrison. Meanwhile Aman-ul-Mulk ruled in Chitral, showing great respect to the wishes of the Government, and in the enjoyment of his subsidy and comparative peace. But in 1892 he died, leaving many sons, all equally ferocious, ambitious and unscrupulous. One of these, Afzal by name, though not the eldest or acknowledged heir, had the good fortune to be on the spot. He seized the reins of power, and having murdered as many if his brothers as he could catch, proclaimed himself Mehtar, and invited the recognition of the Indian Government. He was acknowledged chief, as he seemed to be "a man of courage and determination," and his rule afforded a prospect of settled government. Surviving brothers fled to neighbouring states.

Nizam, the eldest, came to Gilgit and appealed to the British. He got no help. The blessing had already been bestowed. But in November, 1892, Sher Afzul, a brother of the late Aman, returned by stealth to Chitral, whence fraternal affection had driven him, and killed the new Mehtar and another brother, both of whom were his nephews. The "wicked uncle" then ascended the throne, or its equivalent. He was, however, opposed. The Indian Government refused to recognise him. Nizam, at Gilgit, urged his claims, and was finally allowed to go and try to regain his inheritance. The moral support of 250 Cashmere rifles brought him many adherents. He was joined by the people. It was the landing of William of Orange on a reduced scale, and with Cashmere troops instead of Dutch Guards. Twelve hundred men sent by Sher Afzul to oppose him, deserted to his side. The avuncular usurper, realising that it might be dangerous to wait longer, fled to Afghanistan, as James II had fled to France, was received by the ruler with hospitality, and carefully preserved as an element of future disorder.

Nizam now became Mehtar according to his desire. But he did not greatly enjoy his power, and may have evolved some trite reflections on the vanity of earthly ambition. From the first he was poor and unpopular. With the support of the Government of India, however, he managed to maintain a weak, squalid rule for a space. To give him countenance, and in accordance with the Policy, Captain Younghusband was sent to the country with a hundred bayonets. The Gilgit garrison was increased by a battalion, and several posts were established between that place and Mastuj.

Thus the Imperial forces had entered Chitral. Their position was soon to become one of danger. They were separated from Gilgit by many miles of bad road, and warlike tribesmen. To move troops from Gilgit would always be slow and difficult. Another route was however possible, the route I have described—a route northwards from Peshawar through Dir—shorter and easier, starting from British territory and the railway. Towards this line of communication the Indian Government now looked. If British troops or agents were to be retained in Chitral, if in other words their recognised policy was to be continued, this route must be opened up. They sounded the Home Government. Lord Kimberley replied, deprecating increase of responsibilities, of territory and expenditure, and declining to pledge himself to support such a scheme. At the same time he sanctioned the temporary retention of the troops, and the agent, in the hopes of strengthening Nizam. [Despatch from Secretary of State, No.34, 1st Sept., 1893.]

At this point Umra Khan must enter the story. The Gilgit agency report, dated 28th April, 1890, speaks of this chief, who was the Khan of Jandul, but whose influence pervaded the whole of Bajaur as "the most important man between Chitral and Pashawar." To this powerful ruler, another of the sons of Aman, named Amir, had fled from the family massacre which followed his father's death. Umra Khan protected him and determined to turn him to his own advantage. In May, 1894, this youth—he was about twenty years of age—returned to Chitral, professing to have escaped from the hands of Umra Khan. He was kindly received by Nizam, who seems to have been much hampered throughout his career by his virtue. On 1st January, 1895, Amir availed himself of his welcome, to murder his brother, and the principal members of the Chitral Cabinet. He proclaimed himself Mentar and asked for recognition. The Imperial officers, though used to frontier politics, refused to commit themselves to any arrangement with such a villain, until the matter had been considered in India.

Umra Khan now advanced with a large force to the head of the Chitral Valley, nominally to assist his dear friend and ally,

Amir, to consolidate his rule, really in the hopes of extending his own territories. But Amir, knowing Umra well, and having won his kingdom, did not desire to share it. Fighting ensued. The Chitrals were beaten. As he could not make any use of Amir, Umra Khan invited the wicked uncle to return. Sher Afzul accepted. A bargain was struck. Sher Afzul claimed to be made Mehtar, Umra supported his claims. Both threatened force in the event of opposition.

But the Imperial Government rose in wrath, refused to have anything to do with the new claimant, informed him that his language was impertinent, and warned Umra Khan to leave Chitral territory forthwith or take the consequences. The answer was war. The scanty garrisons and scattered parties of British troops were attacked. A company of the 14th Sikhs was cut to pieces. Lieutenants Fowler and Edwards were taken prisoners. Fort Chitral, into which the rest of the Chitral mission and their escort had thrown themselves, was closely and fiercely besieged. To rescue them was imperative. The 1st Division of the Field Army was mobilised. A force of nearly 16,000 men crossed the frontier on the 1st April, from Mardan, to advance to the relief by the shortest route—the route through Swat and Dir—the line of the present Chitral road. The command of the expedition was confided to Sir Robert Low. Sir Bindon Blood was Chief of the Staff.

So far the tale has been of the steady increase of British influence, in accordance with an avowed and consistent policy—primarily in Chitral, and ultimately throughout the border tribes. One movement has been followed by another. All have been aimed at a common end. Now suddenly we are confronted with an act by which the Government of India with open eyes placed an obstacle in the path, which they had so long pursued, to follow which they had made so many efforts themselves and demanded so many sacrifices from their subjects. Perhaps from compunction, but probably to soothe the Liberal Government, by appearing to localise the disturbances, and disclaiming any further acquisition of territory, they issued a proclamation to "all the people of Swat and the people of Bajaur, who do not side with Umra Khan," in which they declared that they had "no intention of permanently occupying any territory through which Umra Khan's misconduct" might "force them to pass, or of interfering with the independence of the tribes." [Proclamation, 14th March, 1895.]

If this proclamation was intended for political purposes in England, it, from one point of view, succeeded most admirably, for there has been nearly as much written about it as about all the soldiers who have been killed and wounded in the war. It had, however, no effect upon the tribesmen, who were infuriated by the sight if the troops and paid no attention to the protestations of the Government. Had they watched with care the long, steady, deliberate advance, which I have so briefly summarised; had they read the avowed and recorded determination of the Indian Administration "to extend and, by degrees, to consolidate their influence" [Letter from Government of India, No.407, 28th February, 1879.] in the whole drainage system of the Indus, they might have even doubted their sincerity. Instead, and being unable to make fine distinctions, they saw only invasion in the military movements.

They gathered accordingly, to oppose the advance of the troops. To the number of 12,000 they occupied the Malakand Pass—a tremendous position. From this they were driven with great slaughter on the 3rd of April, by the two leading brigades of Sir Robert Low's force. Further operations resulted in the passage of the Swat and Panjkora Rivers being effected. The road to Chitral was open. The besiegers of the fort fled, and a small relieving force was able to push through from Gilgit under Colonel Kelly. Umra Khan fled to Afghanistan, and the question of future policy came before the Government of India.

Two alternatives presented themselves: either they must "abandon the attempt to keep up any effective control" over Chitral, or they must put a sufficient garrison there. In pursuance of their recognised policy, the Council decided unanimously that to maintain British influence in Chitral was "a matter of first importance." In a despatch [Despatch of Government of India, No.240, 8th May, 1895.] to the Home Government they set forth all their reasons, and at the same time declared that it was impossible to garrison Chitral without keeping up the road from Peshawar, by which the Relief force had advanced.

On the 13th of June Lord Rosebery's Cabinet replied decisively, with courage if not with wisdom, that "no military force or European agent should be kept at Chitral, that Chitral should not be fortified, and that no road should be made between Peshawar and Chitral." By this they definitely and finally repudiated the policy which had been consistently followed since 1876. They left Chitral to stew in its own juice. They over-ruled the Government of India. It was a bold and desperate attempt to return to the old frontier line. The Indian Government replied: "We deeply regret but loyally accept decision," and began to gather up the severed strings of their policy and weave another web.

But in the nick of time the Liberal Administration fell, and Lord Salisbury's Cabinet reversed their decision. It is interesting, in reading the Blue Books on Indian questions, to watch the emotions of party principles, stirring beneath the uniform mask of official responsibility—which the most reckless of men are compelled to wear as soon as they become ministers. The language, the style, the tone of the correspondence is the same. It is always a great people addressing and instructing their pro-consuls and administrators. But the influence inclines backwards and forwards as the pendulum of politics swings. And as the swing in 1895 was a very great one, a proportionate impulse was given to the policy of advance. "It seemed" to the new ministry "that the policy . . . continuously pursued by successive Governments ought not to be lightly abandoned unless its maintenance had become clearly impossible." [Despatch, Secretary of State, No.30, 16th Aug., 1895.] Thus the retention of Chitral was sanctioned, and the road which that retention necessitated was completed.

I approach with nervousness so great a matter as the "Breach of Faith" question. In a book devoted chiefly to the deeds of soldiers it seems almost presumptuous to discuss an affair which involves the political honour of statesmen. In their unnecessary and gratuitous proclamation the Government of India declared, that they had no intention of interfering with the tribes, or of permanently occupying any territory, the troops might march through; whereas now they do interfere with the tribesmen, and have established garrisons at Dargai, Malakand and Chakdara, all of which are in the territory through which the troops passed. But it takes two to make a bargain or a breach of faith. The tribes took no notice of the proclamation. They did not understand it. They did not believe it. Where there is no faith there can be no breach of faith. The border peoples resisted the advance. That position annulled the proclamation, and proved that it was not credited by the tribesmen. They do not think they have been tricked. They do not regard the road as a "breach of faith." What they do regard it as, is a menace to their independence, and a prelude to annexation. Nor are they wrong. Looking at the road, as I have seen it, and have tried to describe it, running broad and white across the valley; at the soldiers moving along it; at the political officers extending their influence in all directions; at the bridge and fort of Chakdara; and at the growing cantonment on the Malakand Pass, it needs no education to appreciate its significance. Nor can any sophistry obscure it.

CHAPTER III:

THE OUTBREAK

Tantum religio potuit suadere malorum.

LUCRETIUS.

The historian of great events is always oppressed by the difficulty of tracing the silent, subtle influences, which in all communities precede and prepare the way for violent outbursts and uprisings. He may discover many causes and record them duly, but he will always be sensible that others have escaped him. The changing tides of public opinion, the undercurrents of interest, partisanship and caprice, the whirlpools of illogical sentiment or ignorant prejudice, exert forces so complex and numerous, that to observe and appreciate them all, and to estimate the effect of each in raising the storm, is a task beyond the intellect and industry of man. The chronicler of small things lies under even greater disabilities. He has fewer facts to guide his judgment, nor is it as easy to read small print as capital letters.

In an attempt to state the causes of the great tribal upheaval of 1897, these difficulties are increased by the fact that no European can gauge the motives or assume the points of view of Asiatics. It is, however, impossible to pass the question by, and ignoring the detail, I shall endeavour to indicate some at least of the most important and apparent forces, which have led to the formidable combination with which the British power in India has been confronted.

The most marked incident in the "Forward Policy" has been the retention of Chitral. The garrisons, the road, the tribal levies have made the tribesmen realise the proximity and the advance of civilisation. It is possible—even probable—that with all their love of independence, the majority of the inhabitants of the mountains would have been willing, until their liberties were actually curtailed, to remain in passive submission, soothed by the increase of material prosperity. During the two years that the British flag had floated over Chakdara and the Malakand the trade of the Swat Valley had nearly doubled. As the sun of civilisation rose above the hills, the fair flowers of commerce unfolded, and the streams of supply and demand, hitherto congealed by the frost of barbarism, were thawed. Most of the native population were content to bask in the genial warmth and enjoy the new-found riches and comforts. For two years reliefs had gone to and from Chitral without a shot being fired. Not a post-bag had been stolen, not a messenger murdered. The political officers riding about freely among the fierce hill men were invited to settle many disputes, which would formerly have been left to armed force.

But a single class had viewed with quick intelligence and intense hostility the approach of the British power. The priesthood of the Afghan border instantly recognised the full meaning of the Chitral road. The cause of their antagonism is not hard to discern. Contact with civilisation assails the ignorance, and credulity, on which the wealth and influence of the Mullah depend. A general combination of the religious forces of India against that civilising, educating rule, which unconsciously saps the strength of superstition, is one of the dangers of the future. Here Mahommedanism was threatened and resisted. A vast, but silent agitation was begun. Messengers passed to and fro among the tribes. Whispers of war, a holy war, were breathed to a race intensely passionate and fanatical. Vast and mysterious agencies, the force of which is incomprehensible to rational minds, were employed. More astute brains than the wild valleys of the North produce conducted the preparations. Secret encouragement came from the South—from India itself. Actual support and assistance was given from Cabul.

In that strange half light of ignorance and superstition, assailed by supernatural terrors and doubts, and lured by hopes of celestial glory, the tribes were taught to expect prodigious events. Something was coming. A great day for their race and faith was at hand. Presently the moment would arrive. They must watch and be ready. The mountains became as full of explosives as a magazine. Yet the spark was lacking.

At length the time came. A strange combination of circumstances operated to improve the opportunity. The victory of the Turks over the Greeks; the circulation of the Amir's book on "Jehad"; his assumption of the position of a Caliph of Islam, and much indiscreet writing in the Anglo-Indian press, [Articles in Anglo-Indian papers on such subjects as "The Recrudescence if Mahommedanism" produce more effect on the educated native mind than the most seditious frothings of the vernacular press.] united to produce a "boom" in Mahommedanism.

The moment was propitious; nor was the man wanting. What Peter the Hermit was to the regular bishops and cardinals of the Church, the Mad Mullah was to the ordinary priesthood of the Afghan border. A wild enthusiast, convinced alike of his Divine mission and miraculous powers, preached a crusade, or Jehad, against the infidel. The mine was fired. The flame ran along the ground. The explosions burst forth in all directions. The reverberations have not yet died away.

Great and widespread as the preparations were, they were not visible to the watchful diplomatic agents who maintained the relations of the Government with the tribesmen. So extraordinary is the inversion of ideas and motives among those people that it may be said that those who know them best, know them least, and the more logical the mind of the student the less he is able to understand of the subject. In any case among these able men who diligently collected information and observed the state of feeling, there were none who realised the latent forces that were being accumulated on all sides. The strange treachery at Maizar in June was a flash in the pan. Still no one saw the danger. It was not until the early days of July that it was noticed that there was a fanatical movement in Upper Swat. Even then its significance was disregarded and its importance underrated. That a Mad Fakir had arrived was known. His power was still a secret. It did not long remain so.

It is, thank heaven, difficult if not impossible for the modern European to fully appreciate the force which fanaticism exercises among an ignorant, warlike and Oriental population. Several generations have elapsed since the nations of the West have drawn the sword in religious controversy, and the evil memories of the gloomy past have soon faded in the strong, clear light of Rationalism and human sympathy. Indeed it is evident that Christianity, however degraded and distorted by cruelty and intolerance, must always exert a modifying influence on men's passions, and protect them from the more violent forms of fanatical fever, as we are protected from smallpox by vaccination. But the Mahommedan religion increases, instead of lessening, the fury of intolerance. It was originally propagated by the sword, and ever since, its votaries have been subject, above the people of all other creeds, to this form of madness. In a moment the fruits of patient toil, the prospects of material prosperity, the fear of death itself, are flung aside. The more emotional Pathans are powerless to resist. All rational considerations are forgotten. Seizing their weapons, they become Ghazis—as dangerous and as sensible as mad dogs: fit only to be treated as such. While the more generous spirits among the tribesmen become convulsed in an ecstasy of religious bloodthirstiness, poorer and more material souls derive additional impulses from the influence of others, the hopes of plunder and the joy of fighting. Thus whole nations are roused to arms. Thus the Turks repel their enemies, the Arabs of the Soudan break the British squares, and the rising on the Indian frontier spreads far and wide. In each case civilisation is confronted with militant Mahommedanism. The forces of progress clash with those of reaction. The religion of blood and war is face to face with that of peace. Luckily the religion of peace is usually the better armed.

The extraordinary credulity of the people is hardly conceivable. Had the Mad Mullah called on them to follow him to attack Malakand and Chakdara they would have refused. Instead he worked miracles. He sat at his house, and all who came to visit him, brought him a small offering of food or money, in return for which he gave them a little rice. As his stores were continually replenished, he might claim to have fed thousands. He asserted that he was invisible at night. Looking into his room, they saw no one. At these things they marvelled. Finally he declared he would destroy the infidel. He wanted no help. No one should share the honours. The heavens would open and an army would descend. The more he protested he did not want them, the more exceedingly they came. Incidentally he mentioned that they would be invulnerable; other agents added arguments. I was shown a captured scroll, upon which the tomb of the Ghazi—he who has killed an infidel—is depicted in heaven, no fewer than seven degrees above the Caaba itself. Even after the fighting—when the tribesmen reeled back from the terrible army they had assailed, leaving a quarter of their number on the field—the faith of the survivors was unshaken. Only those who had doubted had perished, said the Mullah, and displayed a bruise which was, he informed them, the sole effect of a twelve-pound shrapnel shell on his sacred person.

I pass with relief from the tossing sea of Cause and Theory to the firm ground of Result and Fact. The rumours and reports which reached the Malakand of the agitation in Upper Swat and among the surrounding tribes were fully appreciated by the Pathan Sepoys of the garrison. As July advanced, several commanding officers were warned by their men, that great events were impending. Major Deane, the political agent, watched with great anxiety the daily progress of the fanatical movement. No one desires to be thought an alarmist, least of all on the frontier where there is always danger. At length, however, he felt compelled to officially report the disquieting signs. Warnings were then issued to the officers in charge of the various posts, and the troops were practised in taking up alarm stations. By the 23rd of July all had been informed that the aspect of affairs was threatening, and ordered to observe every precaution. But to the last everybody doubted that there would be a rising, nor did any one imagine that even should one occur, it would lead to more than a skirmish. The natives were friendly and respectful. The valley smiled in fertile prosperity. It was not strange, that none could foresee the changes a week would bring, or guess that in a few days they would be fighting for their lives; that they would carry fire and sword through the peaceful landscape; that the polo ground would be the scene of a cavalry charge, or that the cheery barbarians among whom they had lived quietly for so many months would become maddened and ferocious savages. Never was transformation of scene more complete, or more rapid.

And all the while the rumours of coming war grew stronger and stronger. The bazaars of India, like the London coffee-houses of the last century, are always full of marvellous tales—the invention of fertile brains. A single unimportant fact is exaggerated, and distorted, till it becomes unrecognisable. From it, a thousand wild, illogical, and fantastic conclusions are drawn. These again are circulated as facts. So the game goes on. But amid all this falsehood, and idle report, there often lies important information. The bazaar stories not only indicate the state of native opinion, but not infrequently contain the germ of truth. In Eastern lands, news travels by strange channels, and often with unaccountable rapidity. As July advanced the bazaar at Malakand became full of tales of the Mad Fakir. His miracles passed from mouth to mouth, with suitable additions.

A great day for Islam was at hand. A mighty man had arisen to lead them. The English would be swept away. By the time of the new moon, not one would remain. The Great Fakir had mighty armies concealed among the mountains. When the moment came these would sally forth—horse, foot and artillery—and destroy the infidel. It was even stated that the Mullah had ordered that no one should go near a certain hill, lest the heavenly hosts should be prematurely revealed. So ran the talk. But among all these frothy fabrications there lay a solemn warning.

Though the British military and political officers were compelled to take official notice of the reports received with reference to the tribal gathering, and to make arrangements for the safety of their posts, they privately scouted the idea that any serious events were impending.

On the afternoon of the 26th July the subalterns and younger officers of the Malakand garrison proceeded to Khar to play polo. Thither also came Lieutenant Rattray, riding over from Chakdara fort. The game was a good one, and the tribesmen of the neighbouring village watched it as usual in little groups, with a keen interest. Nothing in their demeanour betrayed their thoughts or intentions. The young soldiers saw nothing, knew nothing, and had they known would have cared less. There would be no rising. If there was, so much the better. They were ready for it. The game ended and the officers cantered back to their camps and posts.

It was then that a strange incident occurred—an incident eminently characteristic of the frontier tribes. As the syces were putting the rugs and clothing on the polo ponies, and loitering about the ground after the game, the watching natives drew near and advised them to be off home at once, for that there was going to be a fight. They knew, these Pathans, what was coming. The wave of fanaticism was sweeping down the valley. It would carry them away. They were powerless to resist. Like one who feels a fit coming on, they waited. Nor did they care very much. When the Mad Fakir arrived, they would fight and kill the infidels. In the meantime there was no necessity to deprive them of their ponies. And so with motives, partly callous, partly sportsmanlike, and not without some faint suspicion of chivalry, they warned the native grooms, and these taking the hint reached the camp in safety.

Late on this same afternoon Major Deane reported to Brigadier-General Meiklejohn, who commanded the Malakand garrison, that matters had assumed a very grave aspect; that a great armed gathering had collected around the Mad Mullah's standard, and that an attack was probable. He advised that the Guides should be called up to reinforce the brigade. A telegram was immediately despatched to Mardan ordering them to march without delay. At 8.30 Lieutenant P. Eliott-Lockhart, who was the senior officer then with the regiment, received the order. At 1.30 A.M. they began their now famous march.

After sending for the Guides, the brigadier, at about seven o'clock, interviewed his different commanding officers, and instructed them to be prepared to turn out at any moment. Major Deane now reported that the Mad Mullah and his gathering were advancing down the valley, and recommended that the Amandara Pass, four miles away, should be held. General Meiklejohn accordingly issued orders for a movable column, to be formed as follows:—

45th Sikhs.
2 Cos. 31st Punjaub Infantry.
2 Guns No. 8 Mountain Battery.
1 Squadron 11th Bengal Lancers.

This force, under command of Lieutenant-Colonel McRae, 45th Sikhs, was to start at midnight and would be supported by the rest of the troops under command of the brigadier at 3 A.M.

All preparations were swiftly made. At 9.45 a telegram from Chakdara—which got through just before the wire was cut—reported that large forces of Pathans were rapidly moving towards the camps. A quarter of an hour later a Jemadar of the Levies galloped in with the news that, to quote the official despatch: "The Fakir had passed Khar and was advancing on Malakand, that neither Levies nor people would act against him, and that the hills to the east of the camp were covered with Pathans."

As soon as the officers had returned from polo, they found plenty of work waiting for them. Bandsmen and boys incapable of carrying arms had to be hurried up to the fort. Indents had to be made out for transport, rations and ammunition. There was much to do, and little time to do it in. At length all was finished, and the troops were in readiness for their early morning start. At 9.30 the officers sat down to dinner, still in their polo kit, which there had been no time to change. At 10 o'clock they were discussing the prospects of the approaching march, and eagerly weighing the chances of a skirmish. The more sanguine asserted that there would be a fight—a small one, it was true—but still a skirmish. Many of those who had never been in action before congratulated themselves on the unlooked-for opportunity. The older and more experienced regarded the matter in the light of a riot. They might have to fire on the tribesmen, but Swatis were such cowards that they would never stand up to the troops. Still it was a chance.

Suddenly in the stillness of the night a bugle-call sounded on the parade ground of the "crater" camp. Everyone sprang up. It was the "Assembly." For a moment there was silence while the officers seized their swords and belts and hurriedly fastened them on. Several, thinking that it was merely the warning for the movable column to fall in, waited to light their cigarettes. Then from many quarters the loud explosion of musketry burst forth, a sound which for six days and nights was to know no intermission.

The attack on the Malakand and the great frontier war had begun.

The noise of firing echoed among the hills. Its echoes are ringing still. One valley caught the waves of sound and passed them to the next, till the whole wide mountain region rocked with the confusion of the tumult. Slender wires and long-drawn cables carried the vibrations to the far-off countries of the West. Distant populations on the Continent of Europe thought that in them they detected the dull, discordant tones of decline and fall. Families in English homes feared that the detonations marked the death of those they loved—sons, brothers or husbands. Diplomatists looked wise, economists anxious, stupid people mysterious and knowledgeable. All turned to have the noise stopped. But that was a task which could not be accomplished until thousands of lives had been sacrificed and millions of money spent.

CHAPTER IV:

THE ATTACK ON THE MALAKAND

Cry "Havoc" and let slip the dogs of war.

"JULIUS CAESAR," Act iii., Sc.i.

It has long been recognised by soldiers of every nation that, to resist a vigorous onslaught by night, is almost the hardest task that troops can be called upon to perform. Panics, against which few brave men are proof, arise in a moment from such situations. Many a gallant soldier has lost his head. Many an experienced officer has been borne down unheeded by a crowd of fugitives. Regiments that have marched unflinchingly to almost certain death on the battlefield, become in an instant terrified and useless.

In the attack on the Malakand camp, all the elements of danger and disorder were displayed. The surprise, the darkness, the confused and broken nature of the ground; the unknown numbers of the enemy; their merciless ferocity; every appalling circumstance was present. But there were men who were equal to the occasion. As soon as the alarm sounded Lieutenant-Colonel McRae of the 45th Sikhs, a holder of the Gold Medal of the Royal Humane Society and of long experience in Afghanistan and on the Indian frontier, ran to the Quarter Guard, and collecting seven or eight men, sent them under command of Major Taylor, of the same regiment, down the Buddhist road to try and check the enemy's advance. Hurriedly assembling another dozen men, and leaving the Adjutant, Lieutenant Barff, with directions to bring on more, he ran with his little party after Taylor in the direction of the entrance gorge of the Kotal camp. Two roads give access to the Malakand camp, from the plain of Khar. At one point the Buddhist road, the higher of the two, passes through a narrow defile then turns a sharp corner. Here, if anywhere, the enemy might be held or at least delayed until the troops got under arms. Overtaking Major Taylor, Colonel McRae led the party, which then amounted to perhaps twenty men, swiftly down the road, It was a race on which the lives of hundreds depended. If the enemy could turn the corner, nothing could check their rush, and the few men who tried to oppose them would be cut to pieces. The Sikhs arrived first, but by a very little. As they turned the corner they met the mass of the enemy, nearly a thousand strong, armed chiefly with swords and knives, creeping silently and stealthily up the gorge, in the hope and assurance of rushing the camp and massacring every soul in it. The whole road was crowded with the wild figures. McRae opened fire at once. Volley after volley was poured into the dense mass, at deadly range. At length the Sikhs fired independently. This checked the enemy, who shouted and yelled in fury at being thus stopped. The small party of soldiers then fell back, pace by pace, firing incessantly, and took up a position in a cutting about fifty yards behind the corner. Their flanks were protected on the left by high rocks, and on the right by boulders and rough ground, over which in the darkness it was impossible to move. The road was about five yards wide. As fast as the tribesmen turned the corner they were shot down. It was a strong position.

> In that strait path a thousand
> Might well be stopped by three

Being thus effectively checked in their direct advance, the tribesmen began climbing up the hill to the left and throwing down rocks and stones on those who barred their path. They also fired their rifles round the corner, but as they were unable to see the soldiers without exposing themselves, most of their bullets went to the right.

The band of Sikhs were closely packed in the cutting, the front rank kneeling to fire. Nearly all were struck by stones and rocks. Major Taylor, displaying great gallantry, was mortally wounded. Several of the Sepoys were killed. Colonel McRae himself was accidentally stabbed in the neck by a bayonet and became covered with blood. But he called upon the men to maintain the good name of "Rattray's Sikhs," and to hold their position till death or till the regiment came up. And the soldiers replied by loudly shouting the Sikh warcry, and defying the enemy to advance.

After twenty minutes of desperate fighting, Lieutenant Barff arrived with thirty more men. He was only just in time. The enemy had already worked round Colonel McRae's right, and the destruction of the few soldiers left alive could not long have been delayed. The reinforcement, climbing up the hillside, drove the enemy back and protected the flank. But the remainder of the regiment was now at hand. Colonel McRae then fell back to a more extended position along a ridge about fifty yards further up the road, and reinforcing Lieutenant Barff's party, repulsed all attacks during the night. About 2 A.M. the tribesmen, finding they could make no progress, drew off, leaving many dead.

The presence of mind, tactical knowledge and bravery displayed in this affair are thus noticed in the official despatches by General Meiklejohn:—

"There is no doubt that the gallant resistance made by this small body in the gorge, against vastly superior numbers, till the arrival of the rest of the regiment, saved the camp from being rushed on that side, and I cannot speak too highly of the behaviour of Lieutenant-Colonel McRae and Major Taylor on this occasion."

While these things were passing on the right, the other attacks of the enemy had met with more success. The camp was assaulted simultaneously on the three sides. The glow of the star shells showed that the north camp was also engaged. The enemy had been checked on the Buddhist road, by Colonel McRae and the 45th Sikhs, but another great mass of men forced their way along the Graded road in the centre of the position. On the first sound of firing the inlying picket of the 24th Punjaub Infantry doubled out to reinforce the pickets on the road, and in the water-gorge. They only arrived in time to find these being driven in by overpowering numbers of the enemy. Hundreds of fierce swordsmen swarmed unto the bazaar and into the serai, a small enclosure which adjoined. Sharpshooters scrambled up the surrounding hills, and particularly from one ragged, rock-strewn peak called Gibraltar, kept up a tremendous fire.

The defence of the left and centre or the camp was confided to the 24th Punjaub Infantry. One company of this regiment under Lieutenant Climo, charging across the football ground, cleared the bazaar at the point of the bayonet. The scene at this moment was vivid and terrible. The bazaar was crowded with tribesmen. The soldiers rushing forward amid loud cheers, plunged their bayonets into their furious adversaries. The sound of the hacking of swords, the screams of the unfortunate shopkeepers, the yells of the Ghazis were plainly heard above the ceaseless roll of musketry. The enemy now tried to force their way back into the bazaar, but the entrance was guarded by the troops and held against all assaults till about 10.45. The left flank of the company was then turned, and the pressure became so severe that they were withdrawn to a more interior line of defence, and took up a position along the edge of the "Sappers' and Miners' enclosure." Another company held the approaches from the north camp. The remainder of the regiment and No.5 company Sappers and Miners, were kept in readiness to reinforce any part of the line.

It is necessary to record the actual movements of the troops in detail, but I am anxious above all things to give the reader a general idea. The enemy had attacked in tremendous strength along the two roads that gave access on the eastern side to the great cup of the Malakand. On the right road, they were checked by the brilliant movement of Colonel McRae and the courage of his regiment. Pouring in overwhelming force along the left road, they had burst into the camp itself, bearing down all opposition. The defenders, unable to hold the extended line of the rim, had been driven to take up a central position in the bottom of the cup. This central position comprised the "Sappers' and Miners' enclosure," the commissariat lines and the Field Engineer Park. It was commanded on every side by the fire from the rim. But the defenders stood at bay, determined at all costs to hold their ground, bad though it was.

Meanwhile the enemy rushed to the attack with wild courage and reckless fury. Careless of life, they charged the slender line of defence. Twice they broke through and penetrated the enclosure. They were met by men as bold as they. The fighting became desperate. The general himself hurried from point to point, animating the soldiers and joining in the defence with sword and revolver. As soon as the enemy broke into the commissariat lines they rushed into the huts and sheds eager for plunder and victims.

Lieutenant Manley, the Brigade Commissariat Officer, stuck stubbornly to his post, and with Sergeant Harrington endeavoured to hold the hut in which he lived. The savage tribesmen burst in the door and crowded into the room. What followed reads like a romance.

The officer opened fire at once with his revolver. He was instantly cut down and hacked to pieces. In the struggle the lamp was smashed. The room became pitch dark. The sergeant, knocking down his assailants, got free for a moment and stood against the wall motionless. Having killed Manley, the tribesmen now began to search for the sergeant, feeling with their hands along the wall and groping in the darkness. At last, finding no one, they concluded he had escaped, and hurried out to look for others. Sergeant Harrington remained in the hut till it was retaken some hours later, and so saved his life.

Another vigorous attack was made upon the Quarter Guard. Lieutenant Watling, who met it with his company of sappers, transfixed a Ghazi with his sword, but such was the fury of the fanatic that as he fell dead he cut at the officer and wounded him severely. The company were driven back. The Quarter Guard was captured, and with it the reserve ammunition of the sappers. Lieutenant Watling was carried in by his men, and, as soon as he reached the dressing station, reported the loss of this important post.

Brigadier-General Meiklejohn at once ordered a party of the 24th to retake it from the enemy. Few men could be spared from the line of defence. At length a small but devoted band collected. It consisted of Captain Holland, Lieutenant Climo, Lieutenant Manley, R.E., the general's orderly, a Sepoy of the 45th Sikhs, two or three sappers and three men of the 24th; in all about a dozen.

The general placed himself at their head. The officers drew their revolvers. The men were instructed to use the bayonet only. Then they advanced. The ground is by nature broken and confused to an extraordinary degree. Great rocks, undulations and trees rendered all movements difficult. Frequent tents, sheds and other buildings increased the intricacies. Amidst such surroundings were the enemy, numerous and well armed. The twelve men charged. The tribesmen advanced to meet them. The officers shot down man after man with their pistols. The soldiers bayoneted others. The enemy drew off discomfited, but half the party were killed or wounded. The orderly was shot dead. A sapper and a havildar of the 24th were severely wounded. The general himself was struck by a sword on the neck. Luckily the weapon turned in his assailant's hand, and only caused a bruise. Captain Holland was shot through the back at close quarters by a man concealed in a tent. The bullet, which caused four wounds, grazed his spine. The party were now too few to effect anything. The survivors halted. Lieutenant Climo took the wounded officer back, and collecting a dozen more men of the 24th, returned to the attack. The second attempt to regain the Quarter Guard was also unsuccessful, and the soldiers recoiled with further loss; but with that undaunted spirit which refuses to admit defeat they continued their efforts, and at the third charge dashed across the open space, bowling over and crushing back the enemy, and the post was recovered. All the ammunition had, however, been carried off by the enemy, and as the expenditure of that night had already been enormous, it was a serious loss. The commissariat lines were at length cleared of the tribesmen, and such of the garrison as could be spared were employed in putting up a hasty defence across the south entrance of the enclosure, and clearing away the cook-houses and other shelters, which might be seized by the enemy.

The next morning no fewer than twenty-nine corpses of tribesmen were found round the cookhouse, and in the open space over which the three charges had taken place. This, when it is remembered that perhaps twice as many had been wounded and had crawled away, enables an estimate to be formed of the desperate nature of the fight for the Quarter Guard.

All this time the fire from rim into the cup had been causing severe and continual losses. The enemy surrounding the enclosure on three sides, brought a cross fire to bear on its defenders, and made frequent charges right up to the breastwork. Bullets were flying in all directions, and there was no question of shelter. Major Herbert, D.A.A.G., was hit early in the night. Later on Lieutenant-Colonel Lamb received the dangerous wound in his thigh which caused his death a few days afterwards. Many Sepoys were also killed and wounded. The command of the 24th Punjaub Infantry devolved upon a subaltern officer, Lieutenant Climo. The regiment, however, will never be in better hands.

At about one o'clock, during a lull in the firing, the company which was lining the east face of the enclosure heard feeble cries of help. A wounded havildar of the 24th was lying near the bazaar. He had fallen in the first attack, shot in the shoulder. The tribesmen, giving him two or three deep sword cuts to finish him, had left him for dead. He now appealed for help. The football ground on which he lay was swept by the fire of the troops, and overrun by the enemy's swordsmen, yet the cry for help did not pass unheeded. Taking two Sepoys with him, Lieutenant E.W. Costello, 24th Punjaub Infantry, ran out into the deadly space, and, in spite of the heavy fire, brought the wounded soldier in safety. For this heroic action he has since received the Victoria Cross.

As the night wore on, the attack of the enemy became so vigorous, that the brigadier decided to call for a reinforcement of a hundred men from the garrison of the fort. This work stood high on a hill, and was impregnable to an enemy unprovided with field guns. Lieutenant Rawlins volunteered to try and reach it with the order. Accompanied by three orderlies, he started. He had to make his way through much broken ground infested by the enemy. One man sprang at him and struck him on the wrist with a sword, but the subaltern, firing his revolver, shot him dead, reached the fort in safety, and brought back the sorely-needed reinforcement.

It was thought that the enemy would make a final effort to capture the enclosure before dawn, that being the hour which Afghan tribesmen usually select. But they had lost heavily, and at about 3.30 A.M. began to carry away their dead and wounded. The firing did not, however, lessen until 4.15 A.M., when the sharpshooters withdrew to the heights, and the fusillade dwindled to "sniping" at long range.

The first night of the defence of the Malakand camp was over. The enemy, with all the advantages of surprise, position and great numbers, had failed to overcome the slender garrison. Everywhere they had been repulsed with slaughter. But the British losses had been severe.

Killed—Hon. Lieutenant L. Manley, Commissariat Department.

Wounded dangerously—Major W.W. Taylor, 45th Sikhs.

Wounded severely—Lieut.-Colonel J. Lamb, 24th P.I.

"   "   Major L. Herbert, D.A.A.G.

"   "   Captain H.F. Holland, 24th P.I.

"   "   Lieutenant F.W. Watling, Q.O. Sappers and Miners.

Of these Lieut.-Colonel Lamb and Major Taylor died of their wounds.

NATIVE RANKS.

Killed 21

Wounded 31

As soon as the first light of morning began to grow in the valley, two companies of the 24th advanced and cleared the bazaar of such of the enemy as had remained behind to plunder. The whole place had been thoroughly ransacked, and everything of value destroyed or carried off. The native manager had had a strange experience, and one which few men would envy. He had remained hidden in the back of a tent during the whole night in equal danger and terror of the bullets of the soldiers and the swords of the enemy. Hearing the friendly voices, he emerged uninjured from his retreat.

Desultory firing was maintained by the tribesmen all day.

While the close and desperate fighting, which has been described, was raging in the south camp, the north camp had not been seriously involved, and had spent a quiet, though anxious night. On the sound of the firing on the Kotal being heard, four guns of No.8 Mountain Battery were moved over to the south-east side of the camp, and several star shells were fired. No large body of the enemy was however discovered. Twice during the night the camp was approached by the tribesmen, but a few rounds of shrapnel were sufficient to drive these away.

When General Meiklejohn found that the garrison of the north camp had not been severely engaged, he ordered a force consisting of two guns and the 31st Punjaub Infantry, under Major Gibbs, covered by forty sowars of the 11th Bengal Lancers, and supported by a wing of the 24th, to move out, reconnoitre the valley and clear it, as much as possible, of the enemy. The column advanced in pursuit as far as Bedford Hill. Here they came upon a large gathering of tribesmen, and as it was now evident that a great tribal rising had broken out, Major Gibbs was ordered to return and to bring his stores and troops into the Kotal camp without delay. The infantry and guns thereupon retired and fell back on the camp, covered by the 24th Punjaub Infantry.

As this regiment was being withdrawn, a sudden attack was made from the high ground above the Buddhist road, and directed against the left flank of the troops. A front was immediately shown, and the 24th advanced to meet their assailants. Lieutenant Climo, who commanded, detached a company to the right, and by this turning movement drove them off, inflicting some loss and capturing a standard. This officer's skill and conduct in this retirement was again the subject of commendation in despatches. The troops reached their respective camps at about 11 o'clock. Meanwhile the cavalry had been ordered to push on, if possible, to Chakdara and reinforce the garrison at that post. The task was one of considerable danger, but by crossing and recrossing the Swat River, the squadron managed to cut their way through the tribesmen and reached the fort with slight loss. This brilliant ride will receive a fuller description in a later chapter.

The evacuation of the north camp proceeded very slowly. The troops packed up their kits with great deliberation, and applications were made for transport. None was, however, available. All the camels were at Dargai, on the Indian side of the mountains. Repeated orders to hurry were sent from the Kotal. All hated leaving their belongings behind, having no confidence in the liberality of a paternal Government. As the afternoon passed, the aspect of the enemy became very threatening and formidable. Great numbers drew near to the camp, and the guns were compelled to fire a good many rounds. At length, at 4 o'clock, imperative orders were sent that the north camp was to be at once abandoned, that the force there was to march to the Kotal, and that all baggage and stores, not yet removed, were to be left where they were.

All the tents were struck, but nothing else could be done, and to the deep disgust of all—officers and men—their property was left to the mercies of the enemy. During the night it was all looted and burnt. Many of the officers thus lost every stitch of clothing they possessed. The flames rising from the scene of destruction were visible far and wide, and the tribesmen in the most distant valleys were encouraged to hurry to complete the slaughter of the accursed infidels.

It cannot be doubted, however, that the concentration of the troops was a wise and judicious step. The garrison of the Kotal and south camp was insufficient, and, whatever happened, it was better for the troops to stand or fall together. The situation was also aggravated by the appearance of large numbers of tribesmen from the Utman Khel country, who crowded the hills to the west of the camp, and thus compelled the defenders to hold a greatly extended line. The abandonment of the north camp was carried out none too soon, for the enemy pressed the withdrawal of the troops, and they reached the south camp under cover of the fire of the 24th Punjaub Infantry, and the Guides Cavalry. These latter had arrived in camp at 8.30 that morning after marching all night. They found plenty of employment.

The telegraph had carried the news of the events of the night to all parts of the world. In England those returning from Goodwood Races read the first details of the fighting on the posters of the evening papers. At Simla, the Government of India awoke to find themselves confronted with another heavy task. Other messages recalled all officers to their regiments, and summoned reinforcements to the scene by road and rail. In the small hours of the 27th, the officers of the 11th Bengal Lancers at Nowshera were aroused by a frantic telegraph operator, who was astounded by the news his machine was clicking out. This man in his shirt sleeves, with a wild eye, and holding an unloaded revolver by the muzzle, ran round waking everyone. The whole country was up. The Malakand garrison was being overwhelmed by thousands of tribesmen. All the troops were to march at once. He brandished copies of the wires he had received. In a few moments official instructions arrived. The 11th Bengal Lancers, the 38th Dogras and the 35th Sikhs started at dawn. No.1 and No.7 British Mountain Batteries were also ordered up. The Guides Cavalry had already arrived. Their infantry under Lieutenant Lockhart reached the Kotal at 7.30 P.M. on the 27th, having, in spite of the intense heat and choking dust, covered thirty-two miles in seventeen and a half hours. This wonderful feat was accomplished without impairing the efficiency of the soldiers, who were sent into the picket line, and became engaged as soon as they arrived. An officer who commanded the Dargai post told me, that, as they passed the guard there, they shouldered arms with parade precision, as if to show that twenty-six miles under the hottest sun in the world would not take the polish off the Corps of Guides. Then they breasted the long ascent to the top of the pass, encouraged by the sound of the firing, which grew louder at every step.

Help in plenty was thus approaching as fast as eager men could march, but meanwhile the garrison had to face the danger as best they could alone. As the 31st Punjaub Infantry, who had been the last to leave the north camp, were arriving at the Kotal, about 1000 tribesmen descended in broad daylight and with the greatest boldness, and threatened their left flank. They drove in two pickets of the 24th, and pressed forward vigorously. Lieutenant Climo with two companies advanced up the hill to meet them, supported by the fire of two guns of the Mountain Battery. A bayonet charge was completely successful. The officers were close enough to make effective use of their revolvers. Nine bodies of the enemy were left on the ground, and a standard was captured. The tribesmen then drew off, and the garrison prepared for the attack, which they knew would come with the dark.

As the evening drew on the enemy were observed assembling in ever-increasing numbers. Great crowds of them could be seen streaming along the Chakdara road, and thickly dotting the hills with spots of white. They all wore white as yet. The news had not reached Buner, and the sombre-clad warriors of Ambeyla were still absent. The glare of the flames from the north camp was soon to summon them to the attack of their ancient enemies. The spectacle as night fell was strange, ominous, but not unpicturesque. Gay banners of every colour, shape and device, waved from the surrounding hills. The sunset caught the flashing of swordblades behind the spurs and ridges. The numerous figures of the enemy moved busily about preparing for the attack. A dropping fire from the sharpshooters added an appropriate accompaniment. In the middle, at the bottom of the cup, was the "crater" camp and the main enclosure with the smoke of the evening meal rising in the air. The troops moved to their stations, and, as the shadows grew, the firing swelled into a loud, incessant roar.

The disposition of the troops on the night of the 27th was as follows:—

1. On the right Colonel McRae, with 45th Sikhs and two guns supported by 100 men of the Guides Infantry, held almost the same position astride the Buddhist road as before.
2. In the centre the enclosure and Graded road were defended by—

    31st Punjaub Infantry.
    No.5 Company Q.O. Sappers and Miners.
    The Guides.
    Two Guns.

3. On the left the 24th Punjaub Infantry, with the two remaining guns under Lieutenant Climo, held the approaches from the abandoned north camp and the fort.

Most of this extended line, which occupied a great part of the rim, was formed by a chain of pickets, detached from one another, and fortified by stone breastworks, with supports in rear. But in the centre the old line of the "Sappers' and Miners' enclosure" was adhered to. The bazaar was left to the enemy, but the serai, about a hundred yards in front of the main entrenchment, was held by a picket of twenty-four men of the 31st Punjaub Infantry, under Subadar Syed Ahmed Shah. Here it was that the tragedy of the night occurred.

At eight o'clock, the tribesmen attacked in tremendous force all along the line. The firing at once became intense and continuous. The expenditure of ammunition by the troops was very great, and many thousands of rounds were discharged. On the right Colonel McRae and his Sikhs were repeatedly charged by the swordsmen, many of whom succeeded in forcing their way into the pickets and perished by the bayonet. Others reached the two guns and were cut down while attacking the gunners. All assaults were however beaten off. The tribesmen suffered terrible losses. The casualties among the Sikhs were also severe. In the morning Colonel McRae advanced from his defences, and, covered by the fire of his two guns, cleared the ground in his front of the enemy.

The centre was again the scene of severe fighting. The tribesmen poured into the bazaar and attacked the serai on all sides. This post was a mud-walled enclosure about fifty yards square. It was loopholed for musketry, but had no flank defences. The enemy made determined efforts to capture the place for several hours. Meanwhile, so tremendous was the fire of the troops in the main enclosure, that the attack upon the serai was hardly noticed. For six hours the picket there held out against all assaults, but the absence of flank defences enabled the enemy to come close up to the walls. They then began to make holes through them, and to burrow underneath. The little garrison rushed from place to place repelling these attacks. But it was like caulking a sieve. At length the tribesmen burst in from several quarters, and the sheds inside caught fire. When all the defenders except four were killed or wounded, the Subadar, himself struck by a bullet, ordered the place to be evacuated, and the survivors escaped by a ladder over the back wall, carrying their wounded with them. The bodies of the killed were found next morning, extraordinarily mutilated.

The defence of this post to the bitter end must be regarded as a fine feat of arms. Subadar Syed Ahmed Shah was originally promoted to a commission for an act of conspicuous bravery, and his gallant conduct on this occasion is the subject of a special paragraph in despatches. [The Subadar and the surviving Sepoys have since received the "Order of Merit."]

On the left, the 24th Punjaub Infantry were also hotly engaged, and Lieutenant Costello received his first severe wound from a bullet, which passed through his back and arm. Towards morning the enemy began to press severely. Whereupon Lieutenant Climo, always inclined to bold and vigorous action, advanced from the breastworks to meet them with two companies. The tribesmen held their ground and maintained a continual fire from Martini-Henry rifles. They also rolled down great stones upon the companies. The 24th continued to advance, and drove the enemy from point to point, and position to position, pursuing them for a distance of two miles. "Gallows Tree" hill, against which the first charge of the counter attack was delivered, was held by nearly 1000 tribesmen. On such crowded masses, the fire of the troops was deadly. The enemy left forty dead in the path of Lieutenant Climo's counter attack, and were observed carrying off many wounded. As they retreated, many took refuge in the village of Jalalkot. The guns were hurried up, and ten shells were thrown into their midst, causing great slaughter. The result of this bold stroke was, that the enemy during the rest of the fighting invariably evacuated the hills before daylight enabled the troops to assume the offensive.

Thus the onslaught of the tribesmen had again been successfully repelled by the Malakand garrison. Many had been killed and wounded, but all the tribes for a hundred miles around were hurrying to the attack, and their number momentarily increased. The following casualties occurred on the night of the 27th:—

BRITISH OFFICER.
Wounded—Lieutenant E.W. Costello.

NATIVE RANKS.
Killed.. 12
Wounded 29

During the day the enemy retired to the plain of Khar to refresh themselves. Great numbers of Bunerwals now joined the gathering. The garrison were able to distinguish these newcomers from the Swatis, Utman Khels, Mamunds, Salarzais and others, by the black or dark-blue clothes they wore. The troops were employed in strengthening the defences, and improving the shelters. The tribesmen kept up a harassing and annoying long-range fire, killing several horses of the Guides Cavalry. Towards evening they advanced to renew the attack, carrying hundreds of standards.

As darkness fell, heavy firing recommenced along the whole front. The enemy had apparently plenty of ammunition, and replied with effect to the heavy fire of the troops. The arrangement of the regiments was the same as on the previous night. On the right, Colonel McRae once more held his own against all attacks. In the centre, severe fighting ensued. The enemy charged again and again up to the breastwork of the enclosure. They did not succeed in penetrating. Three officers and several men were however wounded by the fire. Lieutenant Maclean, of the Guides Cavalry, who was attached temporarily to the 31st Punjaub Infantry, had a wonderful escape. A bullet entered his mouth and passed through his cheek without injuring the bone in any way. He continued on duty, and these pages will record his tragic but glorious death a few weeks later at Landakai.

Lieutenant Ford was dangerously wounded in the shoulder. The bullet cut the artery, and he was bleeding to death when Surgeon-Lieutenant J.H. Hugo came to his aid. The fire was too hot to allow of lights being used. There was no cover of any sort. It was at the bottom of the cup. Nevertheless the surgeon struck a match at the peril of his life and examined the wound. The match went out amid a splutter of bullets, which kicked up the dust all around, but by its uncertain light he saw the nature of the injury. The officer had already fainted from the loss of blood. The doctor seized the artery, and, as no other ligature was forthcoming, he remained under fire for three hours holding a man's life, between his finger and thumb. When at length it seemed that the enemy had broken into the camp he picked up the still unconscious officer in his arms, and, without relaxing his hold, bore him to a place of safety. His arm was for many hours paralysed with cramp from the effects of the exertion of compressing the artery.

I think there are few, whatever may be their views or interests, who will not applaud this splendid act of devotion. The profession of medicine, and surgery, must always rank as the most noble that men can adopt. The spectacle of a doctor in action among soldiers, in equal danger and with equal courage, saving life where all others are taking it, allaying pain where all others are causing it, is one which must always seem glorious, whether to God or man. It is impossible to imagine any situation from which a human being might better leave this world, and embark on the hazards of the Unknown.

All through the night, the enemy continued their attacks. They often succeeded in reaching the breastworks—only to die on the bayonets of the defenders. The guns fired case shot, with terrible effect, and when morning dawned the position was still held by the Imperial Forces. The casualties of the night were as follows:—

BRITISH OFFICERS.
Wounded severely—Lieutenant H.B. Ford, 31st Punjaub Infantry.
"   H.L.S. Maclean, the Guides.
Wounded slightly—Lieutenant G. Swinley, 31st Punjaub Infantry.

NATIVE RANKS.

Killed 2

Wounded 13

On the morning of the 29th signalling communication with Chakdara was for a few moments re-established. The garrison of that post announced their safety, and that all attacks had been repulsed with heavy loss, but they reported that ammunition and food were both running short. During the day the enemy again retired to the plain to rest, and prepare for the great attack, which they intended making that night. The hour would be propitious. It was Jumarat, on which day the prophet watches with especial care over the interests of those who die for the faith. Besides, the moon was full, and had not the Great Fakir declared that this should be the moment of victory? The Mullah exhorted them all to the greatest efforts, and declared that he would himself lead the assault. To-night the infidels would be utterly destroyed.

Meanwhile the troops were busily employed, in spite of their terrible fatigues, in strengthening the defences. The bazaar and the serai were levelled. Trees were blown up, and a clear field of fire was obtained in front of the central enclosure. Great bonfires were also prepared on the approaches, to enable the soldiers to take good aim at their assailants, while they were silhouetted against the light. In such occupations the day passed.

The tribesmen continued to fire at long range and shot several horses and mules. These sharpshooters enjoyed themselves immensely. After the relief of Chakdara, it was found that many of them had made most comfortable and effective shelters among the rocks. One man, in particular, had ensconced himself behind an enormous boulder, and had built a little wall of stone, conveniently loopholed, to protect himself when firing. The overhanging rock sheltered him from the heat of the sun. By his side were his food and a large box of cartridges. Here for the whole week he had lived, steadily dropping bullets unto the camp and firing at what an officer described as all "objects of interest." What could be more attractive?

At four o'clock in the afternoon Major Stuart Beatsen, commanding the 11th Bengal Lancers, arrived with his leading squadron. He brought a small supply of ammunition, which the garrison was in sore need of, the expenditure each night being tremendous, some regiments firing as much as 30,000 rounds. The 35th Sikhs and 38th Dogras under Colonel Reid arrived at Dargai, at the foot of the pass, in the evening. They had marched all day in the most intense heat. How terrible that march must have been, may be judged from the fact, that in the 35th Sikhs twenty-one men actually died on the road of heat apoplexy. The fact that these men marched till they dropped dead, is another proof of the soldierly eagerness displayed by all ranks to get to the front. Brigadier-General Meiklejohn, feeling confidence in his ability to hold his own with the troops he had, ordered them to remain halted at Dargai, and rest the next day.

The attack came with the night, but the defences in the centre had been much improved, and the tribesmen were utterly unable to cross the cleared glacis, which now stretched in front of the enclosure. They, however, assailed both flanks with determination, and the firing everywhere became heavy. At 2 A.M. the great attack was delivered. Along the whole front and from every side enormous numbers swarmed to the assault. On the right and left, hand-to-hand fighting took place. Colonel McRae again held his position, but many of the tribesmen died under the very muzzles of the rifles. The 24th Punjaub Infantry on the left were the most severely engaged. The enemy succeeded in breaking into the breastworks, and close fighting ensued, in which Lieutenant Costello was again severely wounded. But the fire of the troops was too hot for anything to live in their front. At 2.30 the Mad Mullah being wounded, another Mullah killed and several hundreds of tribesmen slain, the whole attack collapsed. Nor was it renewed again with vigor. The enemy recognised that their chance of taking the Malakand had passed.

The casualties were as follows on the night of the 29th:—

BRITISH OFFICERS.

Wounded severely—Lieutenant E.W. Costello, 24th P.I., who had already been severely wounded, but continued to do duty.

"   "   Lieutenant F.A. Wynter, R.A.

NATIVE RANKS.

Killed.. 1
Wounded 17

All the next day the enemy could be seen dragging the dead away, and carrying the wounded over the hills to their villages. Reinforcements, however, joined them, and they renewed their attack, but without much spirit, at 9.30 P.M. They were again repulsed with loss. Once, during a thunderstorm that broke over the camp, they charged the 45th Sikhs' position, and were driven off with the bayonet. Only two men were wounded during the night.

In the morning the 38th Dogras and 35th Sikhs marched into the camp. The enemy continued firing into the entrenchments at long range, but without effect. They had evidently realised that the Malakand was too strong to be taken. The troops had a quiet night, and the weary, worn-out men got a little needed sleep. Thus the long and persistent attack on the British frontier station of Malakand languished and ceased. The tribesmen, sick of the slaughter at this point, concentrated their energies on Chakdara, which they believed must fall into their hands. To relieve this hard-pressed post now became the duty of the garrison of Malakand.

The chapter, which may now appropriately end, has described in detail, and, necessarily, at length, the defence of an outpost of our Empire. A surprise, followed by a sustained attack, has been resisted. The enemy, repulsed at every point, have abandoned the attempt, but surround and closely watch the defences. The troops will now assume the offensive, and the hour of reprisals will commence.

The casualties sustained by the Malakand garrison between 26th July and 1st August were as follows:—

BRITISH OFFICERS KILLED AND DIED OF WOUNDS—3.
Lieutenant-Colonel J. Lamb, 24th Punjaub Infantry.
Major W.W. Taylor, 45th Sikhs.
Lieutenant L. Manley, Commissariat.

WOUNDED—10.

Major L. Herbert, D.A.A.G.

Captain G. Baldwin, D.S.O., Guides Cavalry.

Captain H.F. Holland, 24th Punjaub Infantry.

Lieutenant F.A. Wynter, R.A.

  " F.W. Watling, R.E.

  " E.W. Costello, 24th Punjaub Infantry.

  " H.B. Ford, 31st Punjaub Infantry.

  " H.L.S. Maclean, Guides Cavalry.

2nd Lieutenant G. Swinley, 31st Punjaub Infantry.

  " C.V. Keyes, Guides Cavalry.

NATIVE OFFICERS WOUNDED—7.

TOTAL OFFICERS KILLED AND WOUNDED—20.

BRITISH NON-COMMISSIONED OFFICER KILLED.

Sergeant F. Byrne, R.E.

NATIVE NON-COMMISSIONED OFFICERS AND PRIVATES.

	Killed.	Wounded.
No.8 Bengal Mountain Battery	0	5
11th Bengal Lancers	0	3
No.5 Company Q.O. Sappers and Miners	3	18
24th Punjaub Infantry	3	14
31st " "	12	32
38th Dogras	0	1
45th Sikhs	4	28
Q.O. Corps of Guides	3	27

TOTAL NON-COMMISSIONED OFFICERS AND MEN KILLED AND WOUNDED—153.

CHAPTER V:

THE RELIEF OF CHAKDARA

While the events described in the last chapter had been watched with interest and attention in all parts of the world, they were the subject of anxious consultation in the Council of the Governor-General. It was only natural that the Viceroy, himself, should view with abhorrence the prospect of military operations on a large scale, which must inevitably lead to closer and more involved relations with the tribes of the Afghan border. He belonged to that party in the State which has clung passionately, vainly, and often unwisely to a policy of peace and retrenchment. He was supported in his reluctance to embark on warlike enterprises by the whole force of the economic situation. No moment could have been less fitting: no man more disinclined. That Lord Elgin's Viceroyalty and the Famine year should have been marked by the greatest Frontier War in the history of the British Empire in India, vividly displays how little an individual, however earnest his motives, however great his authority, can really control the course of public affairs.

The Council were called upon to decide on matters, which at once raised the widest and most intricate questions of frontier policy; which might involve great expense; which might well influence the development and progress of the great populations committed to their charge. It would be desirable to consider such matters from the most lofty and commanding standpoints; to reduce detail to its just proportions; to examine the past, and to peer into the future. And yet, those who sought to look thus on the whole situation, were immediately confronted with the picture of the rock of Chakdara, fringed and dotted with the white smoke of musketry, encircled by thousands of fierce assailants, its garrison fighting for their lives, but confident they would not be deserted. It was impossible to see further than this. All Governments, all Rulers, meet the same difficulties. Wide considerations of principle, of policy, of consequences or of economics are brushed aside by an impetuous emergency. They have to decide off-hand. The statesman has to deal with events. The historian, who has merely to record them, may amuse his leisure by constructing policies, to explain instances of successful opportunism.

On the 30th of July the following order was officially published: "The Governor-General in Council sanctions the despatch of a force, to be styled the Malakand Field Force, for the purpose of holding the Malakand, and the adjacent posts, and of operating against the neighbouring tribes as may be required."

The force was composed as follows:—

1st Brigade.

Commanding—Colonel W.H. Meiklejohn, C.B., C.M.G., with the local rank of Brigadier-General.
    1st Battalion Royal West Kent Regiment.
    24th Punjaub Infantry.
    31st Punjaub Infantry.
    45th (Rattray's) Sikhs.
    Sections A and B of No.1 British Field Hospital.
    No.38 Native Field Hospital.
    Sections A and B of No.50 Native Field Hospital.

2nd Brigade.

Commanding—Brigadier-General P.D. Jeffreys, C.B.
    1st Battalion East Kent Regiment (the Buffs).
    35th Sikhs.
    38th Dogras.
    Guides Infantry.
    Sections C and D of No.1 British Field Hospital.
    No.37 Native Field Hospital.
    Sections C and D of No.50 Native Field Hospital.

Divisional Troops.

4 Squadrons 11th Bengal Lancers.
1   "   10th   "   "
2   "   Guides Cavalry.

22nd Punjaub Infantry.
2 Companies 21st Punjaub Infantry.
10th Field Battery.
6 Guns No.1 British Mountain Battery.
6   "   No.7   "   "   "
6   "   No.8 Bengal   "   "
No.5 Company Madras Sappers and Miners.
No.3   "   Bombay   "   "   "
Section B of No.13 British Field Hospital.
Sections A and B of No.35 Native Field Hospital.

Line of Communications.
No.34 Native Field Hospital.
Section B of No.1 Native Field Hospital.

[This complete division amounted to a total available field strength of 6800 bayonets, 700 lances or sabres, with 24 guns.]

The command of this powerful force was entrusted to Brigadier-General Sir Bindon Blood, K.C.B., who was granted the local rank of Major-General.

As this officer is the principal character in the tale I have to tell, a digression is necessary to introduce him to the reader. Born of an old Irish family, a clan that has been settled in the west of Ireland for 300 years, and of which he is now the head, Sir Bindon Blood was educated privately, and at the Indian Military College at Addiscombe, and obtained a commission in the Royal Engineers in December, 1860. For the first eleven years he was stationed in England, and it was not until 1871 that he proceeded to India, where he first saw active service in the Jawaki Afridi Expedition (medal with clasp). In 1878 he returned home, but the next year was ordered to the Zulu War. On the conclusion of hostilities, for which he received a second medal and clasp, he again sailed for India and served throughout the Afghan war of 1880, being for some time with the troops at Cabul. In 1882 he accompanied the Army to Egypt, and was with the Highland Brigade, which was the most severely engaged at Tel-el-Kebir. He received the medal and clasp, Khedive's star and the 3rd class of the Medjidie. After the campaign he went home for two years, and in 1885 made another voyage to the East, over which the Russian war-cloud was then hanging. Since then the general has served in India, at first with the Sappers and Miners, with whose reorganisation he was closely associated, and latterly in command of the Agra District. In 1895 he was appointed Chief of the Staff to Sir Robert Low in the Chitral Expedition, and was present at all the actions, including the storming of the Malakand Pass. For his services he received a degree of knighthood of the Military Order of the Bath and the Chitral medal and clasp. He was now marked as a man for high command on the frontier at the first opportunity. That opportunity the great rising of 1897 has presented.

Thirty-seven years of soldering, of war in many lands, of sport of every kind, have steeled alike muscle and nerve. Sir Bindon Blood, himself, till warned by the march of time, a keen polo player, is one of those few officers of high rank in the army, who recognise the advantages to soldiers of that splendid game. He has pursued all kinds of wild animals in varied jungles, has killed many pig with the spear and shot every species of Indian game, including thirty tigers to his own rifle.

It would not be fitting for me, a subaltern of horse, to offer any criticism, though eulogistic, on the commander under whom I have had the honour to serve in the field. I shall content myself with saying, that the general is one of that type of soldiers and administrators, which the responsibilities and dangers of an Empire produce, a type, which has not been, perhaps, possessed by any nation except the British, since the days when the Senate and the Roman people sent their proconsuls to all parts of the world.

Sir Bindon Blood was at Agra, when, on the evening of the 28th of July, he received the telegram from the Adjutant-General in India, appointing him to the command of the Malakand Field Force, and instructing him to proceed at once to assume it. He started immediately, and on the 31st formally took command at Nowshera. At Mardan he halted to make arrangements for the onward march of the troops. Here, at 3 A.M. on the 1st of August, he received a telegram from Army Headquarters informing him, that Chakdara Fort was hard pressed, and directing him to hurry on to Malakand, and attempt its relief at all costs. The great numbers of the enemy, and the shortness of ammunition and supplies from which the garrison were suffering, made the task difficult and the urgency great. Indeed I have been told, that at Simla on the 1st of August it was feared, that Chakdara was doomed, and that sufficient troops to fight their way to its relief could not be concentrated in time. The greatest anxiety prevailed. Sir Bindon Blood replied telegraphically that "knowing the ground" as he did, he "felt serenely confident." He hurried on at once, and, in spite of the disturbed state of the country, reached the Malakand about noon on the 1st of August.

The desperate position of the garrison of Chaldara was fully appreciated by their comrades at the Malakand. As the night of the 31st had been comparatively quiet, Brigadier-General Meiklejohn determined to attempt to force his way to their relief the next day. He accordingly formed a column as follows:—

45th Sikhs.
24th Punjaub Infantry.
No.5 Company Sappers and Miners.
4 Guns of No.8 Mountain Battery.

At 11 A.M. he sent the cavalry, under Lieutenant-Colonel Adams of the Guides, to make a dash for the Amandara Pass, and if it were unoccupied to seize it. The three squadrons started by the short road to the north camp. As soon as the enemy saw what was going on, they assembled in great numbers to oppose the advance. The ground was most unsuitable for cavalry. Great boulders strewed the surface. Frequent nullahs intersected the plain, and cramped the action of the horsemen. The squadrons soon became hotly engaged. The Guides made several charges. The broken nature of the ground favoured the enemy. Many of them were, however, speared or cut down. In one of these charges Lieutenant Keyes was wounded. While he was attacking one tribesman, another came up from behind, and struck him a heavy blow on the shoulder with a sword. Though these Swatis keep their swords at razor edge, and though the blow was sufficiently severe to render the officer's arm useless for some days, it raised only a thin weal, as if from a cut of a whip. It was a strange and almost an inexplicable escape.

The enemy in increasing numbers pressed upon the cavalry, who began to get seriously involved. The tribesmen displayed the greatest boldness and determination. At length Lieut.-Colonel Adams had to order a retirement. It was none too soon. The tribesmen were already working round the left flank and thus threatening the only line of retreat. The squadrons fell back, covering each other by dismounted fire. The 24th Punjaub Infantry protected their flank as they reached the camp. The cavalry losses were as follows:—

BRITISH OFFICERS.

Wounded severely—Captain G.M. Baldwin, the Guides.
" slightly—Lieutenant C.V. Keyes, the Guides.

NATIVE RANKS.

	Killed	Wounded
11th Bengal Lancers 0	3
Horses... 1	4
Guides Cavalry 1	10
Horses... 3	18

Total casualties—16 men and 26 horses.

The vigorous resistance which the cavalry had encountered, and the great numbers and confidence that the enemy had displayed, effectually put an end to any idea of relieving Chakdara that day. The tribesmen were much elated by their temporary success, and the garrison, worn and wearied by the incessant strain, both mental and physical, were proportionately cast down. Every one anticipated tremendous fighting on the next day. Make the attempt, they must at all hazards. But there were not wanting those who spoke of "forlorn hopes" and "last chances." Want of sleep and rest had told on all ranks. For a week they had grappled with a savage foe. They were the victors, but they were out of breath.

It was at this moment, that Sir Bindon Blood arrived and assumed the command. He found General Meiklejohn busily engaged in organising a force of all arms, which was to move to the relief of Chakdara on the following day. As it was dangerous to denude the Malakand position of troops, this force could not exceed 1000 rifles, the available cavalry and four guns. Of these arrangements Sir Bindon Blood approved. He relieved Brigadier-General Meiklejohn of the charge of the Malakand position, and gave him the command of the relieving column. Colonel Reid was then placed in command of Malakand, and instructed to strengthen the pickets at Castle Rock, as far as possible, and to be ready with a force taken from them, to clear the high ground on the right of the Graded road. The relieving column was composed as follows:—

400 Rifles 24th Punjaub Infantry.
400　　"　　45th Sikhs.
200　　"　　Guides Infantry.
2 Squadrons 11th Bengal Lancers (under Lieut.-Col. R.B. Adams.)
2　　　"　　Guides Cavalry　　　"　　　"　　　"
4 Guns No.8 Mountain Battery.
50 Sappers of No.5 Company.
Hospital details.

Sir Bindon Blood ordered General Meiklejohn to assemble this force before dark near the centre of the camp at a grove of trees called "Gretna Green," to bivouac there for the night, and to be ready to start with the first light of morning. During the afternoon the enemy, encouraged by their success with the cavalry in the morning, advanced boldly to the pickets and the firing was continuous. So heavy indeed did it become between eleven and twelve o'clock at night, that the force at "Gretna Green" got under arms. But towards morning the tribesmen retired.

The reader may, perhaps, have in his mind the description of the Malakand as a great cup with jagged clefts in the rim. Much of this rim was still held by the enemy. It was necessary for any force trying to get out of the cup, to fight their way along the narrow roads through the clefts, which were commanded by the heights on either side. For a considerable distance it was impossible to deploy. Therein lay the difficulty of the operation, which the General had now to perform. The relieving column was exposed to the danger of being stopped, just as Colonel McRae had stopped the first attack of the tribesmen along the Buddhist road. On the 1st of August the cavalry had avoided these difficulties by going down the road to the North camp, and making a considerable detour. But they thus became involved in bad ground and had to retire. The "Graded" road, if any, was the road by which Chakdara was to be relieved. Looking at the tangled, rugged nature of the country, it seems extraordinary to an untrained eye, that among so many peaks and points, one should be of more importance than another. Yet it is so. On the high ground, in front of the position that Colonel McRae and the 45th Sikhs had held so well, was a prominent spur. This was the key which would unlock the gate and set free the troops, who were cramped up within. Every one realised afterwards how obvious this was and wondered they had not thought of it before. Sir Bindon Blood selected the point as the object of his first attack, and it was against this that he directed Colonel Goldney with a force of about 300 men to move, as soon as he should give the signal to advance.

At half-past four in the morning of the 2nd of August he proceeded to "Gretna Green" and found the relieving column fallen in, and ready to march at daybreak. All expected a severe action. Oppressed with fatigue and sleeplessness, there were many who doubted that it would be successful. But though tired, they were determined, and braced themselves for a desperate struggle. The General-in-chief was, as he had said, confident and serene. He summoned the different commanding officers, explained his plans, and shook hands all round. It was a moment of stern and high resolve. Slowly the first faint light of dawn grew in the eastern sky. The brightness of the stars began to pale. Behind the mountains was the promise of the sun. Then the word was given to advance. Immediately the relieving column set off, four deep, down the "Graded" road. Colonel Goldney simultaneously advanced to the attack of the spur, which now bears his name, with 250 men of the 35th Sikhs and 50 of the 38th Dogras. He moved silently towards the stone shelters, that the tribesmen had erected on the crest. He got to within a hundred yards unperceived. The enemy, surprised, opened an irregular and ineffective fire. The Sikhs shouted and dashed forward. The ridge was captured without loss of any kind. The enemy fled in disorder, leaving seven dead and one prisoner on the ground.

Then the full significance of the movement was apparent alike to friend and foe. The point now gained, commanded the whole of the "Graded" road, right down to its junction with the road to the North camp. The relieving column, moving down the road, were enabled to deploy without loss or delay. The door was open. The enemy, utterly surprised and dumfounded by this manoeuvre, were seen running to and fro in the greatest confusion: in the graphic words of Sir Bindon Blood's despatch, "like ants in a disturbed ant-hill." At length they seemed to realise the situation, and, descending from the high ground, took up a position near Bedford Hill in General Meiklejohn's front, and opened a heavy fire at close range. But the troops were now deployed and able to bring their numbers to bear. Without wasting time in firing, they advanced with the bayonet. The leading company of the Guides stormed the hill in their front with a loss of two killed and six wounded. The rest of the troops charged with even less loss. The enemy, thoroughly panic-stricken, began to fly, literally by thousands, along the heights to the right. They left seventy dead behind them. The troops, maddened by the remembrance of their fatigues and sufferings, and inspired by the impulse of victory, pursued them with a merciless vigour.

Sir Bindon Blood had with his staff ascended the Castle Rock, to superintend the operations generally. From this position the whole field was visible. On every side, and from every rock, the white figures of the enemy could be seen in full flight. The way was open. The passage was forced. Chakdara was saved. A great and brilliant success had been obtained. A thrill of exultation convulsed every one. In that moment the general, who watched the triumphant issue of his plans, must have experienced as fine an emotion as is given to man on earth. In that moment, we may imagine that the weary years of routine, the long ascent of the lower grades of the service, the frequent subordination to incompetence, the fatigues and dangers of five campaigns, received their compensation. Perhaps, such is the contrariness of circumstances, there was no time for the enjoyment of these reflections. The victory had been gained. It remained to profit by it. The enemy would be compelled to retire across the plain. There at last was the chance of the cavalry. The four squadrons were hurried to the scene.

The 11th Bengal Lancers, forming line across the plain, began a merciless pursuit up the valley. The Guides pushed on to seize the Amandara Pass and relieve Chakdara. All among the rice fields and the rocks, the strong horsemen hunted the flying enemy. No quarter was asked or given, and every tribesman caught, was speared or cut down at once. Their bodies lay thickly strewn about the fields, spotting with black and green patches, the bright green of the rice crop. It was a terrible lesson, and one which the inhabitants of Swat and Bajaur will never forget. Since then their terror of Lancers has been extraordinary. A few sowars have frequently been sufficient to drive a hundred of these valiant savages in disorder to the hills, or prevent them descending into the plain for hours.

Meanwhile the infantry had been advancing swiftly. The 45th Sikhs stormed the fortified village of Batkhela near the Amandara Pass, which the enemy held desperately. Lieut.-Colonel McRae, who had been relieved from the command of the regiment by the arrival of Colonel Sawyer, was the first man to enter the village. Eighty of the enemy were bayoneted in Batkheka alone. It was a terrible reckoning.

I am anxious to finish with this scene of carnage. The spectator, who may gaze unmoved on the bloodshed of the battle, must avert his eyes from the horrors of the pursuit, unless, indeed, joining in it himself, he flings all scruples to the winds, and, carried away by the impetus of the moment, indulges to the full those deep-seated instincts of savagery, over which civilisation has but cast a veil of doubtful thickness.

The casualties in the relief of Chakdara were as follows:—

11th Bengal Lancers—killed and died from wounds, 3; wounded,3.

	Killed.	Wounded.
Guides Infantry	2	7
35th Sikhs	2	3
45th Sikhs	0	7
24th Punjaub Infantry	0	5
No.8 Bengal Mountain Battery	0	1
Total Casualties—33		

The news of the relief of Chakdara was received with feelings of profound thankfulness throughout India. And in England, in the House of Commons, when the Secretary of State read out the telegram, there were few among the members who did not join in the cheers. Nor need we pay much attention to those few.

CHAPTER VI:

THE DEFENCE OF CHAKDARA

... That tower of strength
Which stood four-square to all the winds that blew.

                              TENNYSON.

The episode with which this chapter is concerned is one that has often occurred on the out-post line of civilisation, and which is peculiarly frequent in the history of a people whose widespread Empire is fringed with savage tribes. A small band of soldiers or settlers, armed with the resources of science, and strengthened by the cohesion of mutual trust, are assailed in some isolated post, by thousands of warlike and merciless enemies. Usually the courage and equipment of the garrison enable them to hold out until a relieving force arrives, as at Rorke's Drift, Fort Chitral, Chakdara or Gulistan. But sometimes the defenders are overwhelmed, and, as at Saraghari or Khartoum, none are left to tell the tale. There is something strangely terrible in the spectacle of men, who fight— not for political or patriotic reasons, not for the sake of duty or glory—but for dear life itself; not because they want to, but because they have to. They hold the dykes of social progress against a rising deluge of barbarism, which threatens every moment to overflow the banks and drown them all. The situation is one which will make a coward valorous, and affords to brave men opportunities for the most sublime forms of heroism and devotion.

Chakdara holds the passage of the Swat River—a rapid, broad, and at most seasons of the year an unfordable torrent. It is built on a rocky knoll that rises abruptly from the plain about a hundred yards from the mountains. Sketches and photographs usually show only the knoll and buildings on it, and any one looking at them will be struck by the picturesque and impregnable aspect of the little fort, without observing that its proportions are dwarfed, and its defences commanded, by the frowning cliffs, under which it stands. In its construction the principles of defilade have been completely ignored. Standing on the mountain ridge, occupied by the signal tower, it is possible to look or fire right into the fort. Every open space is commanded. Every parapet is exposed. Against an enemy unprovided with artillery, however, it could be held indefinitely; but the fact that all interior communications are open to fire, makes its defence painful to the garrison, and might, by gradually weakening their numbers, lead to its capture.

The narrow, swinging, wire bridge across the Swat is nearly 500 yards long. At the southern end it is closed by a massive iron door, loopholed for musketry, and flanked by two stone towers, in one of which a Maxim gun is mounted. On the further side is the fort itself, which consists of the fortified knoll, a strong stone horn-work, an enclosure for horses, protected by a loopholed wall and much tangled barbed wire, and the signal tower, a detached post 200 yards up the cliff.

The garrison of the place consisted at the time of the outbreak of twenty sowars of the 11th Bengal Lancers and two strong companies of the 45th Sikhs, in all about 200 men, under the command of Lieutenant H.B. Rattray. [The actual strength was as follows: 11th Bengal Lancers, 20 sabres; 45th Sikhs, 180 rifles; 2 British telegraphists; 1 Hospital Havildar; 1 Provost Naick (24th Punjaub Infantry); 1 Jemadar (Dir Levies). British officers—45th Sikhs, Lieutenants Rattray and Wheatley; Surgeon-Captain V. Hugo; Political Agent, Lieutenant Minchin.] As the rumours of an impending rising grew stronger and stronger, and the end of July approached, this officer practised his men in taking stations in the event of an alarm, and made such preparations as he thought necessary for eventualities. On the 23rd he received an official warning from the D.A.A.G. [Deputy-Assistant-Adjutant-General. Surely this astounding title, with that of the Deputy-Assistant-Quarter-Master-General, might be replaced with advantage by the more sensible and appropriate terms "Brigade Adjutant" and "Brigade Quartermaster"!], Major Herbert, that a tribal rising was "possible but not probable." Every precaution was henceforth taken in the fort. On the 26th, a Sepoy, who was out sketching, hurried in with the news that a large body of tribesmen were advancing down the valley, and that he himself had been robbed of his compass, his field-glasses and some money.

But, in spite of the disturbed and threatening situation, the British officers of the Malakand garrison, though they took all military precautions for the defence of their posts, did not abandon their practice of riding freely about the valley, armed only with revolvers. Nor did they cease from their amusements. On the evening of the 26th, Lieutenant Rattray went over to Khar as usual to play polo. Just as the game was ended, he received a letter, brought in haste by two sowars, from Lieutenant Wheatley, the other subaltern at Chakdara, warning him that a great number of Pathans with flags were advancing on the fort. He at once galloped back at full speed, passing close to one large gathering of tribesmen, who for some reason of their own took no notice of him, and so reached the fort in safety, and just in time. Formidable masses of men were then closing in on it. He telegraphed to the staff officer at the Malakand reporting the impending attack. Immediately afterwards the wire was cut by the enemy and the little garrison got under arms.

A havildar of the Khan of Dir's Levies had promised the political agent to give warning of any actual assault, by lighting a fire on the opposite hills. At 10.15 a solitary flame shot up. It was the signal. The alarm was sounded. The garrison went to their posts. For a space there was silence, and then out of the darkness began a fusillade, which did not stop until the 2nd of August. Immediately the figures of the tribesmen, as they advanced to the attack on the western face of the fort, became visible. The defenders opened fire with effect. The enemy pressed on vigorously. Their losses were severe. At length they retreated repulsed.

A second attack was immediately delivered against the north-east corner and again beaten off by the garrison. At 4 A.M. a third assault was made upon the cavalry enclosure. The tribesmen, carrying scaling ladders, advanced with great determination. They were received with a deadly fire. They then drew off, and the first night of the siege was terminated by desultory firing. The garrison remained at their posts all night, and when it became day the enemy were seen to have retired, to the hills to the north-west, whence they maintained a ceaseless fire. Although the defenders were protected by their stone walls, many had strange escapes from the bullets, which fell incessantly into the interior.

Meanwhile, in spite of the vigorous attack that was being made on the Malakand, it had been decided to send some assistance to the little band at Chakdara. Captain Wright and forty sowars of the 11th Bengal Lancers with Captain Baker of the 2nd Bombay Grenadiers and transport officer at the Malakand, started at dawn on the 27th, by the road from the north camp. Before they had gone very far they came under the fire of the enemy on the hills. These did not dare to venture into the plain, but availed themselves of the broken nature of the country. As the squadron reached the road leading to the polo ground, Captain Wright received information that the enemy were collected on the plain and immediately the pace was quickened in the hopes of a charge being possible. But the tribesmen ran to the hills at the sight of the Lancers, and maintained a constant, though luckily, an ill-aimed fire. At length the village of Batkhela was reached, and beyond it the Amandara Pass came in sight. This is a gap in a long spur, which runs from the southern side of the valley to the rapid river in the middle. As the river was then in full flood and unfordable, the only road to Chakdara lay over or through the spur. But the pass was held by the enemy.

Captain Wright had by this time realised, what probably no one at the Malakand then knew, that the enemy's numbers were enormous. The whole way from Malakand to Amandara—every ridge and hill was crowned with their banners. Wherever the ground protected them from the horsemen they gathered thickly. Cemeteries [Cemeteries are frequent and prominent features of Frontier landscapes. Some of them are of great extent: all of remarkable sanctity.], nullahs and villages swarmed with men. Their figures could be seen in all directions. Far beyond the Amandara Pass bands of tribesmen, of varying strengths, could be observed hurrying with their standards to the attack. But these formidable signs, far from deterring the cavalry soldier, only added, by displaying how great was the need of Chakdara, to his determination to force his way through at all costs.

Under a dropping fire from the cemetery on the right of the road, a brief consultation was held. The Amandara defile was occupied on both sides by the enemy. With the loss of perhaps a dozen men the squadron might gallop through. But this meant leaving all who fell, to perish miserably, by torture and mutilation. To attempt to pick up the wounded, would lead to the annihilation of the squadron. Any alternative was preferable, though if there were no other way, the dash would have to be made, and the wounded left. A Sowar now said there was a path round the rock by the bank of the river. Captain Wright determined to take it.

The path was bad. After about half the spur had been passed, it ended abruptly in a steep white rock. It was, in fact, a path leading to a point where the natives were in the habit of floating across the river upon "mussucks" (inflated skins). To go back now was to fail. Without hesitation, the horsemen turned to the right up the hill and among the rocks, trusting to get through somehow. After passing over ground which would be difficult to move across on foot, they saw a gorge to their left which appeared as if it would lead to the open plain, on the other side of the ridge. Down this gorge forty horses huddled together, with no room to pick their way, were scrambling and jumping from rock to rock, apparently as conscious as their riders that their lives depended on their cleverness—when, suddenly, the enemy appeared.

As soon as the tribesmen, who were holding the pass, saw the squadron trot off to their right towards the river, they realised that they intended to make a desperate effort to get through to Chakdara. They knew what the ground was like, and confident they would kill them all, if they could get there soon enough, ran swiftly along the spur. It was a race. The leading tribesmen arrived in time to fire on the cavalry, while they were in the gorge. So close were they, that the officers used their revolvers. But the Pathans were out of breath and shot badly. Several horses were hit, including Captain Wright's, but though the large thigh bone was penetrated, the gallant beast held on, and carried his rider to Chakdara safely.

By the extraordinary activity of the horses the rocks were cleared before the enemy could collect in any strength. But, to the dismay of all, the gorge was found to lead, not to the plain, but to a branch of the river. A broad, swift channel of water of unknown depth confronted the cavalry. To go back was now, however, out of the question. They plunged in. The 11th Bengal Lancers are perhaps better mounted than any native cavalry regiment in India.

Their strong horses just held their own against the current. Several were nearly swept away. Captain Wright was the last to cross. All this time the enemy were firing and approaching. At length the passage was made and the squadron collected on an island of flooded rice fields, in which the horses sank up to their hocks. Beyond this ran another arm of the river about fifty yards wide, and apparently almost as deep as the first. The bullets of the enemy made "watery flashes" on all sides. After passing this second torrent the squadron found themselves again on the same bank of the river as the enemy. They were in swampy ground. Captain Wright dismounted his men and returned the fire. Then he turned back himself, and riding into the stream again, rescued the hospital assistant, whose pony, smaller than the other horses, was being carried off its legs by the force of the water. After this the march was resumed. The squadron kept in the heavy ground, struggling along painfully. The enemy, running along the edge of the rice fields, maintained a continual fire, kneeling down to take good aim. A sowar threw up his hands and fell, shot through the back. Several more horses were hit. Then another man reeled in his saddle and collapsed on the ground. A halt was made. Dismounted fire was opened upon the enemy. The wounded were picked up, and by slow degrees Chakdara was approached, when the Bridgehead Maxim gun compelled the tribesmen to draw off. [For the particulars of this affair I am indebted to Captain Baker, 2nd Bombay Grenadiers, who shared its perils.]

Thus the garrison of the fort received a needed reinforcement. I have given a somewhat long description of this gallant ride, because it shows that there are few obstacles that can stop brave men and good horses. Captain Wright now assumed command of Chakdara, but the direction of the defense he still confided to Lieutenant Rattray, as fighting behind walls is a phase of warfare with which the cavalry soldier is little acquainted.

At 11.30, in the heat of the day the tribesmen attacked again. They surrounded the north and east sides of the fort, and made strenuous efforts to get in. They suffered heavy losses from the musketry of the defence, and their dead lay scattered thickly on the approaches. Nor were they removed till nightfall. Many Ghazis, mad with fanaticism, pressed on carrying standards, heedless of the fire, until they fell riddled with bullets under the very walls.

To communicate with the Malakand was now almost impossible. To heliograph, it was necessary that the operator should be exposed to a terrible fire. In the evening the signal tower was surrounded by men in stone sungars, who kept up an incessant fusillade, and made all exposure, even for an instant, perilous.

At midday, after the repulse of the main attack, the guard of the signal tower was reinforced by six men, and food and water were also sent up. This difficult operation was protected by the fire of both the Maxims, and of all the garrison who could be spared from other points. Until the 1st of August, water was sent up daily to the signal tower in this way. The distance was long and the road steep. The enemy's fire was persistent. Looking at the ground it seems wonderful that supplies could have been got through at all.

As night approached, the defenders prepared to meet a fresh attack. Lieutenant Wheatley, observing the points behind which the enemy usually assembled, trained the fort Maxim and the 9-pounder gun on them, while daylight lasted. At 11 P.M. the tribesmen advanced with shouts, yells and the beating of drums. The gun and the Maxims were fired, and it is said that no fewer than seventy men perished by the single discharge. At any rate the assault was delayed for an hour and a half. All day long the garrison had remained at their posts. It was hoped they would now get a little rest. But at 1 o'clock the attack was renewed on the north-east corner. Again the enemy brought up scaling ladders and charged with desperate ferocity. They were shot down.

Meanwhile every spare moment was devoted to improving the cover of the garrison. Captain Baker applied himself to this task, and used every expedient. Logs, sand bags, stones, boxes filled with earth were piled upon the walls. It is due to these precautions that the loss of life was no larger.

Continuous firing occupied the 28th, and at 5.30 P.M. the enemy again assaulted. As in previous attacks, they at first advanced by twos and threes, making little dashes over the open ground, for bits of natural cover, and for the stone sungars they had built all round the fort under cover of darkness. Some of these were within 200 yards of the wall. As they advanced the fire became intense. Then the main rush was delivered. In a great semi-circle round the face of the fort held by the cavalry, and displaying nearly 200 standards whose gay colours were representative of every tribe on the border, they charged right up to the walls. Some of them actually got across the tangled barbed wire and were destroyed in the enclosure. But all efforts were defeated by the garrison, and towards morning the attack melted away, and only the usual sharpshooters remained. Some of these displayed a singular recklessness. One man climbed up into the barbed wire and fired three shots at the defenders at close quarters before he was killed.

Thursday morning dawned on similar scenes. The garrison employed such intervals as occurred in strengthening their defences and improving their cover, particularly in the approaches to the Maxim and field gun platforms. At 3 P.M. the enemy came out of Chakdara village, and, carrying ladders to scale the walls, and bundles of grass to throw on the barbed wire, made a formidable effort. They directed the attack mainly against the signal station. This building is a strong, square, stone tower. Its entrance is above six feet from the ground. All around the top runs a machiconlis gallery, a kind of narrow balcony, with holes in the floor to fire through. It is well provided with loopholes. At 4 o'clock it was closely assailed. The garrison of the fort aided the tower guard by their fire. So bold were the enemy in their efforts, that they rushed in under the musketry of the defence, and lighted a great heap of grass about three yards from the doorway. The flames sprang up. A howl of ferocious delight arose. But the tribesmen relapsed into silence, when they saw that no real harm was done. At sunset the fore sight of the fort Maxim was shot away, and the defenders were temporarily deprived of the service of that powerful weapon. They soon managed, however, to rig up a makeshift, which answered all practical purposes. At 8 P.M. the enemy wearied of the struggle, and the firing died away to desultory skirmishing. They toiled all night carrying away their dead, but next morning over fifty bodies were still lying around the signal tower. Their losses had been enormous.

The morning of the 30th brought no cessation of the fighting, but the enemy, disheartened by their losses of the previous night, did not attack until 7 P.M. At that hour they advanced and made a fresh effort. They were again repulsed. Perhaps the reader is tired of the long recital of the monotonous succession of assaults and repulses. What must the garrison have been by the reality? Until this day—when they snatched a few hours' sleep—they had been continually fighting and watching for ninety-six hours. Like men in a leaking ship, who toil at the pumps ceaselessly and find their fatigues increasing and the ship sinking hour by hour, they cast anxious, weary eyes in the direction whence help might be expected. But none came. And there are worse deaths than by drowning.

Men fell asleep at the loopholes and at the service of the field gun. Even during the progress of the attacks, insulted nature asserted itself, and the soldiers drifted away from the roar of the musketry, and the savage figures of the enemy, to the peaceful unconsciousness of utter exhaustion. The officers, haggard but tireless, aroused them frequently.

At other times the brave Sepoys would despair. The fort was ringed with the enemy. The Malakand, too, was assailed. Perhaps it was the same elsewhere. The whole British Raj seemed passing away in a single cataclysm. The officers encouraged them. The Government of the Queen-Empress would never desert them. If they could hold out, they would be relieved. If not, they would be avenged. Trust in the young white men who led them, and perhaps some dim half-idolatrous faith in a mysterious Sovereign across the seas, whose soldiers they were, and who would surely protect them, restored their fainting strength. The fighting continued.

During the whole time of the siege the difficulty of maintaining signalling communication with the Malakand was extreme. But for the heroism of the signallers, it would have been insuperable. One man in particular, Sepoy Prem Singh, used every day at the risk of his life to come out through a porthole of the tower, establish his heliograph, and, under a terrible fire from short range, flash urgent messages to the main force. The extreme danger, the delicacy of the operation of obtaining connection with a helio, the time consumed, the composure required, these things combined to make the action as brave as any which these or other pages record. [A proposal has recently been made, to give the Victoria Cross to native soldiers who shall deserve it. It would seem that the value of such a decoration must be enhanced by making it open to all British subjects. The keener the competition, the greater the honor of success. In sport, in courage, and in the sight of heaven, all men meet on equal terms.] Early on Saturday morning a supply of water was sent to the guard of the signal tower. It was the last they got until 4.30 on Monday afternoon.

When the attack on the fort began, the enemy numbered perhaps 1500 men. Since then they had been increasing every day, until on the 1st and 2nd, they are estimated to have been between 12,000 and 14,000 strong. Matters now began to assume a still graver aspect. At 5 o'clock on the evening of the 31st a renewed attack was made in tremendous force on the east side of the fort. But it was beaten back with great loss by the Maxims and the field gun. All night long the firing continued, and Sunday morning displayed the enemy in far larger numbers than hitherto. They now captured the Civil Hospital, a detached building, the walls of which they loopholed, and from which they maintained a galling fire. They also occupied the ridge, leading to the signal tower, thus cutting off all communication with its guard. No water reached those unfortunate men that day. The weather was intensely hot. The fire from the ridge made all interior communication difficult and dangerous. The enemy appeared armed to a great extent with Martini-Henry rifles and Sniders, and their musketry was most harassing. The party in the tower kept sending by signal pressing requests for water, which could not be supplied. The situation became critical. I quote the simple words of Lieutenant Rattray's official report:—

"Matters now looked so serious that we decided to send an urgent appeal for help, but owing to the difficulty and danger of signalling we could not send a long message, and made it as short as possible, merely sending the two words, 'Help us.'"

Still the garrison displayed a determined aspect, and though the tribesmen occupied the ridge, the Civil Hospital and an adjoining nullah, none set foot within the defences.

At length the last day of the struggle came. At daybreak the enemy in tremendous numbers came on to the assault, as if resolute to take the place at any cost. They carried scaling ladders and bundles of grass. The firing became intense. In spite of the cover of the garrison several men were killed and wounded by the hail of bullets which was directed against the fort, and which splashed and scarred the walls in every direction.

Then suddenly, as matters were approaching a crisis, the cavalry of the relieving column appeared over the Amandara ridge. The strong horsemen mercilessly pursued and cut down all who opposed them. When they reached the Bridgehead on the side of the river remote from the fort, the enemy began to turn and run. The garrison had held out stubbornly and desperately throughout the siege. Now that relief was at hand, Lieutenant Rattray flung open the gate, and followed by half a dozen men charged the Civil Hospital. Captain Baker and Lieutenant Wheatley followed with a few more. The hospital was recaptured. The enemy occupying it, some thirty in number, were bayoneted. It was a finish in style. Returning, the sallying party found the cavalry—the 11th Bengal Lancers—checked by a sungar full of tribesmen. This they charged in flank, killing most of its occupants, and driving the rest after their comrades in rout and ruin. The last man to leave the sungar shot Lieutenant Rattray in the neck, but that officer, as distinguished for physical prowess as for military conduct, cut him down. This ended the fighting. It is not possible to think of a more fitting conclusion.

The casualties in the siege were as follows:—

	Killed	Wounded
11th B.L.	1	1
45th Sikhs	4	10
Dir Levies	1	0
Followers	1	2
Total, all ranks—20		

This was the loss; but every man in the fort had held death at arm's length, for seven nights, and seven days.

It is a significant fact, that, though the cavalry horses were exposed to the enemy's fire the whole time, hardly any were killed or wounded. The tribesmen, feeling sure that the place was theirs, and hoping that these fine beasts would fall unto their hands alive, had abstained from shooting them.

As far as could be ascertained by careful official inquiries the enemy lost over 2000 men in the attack upon Chakdara.

[The following statistics as to the expenditure of ammunition may be of interest:—

		Rounds.
28th July.	Maxim	843
"	Martini-Henry	7170
29th July.	Maxim	667
"	Martini-Henry	4020
30th July.	Maxim	200
"	Martini-Henry	5530
31st July.	Maxim	180
"	Martini-Henry	2700

This is approximately twenty rounds per man per diem. The fire control must have been excellent.]

CHAPTER VII:

THE GATE OF SWAT

The Malakand Pass gives access to the valley of the Swat, a long and wide trough running east and west, among the mountains. Six miles further to the east, at Chakdara, the valley bifurcates. One branch runs northward towards Uch, and, turning again to the west, ultimately leads to the Panjkora River and beyond to the great valley of Nawagai. For some distance along this branch lies the road to Chitral, and along it the Malakand Field Force will presently advance against the Mohmands. The other branch prolongs the valley to the eastward. A few miles beyond Chakdara a long spur, jutting from the southern mountains, blocks the valley. Round its base the river has cut a channel. The road passes along a narrow stone causeway between the river and the spur. Here is the Landakai position, or as the tribesmen have for centuries called it, the "Gate of Swat." Beyond this gate is Upper Swat, the ancient, beautiful and mysterious "Udyana." This chapter will describe the forcing of the gate and the expedition to the head of the valley.

The severe fighting at the Malakand and Chakdara had shown how formidable was the combination, which had been raised against the British among the hill tribes. The most distant and solitary valleys, the most remote villages, had sent their armed men to join in the destruction of the infidels. All the Banjaur tribes had been well represented in the enemy's ranks. The Bunerwals and the Utman Khels had risen to a man. All Swat had been involved. Instead of the two or three thousand men that had been estimated as the extreme number, who would follow the Mad Fakir, it was now known that over 12,000 were in arms. In consequence of the serious aspect which the military and political situation had assumed, it was decided to mobilise a 3rd and Reserve Brigade composed as follows:—

3rd Brigade.
Commanding—Brigadier-General J.H. Wodehouse, C.B., C.M.G.
2nd Battalion Highland Light Infantry.
1st   "   Gordon Highlanders.
21st Punjaub Infantry.
2nd Battalion 1st Gurkhas.
No. 3 Company Bombay Sappers and Miners.
" 14 British Field Hospital.
" 45 Native   "   "
"   1 Field Medical Depot.

The fighting of the preceding fortnight had left significant and terrible marks on the once smiling landscape. The rice crops were trampled down in all directions. The ruins of the villages which had been burned looked from a distance like blots of ink. The fearful losses which the enemy had sustained, had made an appreciable diminution, not of an army, but of a population. In the attacks upon the Malakand position, about 700 tribesmen had perished. In the siege of Chakdara, where the open ground had afforded opportunity to the modern weapons and Maxim guns, over 2000 had been killed and wounded. Many others had fallen in the relief of Chakdara and in the cavalry pursuit. For days their bodies lay scattered about the country. In the standing crops, in the ruins of villages, and among the rocks, festering bodies lay in the blazing sun, filling the valley with a dreadful smell. To devour these great numbers of vultures quickly assembled and disputed the abundant prey with the odious lizards, which I have mentioned in an earlier chapter, and which emerged from holes and corners to attack the corpses. Although every consideration of decency and health stimulated the energy of the victors in interring the bodies of their enemies, it was some days before this task could be accomplished, and even then, in out-of-the-way places, there remained a good many that had escaped the burying parties.

Meanwhile the punishment that the tribesmen of the Swat Valley had received, and their heavy losses, had broken the spirit of many, and several deputations came to make their submission.

The Lower Swatis surrendered unconditionally, and were allowed to return to their villages. Of this permission they at once availed themselves, and their figures could be seen moving about their ruined homes and endeavouring to repair the damage. Others sat by the roadside and watched in sullen despair the steady accumulation of troops in their valley, which had been the only result of their appeal to arms.

It is no exaggeration to say, that perhaps half the tribesmen who attacked the Malakand, had thought that the soldiers there, were the only troops that the Sirkar [The Government] possessed. "Kill these," they said, "and all is done." What did they know of the distant regiments which the telegraph wires were drawing, from far down in the south of India? Little did they realise they had set the world humming; that military officers were hurrying 7000 miles by sea and land from England, to the camps among the mountains; that long trains were carrying ammunition, material and supplies from distant depots to the front; that astute financiers were considering in what degree their action had affected the ratio between silver and gold, or that sharp politicians were wondering how the outbreak in Swat might be made to influence the impending bye-elections. These ignorant tribesmen had no conception of the sensitiveness of modern civilisation, which thrills and quivers in every part of its vast and complex system at the slightest touch.

They only saw the forts and camps on the Malakand Pass and the swinging bridge across the river.

While the people of Lower Swat, deserted by the Mad Mullah, and confronted with the two brigades, were completely humbled and subdued, the Upper Swatis, encouraged by their priests, and, as they believed, safe behind their "gate," assumed a much more independent air. They sent to inquire what terms the Government would offer, and said they would consider the matter. Their contumacious attitude, induced the political officers to recommend the movement of troops through their country, to impress them with the determination and power of the Sirkar.

The expedition into the Upper Swat Valley was accordingly sanctioned, and Sir Bindon Blood began making the necessary preparations for the advance. The prospects of further fighting were eagerly welcomed by the troops, and especially by those who had arrived too late for the relief of Chakdara, and had had thus far, only long and dusty marches to perform. There was much speculation and excitement as to what units would be selected, every one asserting that his regiment was sure to go; that it was their turn; and that if they were not taken it would be a great shame.

Sir Bindon Blood had however already decided. He had concentrated a considerable force at Amandara in view of a possible advance, and as soon as the movement was sanctioned organised the column as follows:—

1st Brigade.
Commanding—Brigadier-General Meiklejohn.
    Royal West Kent Regiment.
    24th Punjaub Infantry.
    31st   "   "
    45th Sikhs
With the following divisional troops:-
    10th Field Battery.
    No.7 British Mountain Battery.
    " 8 Bengal   "   "
    " 5 Company Madras Sappers and Miners.
    2 Squadrons Guides Cavalry.
    4   "   11th Bengal Lancers.

This force amounted to an available fighting strength of 3500 rifles and sabres, with eighteen guns. Supplies for twelve days were carried, and the troops proceeded on "the 80 lb. scale" of baggage, which means, that they did not take tents, and a few other comforts and conveniences.

Before the force started, a sad event occurred. On the 12th of August, Lieut.-Colonel J. Lamb, who had been wounded on the night of the 26th of July, died. An early amputation might have saved his life; but this was postponed in the expectation that the Rontgen Rays would enable the bullet to be extracted. The Rays arrived from India after some delay. When they reached Malakand, the experiment was at once made. It was found, however, that the apparatus had been damaged in coming up, and no result was obtained. Meanwhile mortification had set in, and the gallant soldier died on the Sunday, from the effects of an amputation which he was then too weak to stand. His thigh bone had been completely shattered by the bullet. He had seen service in Afghanistan and the Zhob Valley and had been twice mentioned in despatches.

On the 14th Sir Bindon Blood joined the special force, and moved it on the 16th to Thana, a few miles further up the valley. At the same time he ordered Brigadier-General Wodehouse to detach a small column in the direction of the southern passes of Buner. The Highland Light Infantry, No.3 Company Bombay Sappers and Miners, and one squadron of the 10th Bengal Lancers accordingly marched from Mardan, where the 3rd Brigade then was, to Rustum. By this move they threatened the Bunerwals and distracted their attention from the Upper Swat Valley. Having thus weakened the enemy, Sir Bindon Blood proceeded to force the "Gate of Swat."

On the evening of the 16th, a reconnaissance by the 11th Bengal Lancers, under Major Beatson, revealed the fact, that the Landakai position was strongly held by the enemy. Many standards were displayed, and on the approach of the cavalry, shots were fired all along the line. The squadron retired at once, and reported the state of affairs. The general decided to attack at day-break.

At 6.30 A.M. on the 17th, the cavalry moved off, and soon came in contact with the tribesmen in some Buddhist ruins near a village, called Jalala. A skirmish ensued. Meanwhile the infantry were approaching. The main position of the enemy was displayed. All along the crest of the spur of Landakai could be seen a fringe of standards, dark against the sky. Beneath them the sword blades of the tribesmen glinted in the sunlight. A long line of stone sungars crowned the ridge, and behind the enemy clustered thickly. It is estimated that over 5000 were present.

It is not difficult to realise what a strong position this was. On the left of the troops was an unfordable river. On their right the mountains rose steeply. In front was the long ridge held by the enemy. The only road up the valley was along the causeway, between the ridge and the river. To advance further, it was necessary to dislodge the enemy from the ridge. Sir Bindon Blood rode forward, reconnoitered the ground, and made his dispositions.

To capture the position by a frontal attack would involve heavy loss. The enemy were strongly posted, and the troops would be exposed to a heavy fire in advancing. On the other hand, if the ridge could once be captured, the destruction of the tribesmen was assured. Their position was good, only as long as they held it. The moment of defeat would be the moment of ruin. The reason was this. The ground behind the ridge was occupied by swampy rice fields, and the enemy could only retire very slowly over it. Their safe line of retreat lay up the spur, and on to the main line of hills. They were thus formed with their line of retreat in prolongation of their front. This is, of course, tactically one of the worst situations that people can get into.

Sir Bindon Blood, who knew what the ground behind the ridge was like, perceived at once how matters stood, and made his plans accordingly. He determined to strike at the enemy's left, thus not only turning their flank, but cutting off their proper line of retreat. If once his troops held the point, where the long ridge ran into the main hills, all the tribesmen who had remained on the ridge would be caught. He accordingly issued orders as follows:—

The Royal West Kent were to mask the front and occupy the attention of the enemy. The rest of the infantry, viz., 24th and 31st Punjaub Infantry and the 45th Sikhs, were to ascend the hills to the right, and deliver a flank attack on the head of the ridge. The cavalry were to be held in readiness to dash forward along the causeway—to repair which a company of sappers was posted—as soon as the enemy were driven off the ridge which commanded it, and pursue them across the rice fields into the open country beyond. The whole of the powerful artillery was to come into action at once.

The troops then advanced. The Royal West Kent Regiment began the fight, by driving some of the enemy from the Buddhist ruins on a small spur in advance of the main position. The 10th Field Battery had been left in rear in case the guns might stick in the narrow roads near Thana village. It had, however, arrived safely, and now trotted up, and at 8.50 A.M. opened fire on the enemy's position and at a stone fort, which they occupied strongly. A few minutes later No.7 Mountain Battery came into action from the spur, which the Royal West Kent had taken. A heavy artillery fire thus prepared the way for the attack. The great shells of the Field Artillery astounded the tribesmen, who had never before witnessed the explosion of a twelve-pound projectile. The two mountain batteries added to their discomfiture. Many fled during the first quarter of an hour of the bombardment. All the rest took cover on the reverse slope and behind their sungars.

Meanwhile the flank attack was developing. General Meiklejohn and his infantry were climbing up the steep hillside, and moving steadily towards the junction of the ridge with the main hill. At length the tribesmen on the spur perceived the danger that was threatening them. They felt the grip on their line of retreat. They had imagined that the white troops would try and force their path along the causeway, and had massed considerable reserves at the lower end of the ridge. All these now realised that they were in great danger of being cut off. They were on a peninsula, as it were, while the soldiers were securing the isthmus. They accordingly began streaming along the ridge towards the left, at first with an idea of meeting the flank attack, but afterwards, as the shell fire grew hotter, and the musketry increased, only in the hope of retreat. Owing to the great speed with which the mountaineers move about the hills, most of them were able to escape before the flank attack could cut them off. Many however, were shot down as they fled, or were killed by the artillery fire. A few brave men charged the 31st Punjaub Infantry, but were all destroyed.

Seeing the enemy in full flight, Sir Bindon Blood ordered the Royal West Kent to advance against the front of the now almost deserted ridge. The British infantry hurrying forward climbed the steep hill and captured the stone sungars. From this position they established touch with the flank attack, and the whole force pursued the flying tribesmen with long-range fire.

The "Gate of Swat" had been forced. It was now possible for troops to advance along the causeway. This had, however, been broken in various places by the enemy. The sappers and miners hastened forward to repair it. While this was being done, the cavalry had to wait in mad impatience, knowing that their chance lay in the plains beyond. As soon as the road was sufficiently repaired to allow them to pass in single file, they began struggling along it, and emerged at the other end of the causeway in twos and threes.

An incident now ensued, which, though it afforded an opportunity for a splendid act of courage, yet involved an unnecessary loss of life, and must be called disastrous. As the cavalry got clear of the broken ground, the leading horsemen saw the tribesmen swiftly running towards the hills, about a mile distant. Carried away by the excitement of the pursuit, and despising the enemy for their slight resistance, they dashed impetuously forward in the hope of catching them before they could reach the hills.

Lieutenant-Colonel Adams, on entering the plain, saw at once that if he could seize a small clump of trees near a cemetery, he would be able to bring effective dismounted fire to bear on the retreating tribesmen. He therefore collected as many men as possible, and with Lieutenant Maclean, and Lord Fincastle, the Times correspondent, rode in the direction of these points. Meanwhile Captain Palmer, who commanded the leading squadron, and Lieutenant Greaves of the Lancashire Fusiliers, who was acting war correspondent of the Times of India, galloped across the rice fields after the enemy. The squadron, unable to keep up, straggled out in a long string, in the swampy ground.

At the foot of the hills the ground was firmer, and reaching this, the two officers recklessly dashed in among the enemy. It is the spirit that loses the Empire many lives, but has gained it many battles. But the tribesmen, who had been outmanoeuvred rather than outfought, turned savagely on their pursuers. The whole scene was witnessed by the troops on the ridge. Captain Palmer cut down a standard-bearer. Another man attacked him. Raising his arm for a fresh stroke, his wrist was smashed by a bullet. Another killed his horse. Lieutenant Greaves, shot through the body, fell at the same moment to the ground. The enemy closed around and began hacking him, as he lay, with their swords. Captain Palmer tried to draw his revolver. At this moment two sowars got clear of the swampy rice fields, and at once galloped, shouting, to the rescue, cutting and slashing at the tribesmen. All would have been cut to pieces or shot down. The hillside was covered with the enemy. The wounded officers lay at the foot. They were surrounded. Seeing this Lieutenant-Colonel Adams and Lord Fincastle, with Lieutenant Maclean and two or three sowars, dashed to their assistance. At their charge the tribesmen fell back a little way and opened a heavy fire. Lord Fincastle's horse was immediately shot and he fell to the ground. Rising, he endeavoured to lift the wounded Greaves on to Colonel Adams' saddle, but at this instant a second bullet struck that unfortunate officer, killing him instantly. Colonel Adams was slightly, and Lieutenant Maclean mortally, wounded while giving assistance, and all the horses but two were shot. In spite of the terrible fire, the body of Lieutenant Greaves and the other two wounded officers were rescued and carried to the little clump of trees.

For this gallant feat of arms both the surviving officers, Colonel Adams and Lord Fincastle, were recommended for, and have since received, the Victoria Cross. It was also officially announced, that Lieutenant Maclean would have received it, had he not been killed. There are many, especially on the frontier, where he was known as a fine soldier and a good sportsman, who think that the accident of death should not have been allowed to interfere with the reward of valour.

The extremes of fortune, which befell Lord Fincastle and Lieutenant Greaves, may well claim a moment's consideration. Neither officer was employed officially with the force. Both had travelled up at their own expense, evading and overcoming all obstacles in an endeavour to see something of war. Knights of the sword and pen, they had nothing to offer but their lives, no troops to lead, no duties to perform, no watchful commanding officer to report their conduct. They played for high stakes, and Fortune never so capricious as on the field of battle, dealt to the one the greatest honour that a soldier can hope for, as some think, the greatest in the gift of the Crown, and to the other Death.

The flight of the enemy terminated the action of Landakai. Thus in a few hours and with hardly any loss, the "Gate of Swat," which the tribesmen had regarded as impregnable, had been forced. One squadron of the Guides cavalry, under Captain Brasier Creagh, pursuing the enemy had a successful skirmish near the village of Abueh, and returned to camp about 6.30 in the evening. [This officer was mentioned in despatches for his skill and judgment in this affair; but he is better known on the frontier for his brilliant reconnaissance towards Mamani, a month later, in which in spite of heavy loss he succeeded in carrying out General Hammond's orders and obtained most valuable information.] During the fight about 1000 tribesmen had threatened the baggage column, but these were but poor-spirited fellows, for they retired after a short skirmish with two squadrons of the 11th Bengal Lancers, with a loss of twenty killed and wounded. The total casualties of the day were as follows:—

BRITISH OFFICERS.

Killed—Lieutenant R.T. Greaves, Lancs. Fusiliers.

"   "   H.L.S. Maclean, Guides.

Wounded severely—Captain M.E. Palmer, Guides.

Wounded slightly—Lieutenant-Colonel R.B. Adams, Guides.

NATIVE RANKS—Wounded—5.

FOLLOWERS—Wounded—2.

Total Casualties—11.

It must be remembered, that but for the incident which resulted in the deaths of the officers, and which Sir Bindon Blood described in his official despatch as an "unfortunate contretemps," the total casualties would have only been seven wounded. That so strong a position should have been captured with so little loss, is due, firstly, to the dispositions of the general; and secondly, to the power of the artillery which he had concentrated. The account of the first attempt to storm the Dargai position on the 20th of October, before it had been shaken by artillery fire, when the Dorsetshire Regiment suffered severe loss, roused many reflections among those who had witnessed the action of Landakai.

The next morning, the 18th, the force continued their march up the valley of the Upper Swat. The natives, thoroughly cowed, offered no further opposition and sued for peace. Their losses at Landakai were ascertained to have exceeded 500, and they realised that they had no chance against the regular troops, when these were enabled to use their powerful weapons.

As the troops advanced up the fertile and beautiful valley, all were struck by the numerous ruins of the ancient Buddhists. Here in former times were thriving cities, and civilised men. Here, we learn from Fa-hien, [Record Of Buddhistic Kingdoms. Translated by James Legge, M.A., LL.D.] were "in all 500 Sangharamas," or monasteries. At these monasteries the law of hospitality was thus carried out: "When stranger bhikshus (begging monks) arrive at one of them, their wants are supplied for three days, after which they are told to find a resting-place for themselves." All this is changed by time. The cities are but ruins. Savages have replaced the civilised, bland-looking Buddhists, and the traveller who should apply for hospitality, would be speedily shown "a resting-place," which would relieve his hosts from further trouble concerning him.

"There is a tradition," continues the intrepid monk, who travelled through some of the wildest countries of the earth in the darkest ages of its history, "that when Buddha came to North India, he came to this country, and that he left a print of his foot, which is long or short according to the ideas of the beholder." Although the learned Fa-hien asserts that "it exists, and the same thing is true about it at the present day," the various cavalry reconnaissances failed to discover it, and we must regretfully conclude that it has also been obliterated by the tides of time. Here too, says this Buddhistic Baedeker, is still to be seen the rock on which "He dried his clothes; and the place where He converted the wicked dragon (Naga)." "The rock is fourteen cubits high and more than twenty broad, with one side of it smooth." This may well be believed; but there are so many rocks of all dimensions that the soldiers were unable to make certain which was the scene of the dragon's repentance, and Buddha's desiccation.

His companions went on ahead towards Jellalabad, or some city in that locality, but Fa-hien, charmed with the green and fertile beauties of "the park," remained in the pleasant valley and "kept the summer retreat." Then he descended into the land of So-hoo-to, which is perhaps Buner.

Even in these busy, practical, matter-of-fact, modern times, where nothing is desirable unless economically sound, it is not unprofitable for a moment to raise the veil of the past, and take a glimpse of the world as it was in other days. The fifth century of the Christian era was one of the most gloomy and dismal periods in the history of mankind. The Great Roman Empire was collapsing before the strokes of such as Alaric the Goth, Attila the Hun, and Genseric the Vandal. The art and valour of a classical age had sunk in that deluge of barbarism which submerged Europe. The Church was convulsed by the Arian controversy. That pure religion, which it should have guarded, was defiled with the blood of persecution and degraded by the fears of superstition. Yet, while all these things afflicted the nations of the West, and seemed to foreshadow the decline or destruction of the human species, the wild mountains of Northern India, now overrun by savages more fierce than those who sacked Rome, were occupied by a placid people, thriving, industrious, and intelligent; devoting their lives to the attainment of that serene annihilation which the word nirvana expresses. When we reflect on the revolutions which time effects, and observe how the home of learning and progress changes as the years pass by, it is impossible to avoid the conclusion, perhaps a mournful one, that the sun of civilisation can never shine all over the world at once.

On the 19th, the force reached Mingaora, and here for five days they waited in an agreeable camp, to enable Major Deane to receive the submission of the tribes. These appeared much humbled by their defeats, and sought to propitiate the troops by bringing in supplies of grain and forage. Over 800 arms of different descriptions were surrendered during the halt. A few shots were fired into the camp on the night of the arrival at Mingaora, but the villagers, fearing lest they should suffer, turned out and drove the "snipers" away. On the 21st a reconnaissance as far as the Kotke Pass afforded much valuable information as to the nature of the country. All were struck with the beauty of the scenery, and when on the 24th the force marched back to Barikot, they carried away with them the memory of a beautiful valley, where the green of the rice fields was separated from the blue of the sky by the glittering snow peaks of the Himalayas.

While the troops rested at Barikot, Sir Bindon Blood personally reconnoitred the Karakar Pass, which leads from the Swat Valley into the country of the Bunerwals. The Bunerwals belong to the Yusaf section, of the Yusafzai tribe. They are a warlike and turbulent people. To their valley, after the suppression of the Indian Mutiny, many of the Sepoys and native officers who had been in revolt fled for refuge. Here, partly by force and partly by persuasion, they established themselves. They married women of the country and made a settlement. In 1863 the Bunerwals came into collision with the British Government and much severe fighting ensued, known to history as the Ambeyla Campaign. The refugees from India renewed their quarrel with the white troops with eagerness, and by their extraordinary courage and ferocity gained the name of the "Hindustani Fanatics." At the cost of thirty-six officers and eight hundred men Buner was subdued. The "Crag Picket" was taken for the last time by the 101st Fusiliers, and held till the end of the operations. Elephants, brought at great expense from India, trampled the crops. Most of the "Hindustani Fanatics" perished in the fighting. The Bunerwals accepted the Government terms, and the troops retired. Since then, in 1868, in 1877 and again in 1884 they raided border villages, but on the threat of an expedition paid a fine and made good the damage. The reputation they have enjoyed since their stout resistance in 1863, has enabled them to take a leading position among the frontier tribes; and they have availed themselves of this to foment and aggravate several outbreaks against the British. Their black and dark-blue clothes had distinguished them from the other assailants of Malakand and Chakdara. They had now withdrawn to their valley and thence defied the Government and refused all terms.

As Sir Bindon Blood and his escort approached the top of the pass, a few shots were fired by the watchers there, but there was no opposition. All the Bunerwals had hurried over to defend the southern entrances to their country, which they conceived were in danger of attack from Brigadier-General Wodehouse's force at Rustum. The general reached the Kotal, and saw the whole valley beneath him. Great villages dotted the plains and the aspect was fertile and prosperous.

The unguarded Karakar Pass was practicable for troops, and if the Government would give their consent, Buner might be reduced in a fortnight without difficulty, almost without fighting.

Telegrams were despatched to India on the subject, and after much delay and hesitation the Viceroy decided against the recommendation of his victorious general. Though the desirability of settling with the Bunerwals was fully admitted, the Government shrank from the risk. The Malakand Field Force thus remained idle for nearly a fortnight. The news, that the Sirkar had feared to attack Buner, spread like wildfire along the frontier, and revived the spirits of the tribes. They fancied they detected a sign of weakness. Nor were they altogether wrong. But the weakness was moral rather than physical.

It is now asserted, that the punishment of Buner is only postponed, and that a few months may see its consummation. [Written in 1897.] The opportunity of entering the country without having to force the passes may not, however, recur.

On the 26th of August the force returned to Thana, and the expedition into Upper Swat terminated.

[The following is the most trustworthy estimate obtainable of loss of life among the tribesmen in the fighting in the Swat Valley from 26th July to 17th August. The figures include wounded, who have since died, and are more than double those killed outright in the actions:—

1. Lower Swat Pathans ....700 Buried in the graveyards.
2. Upper   "   "...................600   "   "   "   "
3. Buner proper.........................500   "   "   "   "
4. Utman Khel............................. 80
5. Yusafzai 50
6. Other tribes 150
           Total—2080.

1, 2 and 3 are the result of recent inquiry on the spot.
4, 5 and 6 are estimates based on native information.

The proportion of killed and died of wounds to wounded would be very high, as the tribes have little surgical or medical knowledge and refused all offers of aid. Assuming that only an equal number were wounded and recovered, the total loss would be approximately 4000. A check is obtained by comparing these figures with the separate estimates for each action:—

Malakand................................. 700
Siege of Chakdara 2000
Relief "   "........................... 500
Action of Landakai 500
          Total—3700.

CHAPTER VIII:

THE ADVANCE AGAINST THE MOHMANDS

The beginning of this chapter must mark a change in the standpoint from which the story is told. Hitherto the course of events has been recorded in the impersonal style of history. But henceforward I am able to rely on my own memory as well as on other people's evidence. [I do not desire to bore the reader or depreciate the story by the introduction of personal matters. It will be sufficient if, in the interests of coherency, I explain my connection with the Malakand Field Force. Having realised, that if a British cavalry officer waits till he is ordered on active service, he is likely to wait a considerable time, I obtained six weeks' leave of absence from my regiment, and on the 2nd of September arrived at Malakand as press correspondent of the PIONEER and DAILY TELEGRAPH, and in the hope of being sooner or later attached to the force in a military capacity.] It may be doubtful whether an historical record gains or loses value when described by an eye-witness. From the personal point of view, all things appear in a gradual perspective, according to the degree in which they affect the individual; and we are so prone to exaggerate the relative importance of incidents, which we see, over those we hear about, that what the narrative gains in accuracy of detail, it may lose in justness of proportion. In so nice a question I shall not pronounce. I remember that the original object with which this book was undertaken, was to present a picture of the war on the North-West Frontier to the Englishmen at home; a picture which should not only exist, but be looked at; and I am inclined to think, that this end will be more easily attained by the adoption of a style of personal narrative. Many facts, too local, too specialised, too insignificant, for an historical record, and yet which may help the reader to form a true impression of the scene and situation, are thus brought within the compass of these pages. The account becomes more graphic if less imposing, more vivid if less judicial. As long as each step down from the "dignity of history" is accompanied by a corresponding increase in interest, we may pursue without compunction that pleasant, if descending, path.

The ninth chapter also introduces a new phase of the operations of the force. The Mohmands now become the enemy and the scene is changed from Swat to Bajaur. Before marching into their country, it will be desirable to consider briefly those causes and events which induced the Government of India to despatch an expedition against this powerful and warlike tribe.

The tidal wave of fanaticism, which had swept the frontier, had influenced the Mohmands, as all other border peoples. Their situation was, however, in several important respects, different from that of the natives of the Swat Valley. These Mohmands had neither been irritated nor interfered with in any way. No military road ran through their territory. No fortified posts stirred their animosity or threatened their independence. Had they respected in others the isolation which they themselves have so long enjoyed, they might have remained for an indefinite period in that state of degraded barbarism which seems to appeal so strongly to certain people in England. They became, however, the aggressors.

In the heart of the wild and dismal mountain region, in which these fierce tribesmen dwell, are the temple and village of Jarobi: the one a consecrated hovel, the other a fortified slum. This obscure and undisturbed retreat was the residence of a priest of great age and of peculiar holiness, known to fame as the Hadda Mullah. His name is Najb-ud-din, but as respect has prevented it being mentioned by the tribesmen for nearly fifty years, it is only preserved in infidel memories and records. The Government of India have, however, had this man's personality brought vividly before them on several occasions. About thirteen years ago he quarrelled with the Amir and raised the Mohmands against him. The Amir replied by summoning his rebellious subject—for Hadda, the Mullah's home and birthplace, is a village of Afghanistan—to answer for his conduct at Cabul. But the crafty priest, who was well acquainted with Afghan legal procedure, declined the invitation, and retired to the independent Mohmand territory, where he has lived ever since.

Content with thus inflicting the punishment of exile, the Amir was disposed to forget the offence. In a letter to his Commander-in-Chief, the "Sipah Salar," a great friend of the Mullah, he described him as a "light of Islam." So powerful a light, indeed, he did not desire to have in his own dominions; but across the border it was fitting that respect should be shown to so holy a man. He therefore directed his officials to cherish and honour him. Thus he retained a powerful weapon—to be used when desirable. Whether by instigation or from personal motives, the Hadda Mullah has long been a bitter foe to the British power. In 1895 he sent the fighting men of the Mohmands to resist the Chitral Relief Force. Since then he has been actively engaged, by preaching and by correspondence with other Mullahs, in raising a great combination against the advancing civilisation.

In 1896 he terminated a long religious controversy with the Manki Mullah of Nowshera and Spinkhara—a comparatively tame Mullah, who now supports the Indian Government—by publishing a book setting forth his views, and demolishing those of his antagonist. This work was printed in Delhi and had an extensive sale among Mahommedans all over India. Complimentary copies were sent to the "Sipah Salar" and other Afghan notabilities, and the fame of the Hadda Mullah was known throughout the land. Besides increasing his influence, his literary success stimulated his efforts.

While the Mad Fakir was rousing Swat and Buner, this powerful priest incited the Mohmands. Though he was known to be a physical coward, his sanctity and the fact that he was their own particular holy man, not less than his eloquence, powerfully moved this savage tribe. A Jehad was proclaimed. How long should Islam be insulted? How long should its followers lurk in the barren lands of the North? He urged them to rise and join in the destruction of the white invaders. Those who fell should become saints; those who lived would be rich, for these Kafirs had money and many other things besides, for which a true believer might find a use.

The combined allurements of plunder and paradise proved irresistible. On the 8th of August a great gathering, nearly 6000 strong, crossed the frontier line, invaded British territory, burned the village of Shankargarh, and attacked the fort of Shabkadr. This place is an advanced post in the defensive system of the frontier, and is situated some nineteen miles to the north-west of Peshawar. Its ordinary garrison consists of about fifty Border Police. It is strongly built, and is intended to attract the attention and delay the advance of a raiding-party, until the Peshawar garrison has had time to take the field. Both of these objects it admirably fulfilled in this case.

As soon as the news of the incursion of the Mohmands was received in Peshawar, a flying column was mobilised and proceeded under the command of Lieut.-Colonel J.B. Woon, 20th Punjaub Infantry, in the direction of the fort. At dawn on the 9th of August they found the tribesmen in force in a strong position near Shabdakr. The force at Colonel Woon's disposal was small. It consisted of:—

4 Guns 51st Field Battery.
2 squadrons 13th Bengal Lancers ....151 lances.
2 Companies Somersetshire Light Infantry........186 rifles.
20th Punjaub Infantry..400   "

A total of about 750 men. The enemy numbered 6000. Nevertheless it was decided to attack at once.

As the action which followed is but remotely connected with the fortunes of the Malakand Field Force, I do not intend to describe it in detail. The infantry in advancing could only attack on a front of 600 yards. The enemy's line, being much longer, quickly turned both flanks. The fire became severe. Numerous casualties occurred. A retirement was ordered. As is usual in Asiatic warfare, it was considerably pressed. The situation at about nine o'clock appeared critical. At this point Brigadier-General Ellis, commanding the Peshawar District, arrived on the field. He immediately ordered the two squadrons of the 13th Bengal Lancers to move well to the right flank, to charge across the front and check the enemy's advance. The "cease fire" sounded as on a field day. Then there was a pause. The movements of the cavalry were concealed from most of the troops, but suddenly all noticed the slackening of the enemy's fire. Then the tribesmen were seen to be in retreat and disorder. The power of cavalry had been strikingly displayed. The two squadrons, ably led, had executed a fine charge over what theorists would call impossible ground for a distance of one and a half miles along the bed of a great nullah, and among rocks and stones that reduced the pace to a trot. The enemy were driven from the field. Sixty were actually speared by the Lancers, and the rest retreated in gloom and disorder to their hills across the frontier.

The casualties were as follows:—

British Officers.

Wounded severely—Major A. Lumb, Somersetshire Light Infantry.

"   "   Captain S.W. Blacker, R.A.

"   "   2nd Lieut. E Drummond, Somersetshire Light Infantry.

Wounded slightly—Lieut. A.V. Cheyne, 13th Bengal Lancers.

British N.C.O.'s and Soldiers.

	Killed.	Wounded.
51st Field Battery, R.A.	0	2
Somersetshire Light Infantry	3	9

Native Ranks.

	Killed.	Wounded.
13th Bengal Lancers	1	12
20th Punjaub Infantry	5	35
Followers	0	1

Total Casualties, all ranks—72.

That such an outrage, as the deliberate violation of British territory by these savages, should remain unpunished, "Forward Policy" or no "Forward Policy," was of course impossible. Yet the vacillation and hesitancy which the Government of India had displayed in the matter of the Bunerwals, and the shocking and disgraceful desertion of the forts in the Khyber Pass, were so fresh in all men's minds, that the order to advance against the Mohmands was received with feelings of the greatest relief throughout the forces. The general plan of the operations as arranged by the Commander-in-Chief was as follows:—

1. Sir Bindon Blood with two brigades of the Malakand Field Force and due proportions of cavalry and guns was to move through South Bajaur to Nawagai, and on the 15th of September invade the Mohmand country from that place.

2. On the same date Major-General Elles with an equal force would leave Shabkadr, and entering the mountains march northeast to effect a junction.

3. This having been done, the combined forces under the supreme command of Sir Bindon Blood would be brought back through the Mohmands' territories to Shabkadr. Incidentally they would deal with the Hadda Mullah's village of Jarobi, and inflict such punishment on the tribesmen as might be necessary to ensure their submission. The troops would then be available for the Tirah Expedition, which it had by this time been decided to organise.

The fact that after leaving Nawagai, nothing was known of the configuration of the country, of which no maps existed; nor of the supplies of food, forage and water available by the way, made the preparations for, and the execution of, these operations somewhat difficult. Wide margins had to be allowed in the matter of rations, and in order to be prepared for all contingencies and obstructions of ground, Sir Bindon Blood equipped his 2nd Brigade entirely with mule transport. The 3rd Brigade with camels would follow if the road was passable.

The following was the composition of the forces employed:—

I. MALAKAND FIELD FORCE.
Commanding—Major-General Sir Bindon Blood.

2nd Brigade.

Brigadier-General Jeffries, C.B.
The Buffs.
35th Sikhs.
38th Dogras.
Guides Infantry.
No.4 Company (Bengal) Sappers and Miners.
No.7 Mountain Battery.

3rd Brigade.

Brigadier-General Wodehouse.
The Queen's Regiment.[This regiment had replaced the Gordon
Highlanders in the 3rd Brigade.]
22nd Punjaub Infantry.
39th Punjaub Infantry.
No.3 Company (Bombay) Sappers and Miners.
No.1 Mountain Battery, R.A.

Cavalry—11th Bengal Lancers.

Line of Communications.   1st Brigade.

Brigadier-General Meiklejohn.
Royal West Kent.
Highland Light Infantry.
31st Punjaub Infantry.
24th Punjaub Infantry.
45th Sikhs.
No.7 British Mountain Battery.
And the following additional troops:—
1 Squadron 10th Bengal Lancers.
2 Squadrons Guides Cavalry.

II.THE MOHMAND FIELD FORCE.
1st Brigade.

1st Battalion Somersetshire Light Infantry.
Maxim Gun Detachment, 1st Battalion Devonshire Regiment.
20th Punjaub Infantry.
2nd Battalion 1st Gurkhas.
Sections A and B No.5 British Field Hospital.
Three Sections No.31 Native   "   "
Section A No.45   "   "   "

2nd Brigade.

2nd Battalion Oxfordshire Light Infantry.
9th Gurkha Rifles.
37th Dogras.
Sections C and D No.5 British Field Hospital.
No.44 Native Field Hospital.

Divisional Troops.

13th Bengal Lancers.
No.3 Mountain Battery, Royal Artillery.
No.5 (Bombay) Mountain Battery.
No.5 Company (Bengal) Sappers and Miners.
28th Bombay Pioneers.
1st Patiala Infantry.
Sections C and D No.63 Native Field Hospital.

To record the actual movements of troops in a campaign, is among the most important duties of one who undertakes to tell its tale. For the sake of clearness, of brevity, and that the reader who is not interested may find convenience in skipping, I shall at once describe the whole of the marches and manoeuvres, by which Sir Bindon Blood moved his brigades across the Panjkora River, and after the Malakand Field Force is safely camped at Ghosam, the reader will be invited to return to examine the scenery, and remark the incidents of the way.

During the end of August, the 2nd Brigade, equipped with mule transport, was at Khar in the Swat Valley. The 3rd Brigade was at Uch. On the 2nd of September, definite orders to advance were received from Simla. In pursuance of these instructions, Sir Bindon Blood ordered Brigadier-General Wodehouse with the 3rd Brigade, which in anticipation had been moved from Uch a few days previously, to take over the bridge across the Panjkora from the Khan of Dir's Levies, and secure the passage. On the 6th, the 3rd Brigade marched from Sarai to Panjkora, and obtained possession of the bridge just in time to prevent it falling into the hands of the enemy, who had already gathered to seize it. The 12-pounder guns of the 10th Field Battery were placed in a strong position commanding the passage, and the brigade camped on the left bank. On the same day, Brigadier-General Jeffries with headquarters marched from Khar to Chakdara. On the 7th he proceeded to Sarai, and on the 8th effected the passage of the Panjkora, and camped on the further bank at Kotkai. On the 10th, both brigades marched to Ghosam, where they concentrated. On the line of communications to the Malakand, stages were established at Chakdara and Sarai, with accommodation for sick and wounded. An advanced depot was formed behind the Panjkora, to guard which and to hold the passage, an additional force was moved from the Swat Valley.

This concentration at Ghosam, of which the details had worked out so mechanically, had been necessitated by the attitude of the tribesmen of Bajaur and the adjoining valleys. Great gatherings had collected, and up to the 7th of September there had been every sign of determined opposition. So formidable did the combination appear, that Sir Bindon Blood arranged to have at his disposal a force of six squadrons, nine battalions and three batteries, in the expectation of an action at or near Ghosam, which would perhaps have been on a larger scale than any British engagement since Tel-el-Kebir. [As so many misconceptions exist as to the British casualties in this victory, it is necessary to state that in the twenty minutes' fighting 11 officers and 43 men were killed and 22 officers and 320 men were wounded.]

These anticipations were however doomed to disappointment. The methodical, remorseless advance of powerful forces filled the tribesmen with alarm. They made a half-hearted attempt to capture the Panjkora bridge, and finding themselves forestalled, fell again to discussing terms. In this scene of indecision the political officers employed all their arts. And then suddenly the whole huge combination, which had been raised in our path, collapsed as an iceberg, when southern waters have melted its base.

Whatever the philanthropist may say, it would appear to have been better policy to have encouraged the tribesmen to oppose the advance in the open, on some well-defined position. Had they done so, there can be no doubt that the two fine brigades, backed by a powerful artillery, and under a victorious commander, who knew and had fought over every inch of the ground, would have defeated them with severe loss. Bajaur would have been settled at a single blow and probably at a far less cost in lives than was afterwards incurred.

Instead of this, it was the aim of our diplomacy to dissipate the opposition. The inflammation, which should have been brought to a head and then operated on, was now dispersed throughout the whole system, with what results future chapters will show.

Having thus brought the brigades peacefully to Gosham, I ask the reader to return to the Malakand and ride thence with the Headquarters Staff along the line of march. On the 5th of September, Sir Bindon Blood and his staff, which I had the pleasure to accompany, started from the Kotal Camp and proceeded across the plain of Khar to Chakdara. Here we halted for the night, and as the scenery and situation of this picturesque fort have already been described, the march may be continued without delay next morning. From Chakdara to Sarai is a stage of twelve miles. The road runs steadily up the valley until the summit of the Catgalla Pass is reached. "Catgalla" means "Cut-throat," and, indeed, it is not hard to believe that this gloomy defile has been the scene of dark and horrid deeds. Thence a descent of two miles leads to Sarai. On the way, we fell in with the 2nd Brigade, and had to leave the road to avoid the long lines of mules and marching men who toiled along it.

The valley at Sarai is about two miles wide, and the mountains rise steeply from it. On every ridge it is possible to distinguish the red brick ruins which were the dwellings of the ancient Buddhists. These relics of an early civilisation, long since overthrown and forgotten, cannot fail to excite interest and awaken reflection. They carry the mind back to the times "when the smoke of sacrifice rose from the Pantheon, and when camelopards and tigers bounded in the Flavian amphitheatre." And they also lead us to speculations of the future, till we wonder whether the traveller shall some day inspect, with unconcerned composure, the few scraps of stone and iron which may indicate the British occupation of India. Few, indeed, the remains would be—for we build for immediate use, not future ostentation in these days, and if we should ever cease to be a force in the world, all traces of us would soon be obliterated by time. Yet, perhaps, if that unborn critic of remote posterity would remember that "in the days of the old British," the rice crop had been more abundant, the number of acres under cultivation greater, the population larger and the death rate lower, than at any period in the history of India—we should not be without a monument more glorious than the pyramids.

We camped with the 2nd Brigade on the night of the 6th, and next morning, while the stars were still shining, resumed the march. Five miles from Sarai the road dwindles to a mule track, and henceforward is not fit for wheeled traffic. In spite of this, the 10th Field Battery had succeeded in getting their guns along it, and had brought them safely to Panjkora. But soldiers will accomplish a good deal to get nearer the enemy. The scenery before the gorge of the river is reached is gloomy, but grand. Great cliffs tower up precipitously on the further bank and the path is cut in the face of the rock. The river, which flows swiftly by, plunges into a narrow cleft about a mile below the bridge, and disappears among the mountains. It abounds in fish, but is rapid and dangerous, and while the troops were encamped near it, two gunners lost their lives by falling in, and being carried down. Indeed, watching the dead bodies of several camels being swept along, swirled around, and buffeted against the rocks, it was not hard to understand these accidents.

At length, the bridge is reached. It is a frail structure, supported on wire ropes. At each end are gates, flanked by little mud towers. The battery was established on a knoll to the right, and the long muzzles of the guns peered through stone embrasures at the opposite hills. It was round the bases of these hills that much hard fighting took place in the Chitral campaign. About half a mile beyond the bridge, I was shown the place where the Guides had been so hard pressed, and for a whole night had had to stand at bay, their colonel killed, the bridge broken, and the river in flood, against the tribesmen in overwhelming numbers.

The field telegraph stopped at the bridge-head, and a small tent with a half-dozen military operators marked the breaking of the slender thread that connected us, across thousands of miles of sea and land, with London. Henceforward a line of signal stations with their flickering helios would be the only links. We were at the end of the wire. I have often stood at the other and watched the tape machine click off the news as it arrives; the movements of the troops; the prospects of action; the fighting; the casualties. How different are the scenes. The club on an autumn evening— its members grouped anxiously around, discussing, wondering, asserting; the noise of the traffic outside; the cigarette smoke and electric lights within. And, only an hour away along the wire, the field, with the bright sunlight shining on the swirling muddy waters; the black forbidding rocks; the white tents of the brigade a mile up the valley; the long streak of vivid green rice crop by the river; and in the foreground the brown-clad armed men. I can never doubt which is the right end to be at. It is better to be making the news than taking it; to be an actor rather than a critic.

To cross the bridge, it was necessary to dismount and lead the horses over in single file. Even then the swinging of the whole structure made it difficult to walk. The passage of the transport under such conditions occupied all the day, and the unfortunate officers in charge of the mule trains were working incessantly. The staff passed quickly, however, and riding on about a mile forded the tributary stream of the Jandol, and reached the camp at Kotkai about noon. Thence we proceeded on the following day to Ghosam, but as the road is uninteresting, and I am beginning to think the reader will readily excuse further description, we need not toil along it in the dust and the heat. The narration of the daily movements of troops, unmarked by variety of incident, is dull and wearying. Yet he who would obtain a true idea of the soldier's life on service, must mentally share the fatigues of the march and the monotony of the camp. The fine deeds, the thrilling moments of war, are but the high lights in a picture, of which the background is routine, hard work, and discomfort.

At Ghosam the 2nd Brigade remained until joined by the 3rd and pending negotiations between the political officers and the tribal Jirgahs.

The use of purely local terms in all writing is to be deprecated. Perhaps the reason that no popular history of India exists, is to be found in the outlandish names of the characters, and the other expressions with which the pages are sprinkled. In this account I have zealously tried to avoid the ugly jargon of a degraded language, and to minimise the use of native names. The term just employed has, however, been so freely used in the newspapers recently, that it is perhaps as well to explain its meaning. A Jirgah is a deputation of tribesmen. It does not necessarily represent the tribe. It may present—and very often does—a minority report. Occasionally it expresses the opinion only of its own members. What has been settled one day is therefore very often overruled the next. The

Jirgah may accept terms of peace in the morning, and the camp may be rushed that night. These were, however, genuine, and spoke in the name and with the authority of the tribes. All day they kept arriving and squatting in rows before Major Deane's tent, to hear the Government terms. The chief condition imposed, was the surrender of rifles. A fixed number, based on calculation of wealth and population, was demanded from each clan. This method of punishment is peculiarly galling to people whose life is so full of war. No other course was, however, open but submission, and, promising that the terms should be complied with, the deputations departed. To stimulate their efforts and zeal in collecting their arms, the combined movements were delayed for three days, and the forces remained encamped at Ghosam, near Manda.

I avail myself of this halt to touch, albeit with no little trepidation, the tangled and obscure subject of tribal politics in Dir and Bajaur. All the people, incited by their priests, are bitterly hostile to the British Government, except those benefited by the subsidies paid. They were now anxious to fight, and were only restrained by a fear which fury or fanaticism might at any moment overcome. Four principal khans exercise an authority which varies locally, from absolute dominion to a shadowy suzerainty, over the whole region. The Khan of Dir, the most important, is a Government nominee. He is supported by the British influence, and is, as I have already noticed, entrusted with the raising of Levies to protect and keep in repair the Chitral road. For these services he receives pay, and a certain allowance of arms and ammunition. His own subjects are strongly opposed to his rule from dislike of his British sympathies, and he only maintains himself by the assistance which the Government gives him in arms and money. In other words he is a puppet.

The Khan of Nawagai is constrained by fear to display a friendly attitude towards the Sirkar. His subjects resent this and his position is insecure. He receives some moral support from the British agents, and as his people are uncertain how far the Government would go to uphold him, and also as they partly realise his difficult position, they have hitherto submitted sullenly to his rule.

The position and attitude of the Khan of Jar are similar, but he is a less influential chief. The fourth potentate, the Khan of

Khar, is perhaps the most honest and trustworthy. He will appear in a later chapter, and the reader will have the opportunity of judging of his character from his conduct. Thus in these valleys, while the people are all hostile, their rulers find it expedient to preserve a friendly demeanour to the British, and for this they are hated by their subjects.

At this stage, the leader of the popular party claims attention. As is usual, he is out of office. After the Chitral expedition of 1895, Umra Khan was expelled from his territories, and escaped to Cabul. There he has remained. The Amir is under an obligation to the British Government to prevent his raising trouble in Bajaur. If the Amir desired war he would send Umra Khan back. This would create a strong faction throughout the whole country—but particularly in the Jandol, Salarzai and Mamund Valleys—hostile to the British and the friendly khans. The Amir hinted at this in a recent letter to the Government of India; and such a step would probably precede his declaration of war, or follow ours. The Afghan sovereign is, however, well aware that he has at present nothing to gain, and many things to lose, by provoking a war with the great power which gave him his throne and has since increased his revenue by subsidies. In the meanwhile, anxious to preserve his influence with the border tribes, and to impress the Indian Government with the fact that he could be a powerful foe, he keeps Umra Khan as a trump card, to be played when the occasion arises. That he may maintain his authority in Bajaur, the exiled khan is well supplied with funds, with which to arm and pay his retainers.

The situation I have thus briefly described has been little altered by the operations with which future chapters are concerned. The friendly khans have been fortified in their allegiance and position by the military demonstration and by the severe punishment inflicted on those tribes who resisted. On the other hand, the hostility of the people has been not unnaturally increased by war, and one tribe in particular has gained a reputation for courage, which will give them the power to cause trouble in the future. I shall not, however, anticipate the tale.

CHAPTER IX:

RECONNAISSANCE

While the infantry of both brigades remained halted at Ghosam, near Manda, the cavalry made daily reconnaissances in all directions. Sometimes the object in view was topographical, sometimes military, and at others diplomatic, or to use the Indian application of the term, "political."

On the 10th, Major Deane visited the various chiefs in the Jandul Valley. I asked and obtained permission to accompany him. A change from the hot and dusty camp was agreeable to all who could be spared, and quite a party was formed, among whom were some whose names have occurred previously in these pages— Major Beatson, Major Hobday, and Lord Fincastle. A squadron of the 11th Bengal Lancers acted as escort.

The valley of the Jandul is about eight miles long and perhaps half as broad. It opens out of the main valley, which extends from the Panjkora to Nawagai, and is on all other sides surrounded by high and precipitous mountains. The bed of the river, although at the time of our visit occupied only by a small stream, is nearly half a mile broad and bordered by rice fields, to which the water is conducted by many artfully contrived dykes and conduits. The plain itself is arid and sandy, but at the winter season yields a moderate crop. The presence of water below the surface is attested by numerous groves of chenar trees.

This valley may, in natural and political features, be taken as typical of the Afghan valleys. Seven separate castles formed the strongholds of seven separate khans. Some of these potentates had been implicated in the attack on the Malakand, and our visit to their fastnesses was not wholly of an amicable nature. They had all four days before been bound by the most sacred oaths to fight to the death. The great tribal combination had, however, broken up, and at the last moment they had decided upon peace. But the Pathan does nothing by halves. No black looks, no sullen reserve, marred the geniality of their welcome. As we approached the first fortified village the sovereign and his army rode out to meet us, and with many protestations of fidelity, expressed his joy at our safe arrival. He was a fine-looking man and sat well on a stamping roan stallion. His dress was imposing. A waistcoat of gorgeous crimson, thickly covered with gold lace, displayed flowing sleeves of white linen, buttoned at the wrist. Long, loose, baggy, linen trousers, also fastened above the ankle, and curiously pointed shoes clothed his nether limbs. This striking costume was completed by a small skull-cap, richly embroidered, and an ornamental sabre.

He sprang from his horse with grace and agility, to offer his sword to Major Deane, who bade him mount and ride with him. The army, four or five rascally-looking men on shaggy ponies, and armed with rifles of widely different patterns, followed at a distance. The fort was an enclosure about a hundred yards square. Its walls were perhaps twenty feet high and built of rough stones plastered together with mud and interspersed with courses of timber. All along the top was a row of loopholes. At each corner a tall flanking tower enfiladed the approaches. At the gate of this warlike residence some twenty or thirty tribesmen were gathered, headed by the khan's own cousin, an elderly man dressed in long white robes. All saluted us gravely. The escort closed up. A troop trotted off to the right out of the line fire of the fort. The advance scouts, passing round the walls, formed on the farther side. These matters of detail complied with, conversation began. It was conducted in Pushtu, and was naturally unintelligible to every one of our party except the two political officers. Apparently Major Deane reproached the two chiefs for their conduct. He accused them of having seized the bridge across the Panjkora and delivered the passage to the fanatic crowds that had gathered to attack the Malakand. This they admitted readily enough. "Well, why not?" said they; "there was a good fair fight." Now they would make peace. They bore no malice, why should the Sirkar?

It was not, however, possible to accept this sportsmanlike view of the situation. They were asked where were the rifles they had been ordered to surrender. At this they looked blank. There were no rifles. There never had been any rifles. Let the soldiers search the fort and see for themselves. The order was given; three or four sowars drew their carbines, dismounted and entered the great and heavy gate, which had been suspiciously opened a little way.

The gate gave access to a small courtyard, commanded on every side by an interior defence. In front was a large low room of uncertain dimensions: a kind of guard-house. It simply hummed with men. The outer walls were nearly five feet thick and would have resisted the fire of mountain guns. It was a strong place.

The Lancers, accustomed to the operation of hunting for arms, hurriedly searched the likely and usual places, but without success. One thing, however, they noticed, which they immediately reported. There were no women and children in the fort. This had a sinister aspect. Our visit was unexpected and had taken them by surprise, but they were prepared for all emergencies. They had hidden their rifles and cleared for action.

The two chiefs smiled in superior virtue. Of course there were no rifles. But matters took, for them, an unexpected turn. They had no rifles—said Major Deane—very well, they should come themselves. He turned to an officer of the Lancers; a section rode forward and surrounded both men. Resistance was useless. Flight was impossible. They were prisoners. Yet they behaved with Oriental composure and calmly accepted the inevitable. They ordered their ponies and, mounting, rode behind us under escort.

We pursued our way up the valley. As we approached each fort, a khan and his retainers advanced and greeted us. Against these there was no definite charge, and the relations throughout were amicable. At the head of the valley is Barwa, the home of the most powerful of these princelets. This fort had belonged to Umra Khan, and attested, by superiority of construction, the intellectual development of that remarkable man. After the Chitral expedition it had been given by the Government to its present owner, who, bitterly hated by the other chieftains of the valley, his near relatives mostly, had no choice but loyalty to the British. He received us with courtesy and invited us to enter and see the fort. This, after taking all precautions and posting sentries, we did. It was the best specimen of Afghan architecture I have seen. In this very fort Lieutenants Fowler and Edwards were confined in 1895, when the prisoners of Umra Khan. The new chief showed their room which opened on a balcony, whence a fine view of the whole valley could be obtained. There are many worse places of durance. The fort is carefully defended and completely commands the various approaches. Judicious arrangements of loopholes and towers cover all dead ground. Inside the walls galleries of brushwood enabled the defenders to fire without exposing themselves. In the middle is the keep, which, if Fortune were adverse, would be the last stronghold of the garrison.

What a strange system of society is disclosed by all this! Here was this man, his back against the mountains, maintaining himself against the rest of the valley, against all his kin, with the fear of death and the chances of war ever in his mind, and holding his own, partly by force of arms, partly by the support of the British agents, and partly through the incessant feuds of his adversaries.

It is "all against all," in these valleys. The two khans who had been arrested would have fled to the hills. They knew they were to be punished. Still they dared not leave their stronghold. A neighbour, a relation, a brother perhaps, would step into the unguarded keep and hold it for his own. Every stone of these forts is blood-stained with treachery; each acre of ground the scene of a murder. In Barwa itself, Umra Khan slew his brother, not in hot anger or open war, but coldly and deliberately from behind. Thus he obtained power, and the moralist might observe with a shudder, that but for the "Forward Policy" he would probably be in full enjoyment to-day. This Umra Khan was a man of much talent, a man intellectually a head and shoulders above his countrymen. He was a great man, which on the frontier means that he was a great murderer, and might have accomplished much with the quick-firing guns he was negotiating for, and the troops he was drilling "on the European model." The career of this Afghan Napoleon was cut short, however, by the intervention of Providence in the guise or disguise of the Indian Government. He might have been made use of. People who know the frontier well, say that a strong man who has felt the grip of the British power is the best tool to work with, and that if Umra Khan, humbled and overawed, had been reinstated, he might have done much to maintain law and order. As long as they fight, these Afghans do not mind much on which side they fight. There are worse men and worse allies helping us to-day. The unpractical may wonder why we, a people who fill some considerable place in the world, should mix in the petty intrigues of these border chieftains, or soil our hands by using such tools at all. Is it fitting that Great Britain should play off one brutal khan against his neighbours, or balance one barbarous tribe against another? It is as much below our Imperial dignity, as it would be for a millionaire to count the lumps in the sugar-basin. If it be necessary for the safety of our possessions that these territories should be occupied, it would be more agreeable to our self-respect that we should take them with a strong hand. It would be more dignified, but nothing costs more to keep up than dignity, and it is perhaps because we have always been guided by sound commercial principles in this respect that we have attained our present proud position.

After looking round the fortress and admiring the skill and knowledge with which it was built, we were conducted by the khan to the shade of some beautiful chenar trees, which grew near a little spring not far from the walls of the fort. Here were a number of charpoys, or native bedsteads, very comfortable, but usually full of bugs, and on these we sat.

Remembering Maizar, and many other incidents of frontier hospitality, sentries were posted on all the approaches and a sufficient guard kept under arms. Then we had breakfast—a most excellent breakfast.

The arrangements for the comfort and convenience of the troops of the Frontier Force are unequalled. They live more pleasantly and with less discomfort on active service than does a British regiment at the Aldershot manoeuvres. Whether the march be long or short, peaceful or opposed, whether the action be successful or the reverse, their commissariat never fails. In fact it is only just to say that they have always lances and bullets for an enemy, and sandwiches and "pegs" for a friend.

On this occasion, our provisions were supplemented by the hospitality of the khan. A long row of men appeared, each laden with food. Some carried fruit,—pears or apples; others piles of chupatties, or dishes of pillau.

Nor were our troopers forgotten. The Mahommedans among them eagerly accepted the proffered food. But the Sikhs maintained a remorseful silence and declined it. They could not eat what had been prepared by Mussulman hands, and so they sat gazing wistfully at the appetising dishes, and contented themselves with a little fruit.

Very austere and admirable they looked, almost painfully conscious of their superior virtue. But I could not help thinking that had we not been spectators the chenar trees might have witnessed the triumph of reason over religious prejudice.

During the heat of the day we rested in this pleasant grove, and with sleep and conversation passed the hours away, while the sentries pacing to and fro alone disturbed the illusion that this was some picnic party in a more propitious land. Then, as the shadows lengthened, we started upon our return to camp.

On arriving, the political officers were pleased, and the soldiers disappointed, to find that the tribesmen were determined to accept the Government terms. A hundred rifles from the Utman Khels had already been surrendered, and now lay outside Major Deane's tent, surrounded by a crowd of officers, who were busily engaged in examining them.

Opinion is divided, and practice has followed opinion as to whether, in a tale of travel or of war, it is preferable to intersperse the narrative with conclusions and discussions, or to collect them all in a final chapter. I shall unhesitatingly embrace the former method. The story shall be told as it happened, and the reader's attention will be directed to such considerations and reflections as arise by the way. It will therefore be convenient to make a digression into the question of the supply of arms to the frontier tribes, while a hundred rifles, probably a representative hundred, are piled in the main street of the camp at Ghosam.

The perpetual state of intestine war, in which the border peoples live, naturally creates a keen demand for deadly weapons. A good Martini-Henry rifle will always command a price in these parts of Rs.400 or about 25 British pounds. As the actual value of such a rifle does not exceed Rs.50, it is evident that a very large margin of profit accrues to the enterprising trader. All along the frontier, and from far down into India, rifles are stolen by expert and cunning thieves. One tribe, the Ut Khels, who live in the Laghman Valley, have made the traffic in arms their especial business. Their thieves are the most daring and their agents the most cunning. Some of their methods are highly ingenious. One story is worth repeating. A coffin was presented for railway transport. The relatives of the deceased accompanied it. The dead man, they said, had desired to be buried across the frontier. The smell proclaimed the corpse to be in an advanced state of decomposition. The railway officials afforded every facility for the passage of so unpleasant an object. No one checked its progress. It was unapproachable. It was only when coffin and mourners were safe across the frontier that the police were informed that a dozen rifles had been concealed in the coffin, and that the corpse was represented by a quarter of "well hung" beef!

I regret to have to state, that theft is not the only means by which the frontier tribes obtain weapons. Of a hundred rifles, which the Utman Khels had surrendered, nearly a third were condemned Government Martinis, and displayed the Government stamp. Now no such rifles are supposed to exist. As soon as they are condemned, the arsenal authorities are responsible that they are destroyed, and this is in every case carried out under European supervision. The fact, that such rifles are not destroyed and are found in the possession of trans-frontier tribesmen, points to a very grave instance of dishonest and illegal traffic being carried on by some person connected with the arsenal. It need hardly be said that a searching inquiry was instituted.

Another point connected with these rifles is that even when they have been officially destroyed, by cutting them in three pieces, the fractions have a marketable value. Several were shown me which had been rejoined by the tribesmen. These were, of course, very dangerous weapons indeed. The rest of the hundred had strange tales to tell. Two or three were Russian military rifles, stolen probably from the distant posts in Central Asia. One was a Snider, taken at Maiwand, and bearing the number of the ill-fated regiment to which it had belonged. Some had come from Europe, perhaps overland through Arabia and Persia; others from the arms factory at Cabul. It was a strange instance of the tireless efforts of Supply to meet Demand.

The importance of the arms question cannot be exaggerated. The long-range rifle fire, which has characterised the great frontier war, is a new feature. Hitherto our troops have had to face bold sword charges but comparatively little firing. Against the former, modern weapons are effective. But no discipline and no efficiency can stop bullets hitting men. This is a small part of the question. In the matter of fighting, what is good enough for the tribesmen should be good enough for the soldier. A more serious consideration is raised than that of casualties, which are after all only the inseparable concomitant of glory. Transport in mountainous countries depends entirely on mules and camels. A great number are needed even to supply one brigade. At night these animals have to be packed closely in an entrenched camp. It is not possible to find camping grounds in the valleys which are not commanded by some hill or assailable from some nullah. It is dangerous to put out pickets, as they may be "rushed" or, in the event of a severe attack, shot down, by the fire of their main body. [This applies to Swat and Bajaur, where the sword charge is still to be apprehended.] The result is that the transport animals must be exposed to long-range fire at night. The reader will observe, as the account proceeds, that on two occasions a large number of transport mules were killed in this way. When a certain number are killed, a brigade is as helpless as a locomotive without coal. It cannot move. Unless it be assisted it must starve. Every year the tribesmen will become better marksmen, more completely armed with better rifles. If they recognise the policy of continually firing at our animals, they may bring all operations to a standstill. And so by this road I reach the conclusion that whatever is to be done on the frontier, should be done as quickly as possible. But to return to the story.

The next day, the 11th of September, the troops remained halted at Ghosam, and another squadron was ordered to escort the Intelligence Officer, Captain H.E. Stanton, D.S.O., while making a topographical reconnaissance of the passes into the Utman Khel country. The opportunity of making fresh maps and of adding to and correcting the detail of existing maps only occurs when troops are passing through the country, and must not be neglected. The route lay up the main valley which leads to Nawagei. We started early, but the way was long and the sun high before we reached the entrance of the pass. The landscape was one of the strangest I shall ever see. On the opposite bank of the river were the dwellings of the Utman Khels, and in an area seven miles by three, I counted forty-six separate castles, complete with moats, towers and turrets. The impression produced was extraordinary. It suggested Grimm's fairy tales. It almost seemed as if we had left the natural earth and strayed into some strange domain of fancy, the resort of giants or ogres.

To reach the pass, we were compelled to traverse a large village, and as the situation in the narrow, winding streets was about as awkward for cavalry as could be imagined, every possible precaution was taken to guard against attack. At length the squadron passed safely through and formed up on the farther side. The steep ascent to the passes became visible. As there were two routes to be reconnoitered, the party was divided, and after a hasty breakfast we commenced the climb. For a considerable distance it was possible to ride. At every difficult turn of the track sowars were posted to secure the retreat, if it should be necessary to come back in a hurry. The head man of the village furnished a guide, a cheery and amusing fellow, who professed much solicitude for our safety. But no reliance could be placed on these people, and on the opposite side of the valley numerous figures could be seen moving along and keeping pace with our advancing party. At length the horses and the greater part of the escort had to be abandoned. I accompanied Captain Stanton, and Captain Cole, who commanded the squadron and was also Reuter's correspondent, with a couple of troopers to the top of the pass. The day was intensely hot, and the arduous climb excited a thirst which there was nothing to allay. At length we gained the summit, and stood on the Kotal.

Far below us was a valley, into which perhaps no white man had looked since Alexander crossed the mountains on his march to India. Numerous villages lay dotted about in its depths, while others nestled against the hills. Isolated forts were distinguishable, while large trees showed there was no lack of water. It was a view that repaid the exertions of the climb, even if it did not quench the thirst they had excited.

While Captain Stanton was making his sketch,—one of those useful view-sketches, now taking the place of all others, in rapid cavalry reconnaissance, we amused our fancy by naming the drinks we should order, were a nice, clean European waiter at hand to get them. I forget what my selection was, but it was something very long and very cold. Alas! how far imagination lags behind reality. The vivid impressions which we conjured up—the deep glasses, and the clinking ice—did little to dissipate the feelings of discomfort.

Our guide meanwhile squatted on the ground and pronounced the names of all the villages, as each one was pointed at. To make sure there was no mistake, the series of questions was repeated. This time he gave to each an entirely different name with an appearance of great confidence and pride. However, one unpronounceable name is as good as another, and the villages of the valley will go down to official history, christened at the caprice of a peasant. But perhaps many records, now accepted as beyond dispute, are derived from such a slender authority.

The sketch finished, we commenced the descent and reached our horses without incident. The squadron concentrated near the village, and we heard that the other sketching party had met with more adventures than had fallen to our lot.

It was commanded by Lieutenant Hesketh, a young officer, who was severely wounded at the storming of the Malakand Pass in 1895, and who, having again volunteered for active service, was attached to the 11th Bengal Lancers. At the foot of the pass he dismounted his troop and, taking a few men with him, began the climb. The pass was occupied by tribesmen, who threatened to fire on the party if they advanced farther. The subaltern replied, that he only wished to see the country on the other side and did not intend to harm any one. At the same time he pursued his way and the tribesmen, not wishing to bring matters to a crisis, fell back slowly, repeatedly taking aim, but never daring to fire. He reached the top of the pass and Captain Walters, the Assistant Intelligence Officer, was able to make a most valuable sketch of the country beyond. It was a bold act and succeeded more through its boldness than from any other cause; for, had the tribesmen once opened fire, very few of the party could have got down alive. Making a detour to avoid the village, which it was undesirable to traverse a second time, the squadron returned and arrived at the camp at Ghosam as the sun was setting.

The service camp of an Anglo-Indian brigade is arranged on regular principles. The infantry and guns are extended in the form of a square. The animals and cavalry are placed inside. In the middle is the camp of the Headquarters staff, with the tent of the brigadier facing that of the general commanding the division. All around the perimeter a parapet is built, varying in height according to the proximity and activity of the enemy. This parapet not only affords cover from random shots, but also makes a line for the men to form on in case of a sudden attack. Behind it the infantry lie down to sleep, a section of each company, as an inlying picket, dressed and accoutred. Their rifles are often laid along the low wall with the bayonets ready fixed. If cavalry have to be used in holding part of the defences, their lances can be arranged in the same way. Sentries every twenty-five yards surround the camp with a line of watchers.

To view the scene by moonlight is alone an experience which would repay much travelling. The fires have sunk to red, glowing specks. The bayonets glisten in a regular line of blue-white points. The silence of weariness is broken by the incessant and uneasy shuffling of the animals and the occasional neighing of the horses. All the valley is plunged in gloom and the mountains rise high and black around. Far up their sides, the twinkling watch-fires of the tribesmen can be seen. Overhead is the starry sky, bathed in the pale radiance of the moon. It is a spectacle that may inspire the philosopher no less than the artist. The camp is full of subdued noises. Here is no place for reflection, for quiet or solemn thought. The day may have been an exciting one. The morrow may bring an action. Some may be killed, but in war-time life is only lived in the present. It is sufficient to be tired and to have time to rest, and the camp, if all the various items that compose it can be said to have a personality, shrugs its shoulders and, regarding the past without regret, contemplates the future without alarm.

CHAPTER X:

THE MARCH TO NAWAGAI

After considering such maps and information as to the nature of the country as were available, Sir Bindon Blood decided to enter the territories of the Mohmands by two routes. (1) The 3rd Brigade through the pass of Nawagai. (2) The 2nd Brigade over the Rambat Pass. This would sweep the country more thoroughly, and afford increased facilities for drawing supplies. As the 3rd Brigade had a greater distance to cover, it passed in front of the 2nd, and on the 12th of September, by a march of twelve miles, reached Shumshuk. The 2nd Brigade, which had hitherto been leading, moved by an easy stage of seven miles to Jar, and there camped within supporting distance.

The Headquarters staff was now transferred to the 3rd Brigade and marched with them. The road lay for the first five or six miles over the ground, which the cavalry had reconnoitered the day before. Again all were struck by the great array of castles on the Utman Khel side of the valley. Many eager spirits would have liked to stop and blow up some of these fine places. But the Government terms had been complied with and the columns moved slowly by, eyeing the forts, which were covered with the white and blue clad figures of their defenders, with a sour disdain.

After riding for a couple of hours, the staff halted for breakfast under a shady tree by the banks of a clear and rapid stream.

Two hundred yards away we observed a large flight of teal sitting tamely on the water. Every one became interested. Rifles there were in plenty; but where could a gun be found? Rigorous and hasty search was made. The political officer of the force, Mr. Davis, being consulted, eventually produced a friendly khan, who was the owner of a shot gun. After further delay this weapon was brought. The teal still floated unconcernedly on the water. A gun awakened no sense of danger. Shots in plenty they had heard in the valley, but they were not usually fired at birds. The exciting moment now arrived. Who should shoot? The responsibility was great. Many refused. At length Veterinary-Captain Mann, who was wounded a few days later at Nawagai, volunteered. He took the gun and began a painful stalk. He crawled along cautiously. We watched with suppressed emotion. Suddenly two shots rang out. They were to be the first of many. The men in the marching column 200 yards away became wide awake. The teal rose hurriedly and flew away, but four remained behind, killed or wounded. These birds we picked up with a satisfaction which was fully justified by their excellence that night at dinner.

Another mile or so brought us to the Watelai River, a stream about thirty yards broad, which flows into the Jandul, and thence into the Panjkora. Crossing this and climbing the opposite bank, the troops debouched on to the wide level plateau of Khar, perhaps ten miles across and sixteen in length. Standing on the high ground, the great dimensions of the valley were displayed. Looking westward it was possible to see the hills behind the Panjkora, the sites of the former camps, and the entrance of the subsidiary valley of the Jandul. In front, at the further end, an opening in the mountain range showed the pass of Nawagai. Towering on the left was the great mass of the Koh-i-mohr, or "Mountain of Peacocks"—a splendid peak, some 8000 feet high, the top of which is visible from both Peshawar and Malakand. Its name is possibly a corruption. Arrian calls it Mount Meros. At its base the city of Nysa stood in former times, and among many others fell before the arms of Alexander. Its inhabitants, in begging for peace, boasted that they conducted their government "with constitutional order," and that "ivy, which did not grow in the rest of India, grew among them." City, ivy, and constitutional order have alike disappeared. The mountain alone remains. A little to the northward the Ramlat Pass was distinguishable. On the right the smooth plain appeared to flow into the hill country, and a wide bay in the mountains, roughly circular in shape and nearly twelve miles across, opened out of the valley. The prominent spurs which ran from the hills formed many dark ravines and deep hollows, as it were gulfs and inlets of the sea.

The entrance was perhaps a mile broad. I remember that, when I first looked into the valley, the black clouds of a passing storm hung gloomily over all, and filled it with a hazy half-light that contrasted with the brilliant sunshine outside. It was the Watelai, or as we got to call it later—the Mamund Valley.

The Khan of Khar met the general on the farther bank of the river. He was a tall, fine-looking man with bright eyes, bushy black whiskers and white teeth, which his frequent smiles displayed. He was richly dressed, attended by a dozen horsemen and mounted on a handsome, though vicious dun horse. He saluted Sir Bindon Blood with great respect and ceremony. Some conversation took place, conducted, as the khan only spoke Pushtu, through the political officer. The khan asserted his loyalty and that of his neighbour the Khan of Jar. He would, he said, do his utmost to secure the peaceful passage of the troops. Such supplies as they might need, he would provide, as far as his resources would go. He looked with some alarm at the long lines of marching men and animals. The general reassured him. If the forces were not interfered with or opposed, if the camps were not fired into at night, if stragglers were not cut off and cut up by his people, payment in cash would be made for all the grain and wood it was necessary to requisition.

The khan accepted this promise with gratitude and relief, and henceforth during the operations which took place at Nawagai and in the Mamund Valley, he preserved a loyal and honourable behaviour. To the best of his power he restrained his young bloods. As much as he was able, he used his influence to discourage the other tribes from joining the revolt. Every night his pickets watched our camps, and much good sleep was obtained by weary men in consequence. At the end of the fighting he was the intermediary between the Government and the Mamund tribesmen. And on one occasion he rendered a signal service, though one which should hardly have been entrusted to him, by escorting with his own retainers an ammunition convoy to the 2nd Brigade, when troops and cartridges were alike few and sorely needed. Had he proved treacherous in this instance the consequences might have been most grave. Throughout, however, he kept his word with the general, and that in the face of opposition from his own people, and threats of vengeance from his neighbours.

He on his part will not complain of British good faith. Although the fighting was continued in the district for nearly a month, not one of his villages was burnt, while all damage done to his crops was liberally compensated. He was guaranteed against reprisals, and at the end of the operations the gift of a considerable sum of money proved to him that the Sirkar could reward its friends, as well as punish its enemies.

The camel transport of the 3rd Brigade lagged on the road, and the troops, tired after their long march, had to wait in the blazing sun for a couple of hours without shelter until the baggage came up. At length it arrived, and we proceeded to camp as far as is possible without tents. Shelters were improvised from blankets, from waterproof sheets supported on sticks, or from the green boughs of some adjacent trees. Beneath these scanty coverings the soldiers lay, and waited for the evening.

Every one has read of the sufferings of the British troops in having to campaign in the hot weather during the Indian Mutiny. September in these valleys is as hot as it is easy to imagine or elegant to describe, and the exposure to the sun tells severely on the British battalions, as the hospital returns show. Of course, since Mutiny days, many salutary changes have been made in the dress and equipment of the soldier. The small cap with its insufficient puggaree is replaced by the pith helmet, the shade of which is increased by a long quilted covering. The high stock and thick, tight uniforms are gone, and a cool and comfortable khaki kit has been substituted. A spine protector covers the back, and in other ways rational improvements have been effected. But the sun remains unchanged, and all precautions only minimise, without preventing the evils.

Slowly the hours pass away. The heat is intense. The air glitters over the scorched plain, as over the funnel of an engine. The wind blows with a fierce warmth, and instead of bringing relief, raises only whirling dust devils, which scatter the shelters and half-choke their occupants. The water is tepid, and fails to quench the thirst. At last the shadows begin to lengthen, as the sun sinks towards the western mountains. Every one revives. Even the animals seem to share the general feeling of relief. The camp turns out to see the sunset and enjoy the twilight. The feelings of savage hatred against the orb of day fade from our minds, and we strive to forget that he will be ready at five o'clock next morning to begin the torment over again.

As there were still several days to spare before the Malakand Field Force was due to enter the Mohmand country, Sir Bindon Blood ordered both brigades to remain halted on the 13th: the 3rd Brigade at Shumshuk; the 2nd at Jar. Meanwhile two reconnaissances were to be sent, one to the summit of the Rambat Pass, and the other up the Watelai Valley.

The night of the 12th was the first occasion of "sniping," since the advance against the Mohmands had begun. About half a dozen shots were fired into camp, without other result than to disturb light sleepers. Still it marked a beginning.

The reconnaissances started next morning. The general accompanied the one to the Rambat pass, to satisfy himself as to the nature of the unexplored country on the other side. Two companies of infantry were ordered to clear the way, and two others remained in support half-way up the pass. Sir Bindon Blood started at six o'clock accompanied by his escort, whose gay pennons combined, with the Union Jack of the Headquarters staff, to add a dash of colour to the scene. After riding for a couple of miles we caught up the infantry and had to halt, to let them get on ahead and work through the broken ground and scrub. A mile further it was necessary to dismount and proceed on foot. No opposition was encountered, though the attitude and demeanour of the natives was most unfriendly. The younger ones retired to the hills. The elder stayed to scowl at, and even curse us. The village cemetery was full of property of all kinds, beds, pitchers, and bags of grain, which the inhabitants had deposited there under the double delusion, that we wanted to plunder, and that in so sacred a spot it would be safe—were such our intention. In spite of their black looks, they were eventually all made to stand up and salute respectfully.

The climb was a stiff one and took at least an hour. But the track was everywhere passable, or capable of easily being made passable for mules. The general, trained and hardened by years of shooting of all kinds in the jungles, arrived at the top first, followed by Brigadier-General Wodehouse, and a panting staff. A fine view of the Ambasar Valley was displayed. It was of arid aspect. Villages in plenty could be seen, but no sign of water. This was serious, as information as to wells was unreliable, and it was desirable to see some tanks and streams, before allowing a column to plunge into the unknown dangers of the valley. After some consideration Sir Bindon Blood decided to modify the original plan and send only two battalions of the 2nd Brigade with one squadron over the pass, while the rest were to march to join him at Nawagai. We then returned, reaching camp in time for luncheon.

Meanwhile the reconnaissance up the Watelai or Mamund Valley had been of a more interesting nature. Two squadrons of the 11th Bengal Lancers, under Major Beatson, and with Mr. Davis, the political officer, were sent to put some pressure on the Mamunds, to make them carry out the terms agreed upon. They had promised to surrender fifty rifles. This they now showed no intention of doing. They had realised, that the brigades were only marching through the country, and that they had no time to stop, and they were determined to keep their arms as long as possible.

As the cavalry approached the first village, about 300 men gathered and, displaying standards, called on the Lancers to stop. An altercation ensued. They were given half an hour to remove their women and children. Then the squadrons advanced. The tribesmen, still menacing, retired slowly towards the hills. Then a small party came up and informed Major Beatson, that in the next village was a troop-horse, which had been captured in the fighting in the Swat Valley. This admission, that the Mamunds had been implicated in the attack on the Malakand, was sufficiently naive. The cavalry rode on to the village. The horse was not to be found, but the officious informers from the first village eagerly pointed out where it had been stabled. In consequence of this information, and to stimulate the tribesmen to carry out the original terms, Mr. Davis decided to make an example and authorised Major Beatson to destroy the house of the owner of the stolen property. This was accordingly done. As soon as the smoke began to rise, the tribesmen, who had waited, half a mile away, opened a dropping fire from Martini-Henry rifles on the cavalry. These, not wishing to engage, retired at a trot. They were followed up, but though the fire was well directed, the range was too great for accurate shooting and the bullets whizzed harmlessly overhead,

As the Lancers left the valley, an incident occurred which illustrates what has been said in an earlier chapter, and is characteristic of the daily life of the natives. The people of the first village had directed the attention of the cavalry to the second. Part of the second had been in consequence burnt. The inhabitants of both turned out to discuss the matter with rifles and, when last seen that night, were engaged in a lively skirmish. Apparently, however, they soon forgot their differences.

The rumour that the cavalry had been fired on preceded them to camp, and the prospects of some opposition were everywhere hailed with satisfaction. Many had begun to think that the Mohmand expedition was going to be a mere parade, and that the tribesmen were overawed by the powerful forces employed. They were soon to be undeceived. I watched the squadrons return. Behind them the Mamund Valley was already dark with the shadows of the evening and the heavy clouds that had hung over it all day. They were vastly pleased with themselves. Nothing in life is so exhilarating as to be shot at without result. The sowars sat their horses with conscious pride. Some of the younger officers still showed the flush of excitement on their cheeks. But they pretended excellently well to have forgotten all about the matter. They believed a few fellows had "sniped" at them; that was all.

But it was by no means all. Whatever is the Afhgan equivalent of the "Fiery Cross" was circulated among the tribes. There was no time for them to gather to attack that night, and the situation of the camp in the open was unsuited to night firing. The other brigade was coming. They would wait. They therefore contented themselves with firing occasional shots, beginning while we were at dinner, and continuing at intervals until daylight. No one was hurt, but we may imagine that the tribesmen, who spent the night prowling about the nullahs, and firing from time to time, returned to their countrymen next morning boasting of what they had done. "Alone, while ye all slumbered and slept, in the night, in the darkness, I, even I, have attacked the camp of the accursed ones and have slain a Sahib. Is it not so, my brothers?" Whereupon the brothers, hoping he would some day corroborate a lie for them, replied, that it was undoubtedly so, and that he had deserved well of the tribe. Such is the reward of the "sniper."

Early next morning the 3rd Brigade and three squadrons of the 11th Bengal Lancers moved on to Nawagai and crossed the pass without opposition. The general and Headquarters staff accompanied them, and we found ourselves in a wide and extensive valley, on the far side of which the Bedmanai Pass could be plainly seen. Here, at last, we got definite information of the Mohmands' intentions. The Hadda Mullah with 1000 tribesmen had gathered to oppose the further advance. After all there would be a fight. In the evening Sir Bindon Blood, taking a squadron of cavalry, rode out to reconnoitre the approaches to the pass and the general configuration of the ground. On his return he sent a despatch to the Government of India, that he would force it on the 18th. The soldiers, especially the British troops, who had not yet been engaged, eagerly looked forward to the approaching action. But events were destined to a different course.

It was already dusk when we returned from the reconnaissance. The evening was pleasant and we dined in the open air. Still the valley was very dark. The mountains showed a velvet black. Presently the moon rose. I repress the inclination to try to describe the beauty of the scene, as the valley was swiftly flooded with that mysterious light. All the suitable words have probably been employed many times by numerous writers and skipped by countless readers. Indeed I am inclined to think, that these elaborate descriptions convey little to those who have not seen, and are unnecessary to those who have. Nature will not be admired by proxy. In times of war, however, especially of frontier war, the importance of the moon is brought home to everybody. "What time does it rise to-night?" is the question that recurs; for other things—attacks, "sniping," rushes,—besides the tides are influenced by its movements.

Meanwhile, as at Nawagai, at a peaceful camp and a quiet dinner we watched the "silvery maiden" swiftly appear over the eastern mountains. She was gazing on a different scene eleven miles away, in the valley we had left.

The 2nd Brigade had marched that morning from Jar to the foot of the Rambat Pass, which it was intended to cross the next day. Brigadier-General Jefferys, in anticipation of this movement, sent the Buffs up to hold the Kotal, and camped at the foot with the rest of his force. The situation of the camp, which had been adopted with a view to the advance at daybreak, favored the approach of an enemy. The ground was broken and intersected by numerous small and tortuous nullahs, and strewn with rocks. Any other site would, however, have necessitated a long march the next day, and no attack was thought likely.

At 8.15, as the officers were finishing dinner, three shots rang out in the silence. They were a signal. Instantly brisk firing broke out from the nullahs on the face of the square occupied by the Guides Infantry. Bullets whistled all about the camp, ripping through the tents and killing and wounding the animals.

The Guides returned the fire with steadiness, and, as the shelter trench they had dug in front of their section of the line was higher than at other parts, no officers or men were hit. At ten o'clock a bugler among the enemy sounded the "Retire," and the fire dwindled to a few dropping shots. All were congratulating themselves on a termination of the event, when at 10.30 the attack was renewed with vigour on the opposite side of the camp, occupied by the 38th Dogras. The enemy, who were largely armed with Martini-Henry rifles, crept up to within 100 yards of the trenches. These were only about eighteen inches high, but afforded sufficient cover to the soldiers. The officers, with a splendid disregard of the danger, exposed themselves freely. Walking coolly up and down in the brilliant moonlight they were excellent targets. The brigadier proceeded himself to the threatened side of the camp, to control the firing and prevent the waste of ammunition. A good many thousand rounds were, however, fired away without much result. Several star shells were also fired by the battery. The ground was so broken that they revealed very little, but the tribesmen were alarmed by the smell they made, thinking it a poisonous gas. The officers were directed to take cover, but the necessity of sending messages and regulating the fire involved a great deal of exposure. And to all who showed above the trench the danger was great. Captain Tomkins of the 38th Dogras was shot through the heart, and a few minutes later the adjutant of the regiment, Lieutenant Bailey, was also killed. In assisting to take these officers to the hospital, where a rough shelter of boxes had been improvised, Lieutenant Harington, an officer attached to the Dogras, received a bullet in the back of the head, which penetrated his brain and inflicted injuries from which he died subsequently. All tents were struck and as much cover as could be made from grain-bags and biscuit-boxes was arranged. At 2.15 the firing ceased and the enemy drew off, taking their killed and wounded with them. They had no mind to be surprised by daylight, away from their hills. But they had already remained a little too long.

As soon as the light allowed, the cavalry squadron under Captain Cole started in pursuit. After a long gallop down the valley, he caught one party making for the mountains. Charging immediately, he succeeded in spearing twenty-one of these before they could reach the rocks. The squadron then dismounted and opened fire with their carbines. But the tribesmen turned at once and made a dash in the direction of the led horses. A sowar was wounded and a couple of horses killed. The cavalrymen, threatened in a vital point, ran hurriedly back, and just got into their saddles in time. In the haste of mounting four horses got loose and galloped away, leaving six dismounted men. Captain Cole placed one of them before him on the saddle, and the troopers followed his example. The squadron thus encumbered, retired, and after getting out of range, succeeded in catching their loose horses again. The enemy, seeing the cavalry mounted once more, took refuge on the hills. But it was evident, they were eager for fighting.

The casualties in the night attack of Markhanai were as follows:—

BRITOFFICERS.
Killed—Capt. W.E. Tomkins, 38th Dogras.
" Lieut. A.W. Bailey, 38th Dogras.
Died of wounds—Lieut. H.A. Harington, attd. 38th Dogras.

NATIVE OFFICER.
Wounded 1

NATIVE SOLDIERS.

	Killed.	Wounded.
No.8 Mountain Battery	1	1
35th Sikhs	1	3
38th Dogras	1	0
Guides Infantry	0	1
Followers	2	2

Total Casualties, 16; and 98 horses and mules.

Meanwhile, the 3rd Brigade had passed a tranquil night at Nawagai. Next morning, however, at about six o'clock, a message was heliographed from the Buffs on the Rambat Pass, to the effect that an attack had been made on General Jeffreys' camp; that heavy firing had continued all night, and that several officers were among the casualties. This news set every one agog. While we were breakfasting, a native officer and ten sowars of the 11th Bengal Lancers arrived at speed with full details: six hours' fighting with the Mamunds: three officers killed or mortally wounded; and nearly a hundred animals hit. In consequence of this information, Sir Bindon Blood cancelled the orders for the passage of the Rambat Pass and instructed General Jeffreys to enter the Mamund Valley and thoroughly chastise the tribesmen.

I was allowed to go back with the native officer's escort to the 2nd Brigade, in order to witness the operations which had been ordered. Judiciously selecting a few things, which could be carried on the saddle, of which the most important were a cloak, some chocolate and a tooth-brush, I hurried after the escort, who had already started, and overtook them just as they had got through the pass of Nawagai.

For the first six miles the road lay through a network of deep ravines, through which the troopers picked their way very carefully. It would have been a bad place for a small party to have been attacked in, but fortunately, though several armed tribesmen were seen, they did not fire at us. At one point the route lay through a deep nullah, along which some of the assailants of the night before had retired. These were probably from the Charmanga Valley. They had evidently suffered losses. Several native beds on which wounded men had been carried lay scattered about. At this place they had probably found some oxen, to which they had transferred their bodies. At length we got clear of the difficult ground, and entering the smooth plain of Nawagai looked out eagerly for the brigade. Seven miles away across the valley was a long brown streak. It was the troops marching from Markhanai to the entrance of the Mamund Valley. The smoke of five burning villages rose in a tall column into the air—blue against the mountains, brown against the sky. An hour's riding brought us to the brigade. Every one was full of the events of the night, and all looked worn from having had no sleep. "You were very lucky to be out of it," they said. "There's plenty more coming."

The cavalry soon returned from their pursuit. The points of their lances were covered with dark smears. A sowar displayed his weapon proudly to some Sikhs, who grinned in appreciation. "How many?" was the question asked on all sides. "Twenty-one," replied the officer. "But they're full of fight."

Orders were now issued for the brigade to camp on the open ground near Inayat Kila, which, translated, means Fort Grant, and is the name of a considerable stone stronghold belonging to the Khan of Khar. Although the troops were very tired from their march, and the fighting of the preceding night, they began entrenching with alacrity. Besides making an outer wall to the camp, about three and a half feet high, everybody scratched a little hole for himself. In these occupations the afternoon passed.

The Buffs came in at sunset, having marched from the top of the Rambat Pass. They had heard the firing of the night and were disappointed at having been absent. It was "just their luck," they said. During the Chitral campaign of 1895, they had had the ill-fortune to miss every engagement. It would be the same now. All tried to reassure them. As soon as it was dark an attack was probable.

A dropping fire began after dinner from the great nullah to the north of the camp, and all lights were put out and the tents struck. Every one retired to the soup-plate he had scooped in the earth. But no attack was made. The enemy had informed the political officer through the friendlies, that they were weary and would rest that night. They sent a few "snipers" to fire into the camp, and these kept up a desultory fusillade until about two o'clock, when they drew off.

Those who had been deprived of their rest the night before soon dropped off to sleep, in spite of the firing. Others, not overpowered by weariness, found no occupation but to lie in their holes and contemplate the stars—those impartial stars which shine as calmly on Piccadilly Circus as on Inayat Kila.

CHAPTER XI:

THE ACTION OF THE MAMUND VALLEY, 16TH SEPTEMBER

Sound as of bugle in camp, how it rings through the chill
air of morning,
Bidding the soldier arise, he must wake and be armed ere
the light.
Firm be your faith and your feet, when the sun's burning
rays shall be o'er you.
When the rifles are ranging in line, and the clear note of
battle is blown.

"A Sermon in Lower Bengal," SIR A. LYALL.

The story has now reached a point which I cannot help
regarding as its climax. The action of the Mamund Valley is recalled
to me by so many vivid incidents and enduring memories, that it
assumes an importance which is perhaps beyond its true historic
proportions. Throughout the reader must make allowances for
what I have called the personal perspective. Throughout he must
remember, how small is the scale of operations. The panorama is
not filled with masses of troops. He will not hear the thunder of a
hundred guns. No cavalry brigades whirl by with flashing swords.
No infantry divisions are applied at critical points. The looker-
on will see only the hillside, and may, if he watches with care,
distinguish a few brown clad men moving slowly about it, dwarfed
almost to invisibility by the size of the landscape. I hope to take
him close enough, to see what these men are doing and suffering;
what their conduct is and what their fortunes are. But I would ask

him to observe that, in what is written, I rigidly adhere to my role of a spectator. If by any phrase or sentence I am found to depart from this, I shall submit to whatever evil things the ingenuity of malice may suggest.

On the morning of the 16th, in pursuance of Sir Bindon Blood's orders, Brigadier-General Jeffreys moved out of his entrenched camp at Inayat Kila, and entered the Mamund Valley. His intentions were, to chastise the tribesmen by burning and blowing up all defensible villages within reach of the troops. It was hoped, that this might be accomplished in a single day, and that the brigade, having asserted its strength, would be able to march on the 17th to Nawagai and take part in the attack on the Bedmanai Pass, which had been fixed for the 18th. Events proved this hope to be vain, but it must be remembered, that up to this time no serious opposition had been offered by the tribesmen to the columns, and that no news of any gathering had been reported to the general. The valley appeared deserted. The villages looked insignificant and defenceless. It was everywhere asserted that the enemy would not stand.

Reveille sounded at half-past five, and at six o'clock the brigade marched out. In order to deal with the whole valley at once, the force was divided into three columns, to which were assigned the following tasks:—

I. The right column, under Lieut.-Col. Vivian, consisting of the 38th Dogras and some sappers, was ordered to attack the village of Domodoloh. II. The centre column, under Colonel Goldney, consisting of six companies Buffs, six companies 35th Sikhs, a half-company sappers, four guns of No.8 Mountain Battery and the squadron of the 11th Bengal Lancers, was ordered to proceed to the head of the valley, and destroy the villages of Badelai and Shahi-Tangi (pronounced Shytungy). III. The left column, under Major Campbell, consisting of five companies of the Guides Infantry, and some sappers, was directed against several villages at the western end of the valley.

Two guns and two companies from each battalion were left to protect the camp, and a third company of the Guides was detached to protect the survey party. This reduced the strength of the infantry in the field to twenty-three companies, or slightly over 1200 men. Deducting the 300 men of the 38th Dogras who were not engaged, the total force employed in the action was about 1000 men of all arms.

It will be convenient to deal with the fortunes of the right column first. Lieut.-Colonel Vivian, after a march of six miles, arrived before the village of Domodoloh at about 9 A.M. He found it strongly held by the enemy, whose aspect was so formidable, that he did not consider himself strong enough to attack without artillery and supports, and with prudence returned to camp, which he reached about 4 P.M. Two men were wounded by long-range fire.

The centre column advanced covered by Captain Cole's squadron of Lancers, to which I attached myself. At about seven o'clock we observed the enemy on a conical hill on the northern slopes of the valley. Through the telescope, an instrument often far more useful to cavalry than field-glasses, it was possible to distinguish their figures. Long lines of men clad in blue or white, each with his weapon upright beside him, were squatting on the terraces. Information was immediately sent back to Colonel Goldney. The infantry, eager for action, hurried their march. The cavalry advanced to within 1000 yards of the hills. For some time the tribesmen sat and watched the gradual deployment of the troops, which was developing in the plain below them. Then, as the guns and infantry approached, they turned and began slowly to climb the face of the mountain.

In hopes of delaying them or inducing them to fight, the cavalry now trotted to within closer range, and dismounting, opened fire at 7.30 precisely. It was immediately returned. From high up the hillside, from the cornfields at the base, and from the towers of the villages, little puffs of smoke darted. The skirmish continued for an hour without much damage to either side, as the enemy were well covered by the broken ground and the soldiers by the gravestones and trees of a cemetery. Then the infantry began to arrive. The Buffs had been detached from Colonel Goldney's column and were moving against the village of Badelai. The 35th Sikhs proceeded towards the long ridge, round the corner of which Shahi-Tangi stands. As they crossed our front slowly—and rather wearily, for they were fatigued by the rapid marching—the cavalry mounted and rode off in quest of more congenial work with the cavalryman's weapon—the lance. I followed the fortunes of the Sikhs. Very little opposition was encountered. A few daring sharpshooters fired at the leading companies from the high corn. Others fired long-range shots from the mountains. Neither caused any loss. Colonel Goldney now ordered one and a half companies, under Captain Ryder, to clear the conical hill, and protect the right of the regiment from the fire—from the mountains. These men, about seventy-five in number, began climbing the steep slope; nor did I see them again till much later in the day. The remaining four and a half companies continued to advance. The line lay through high crops on terraces, rising one above the other. The troops toiled up these, clearing the enemy out of a few towers they tried to hold. Half a company was left with the dressing station near the cemetery, and two more were posted as supports at the bottom of the hills. The other two commenced the ascent of the long spur which leads to Shahi-Tangi.

It is impossible to realise without seeing, how very slowly troops move on hillsides. It was eleven o'clock before the village was reached. The enemy fell back "sniping," and doing hardly any damage. Everybody condemned their pusillanimity in making off without a fight. Part of the village and some stacks of bhoosa, a kind of chopped straw, were set on fire, and the two companies prepared to return to camp.

But at about eight the cavalry patrols had reported the enemy in great strength at the northwest end of the valley. In consequence of this Brigadier-General Jeffreys ordered the Guides Infantry to join the main column. [Copy of message showing the time:—"To Officer, Commanding Guides Infantry.—Despatched 8.15 A.M. Received 8.57 A.M. Enemy collecting at Kanra; come up at once on Colonel Goldney's left. C. Powell, Major, D.A.Q.M.G."] Major Campbell at once collected his men, who were engaged in foraging, and hurried towards Colonel Goldney's force. After a march of five miles, he came in contact with the enemy in strength on his left front, and firing at once became heavy. At the sound of the musketry the Buffs were recalled from the village of Badelai and also marched to support the 35th Sikhs.

While both these regiments were hurrying to the scene, the sound of loud firing first made us realise that our position at the head of the spur near Shahi-Tangi was one of increasing danger. The pressure on the left threatened the line of retreat, and no supports were available within a mile. A retirement was at once ordered. Up to this moment hardly any of the tribesmen had been seen. It appeared as if the retirement of the two companies was the signal for their attack. I am inclined to think, however, that this was part of the general advance of the enemy, and that even had no retirement been ordered the advanced companies would have been assailed. In any case the aspect of affairs immediately changed. From far up the hillsides men came running swiftly down, dropping from ledge to ledge, and dodging from rock to rock. The firing increased on every hand. Half a company was left to cover the withdrawal. The Sikhs made excellent practice on the advancing enemy, who approached by twos and threes, making little rushes from one patch of cover to another. At length a considerable number had accumulated behind some rocks about a hundred yards away. The firing now became heavy and the half-company, finding its flank threatened, fell back to the next position.

A digression is necessary to explain the peculiar configuration of the ground.

The spur, at the top of which the village stands, consists of three rocky knolls, each one higher than the other, as the main hill is approached. These are connected by open necks of ground, which are commanded by fire from both flanks. In section the ground resembles a switchback railway.

The first of these knolls was evacuated without loss, and the open space to the next quickly traversed. I think a couple of men fell here, and were safely carried away. The second knoll was commanded by the first, on to which the enemy climbed, and from which they began firing. Again the companies retired. Lieutenant Cassells remained behind with about eight men, to hold the knoll until the rest had crossed the open space. As soon as they were clear they shouted to him to retire. He gave the order.

Till this time the skirmishing of the morning might have afforded pleasure to the neuropath, experience to the soldier, "copy" to the journalist. Now suddenly black tragedy burst upon the scene, and all excitement died out amid a multitude of vivid trifles. As Lieutenant Cassells rose to leave the knoll, he turned sharply and fell on the ground. Two Sepoys immediately caught hold of him. One fell shot through the leg. A soldier who had continued firing sprang into the air, and, falling, began to bleed with strange and terrible rapidity from his mouth and chest. Another turned on his back kicking and twisting. A fourth lay quite still. Thus in the time it takes to write half the little party were killed or wounded. The enemy had worked round both flanks and had also the command. Their fire was accurate.

Two officers, the subadar major, by name Mangol Singh, and three or four Sepoys ran forward from the second knoll, to help in carrying the wounded off. Before they reached the spot, two more men were hit. The subadar major seized Lieutenant Cassells, who was covered with blood and unable to stand, but anxious to remain in the firing line. The others caught hold of the injured and began dragging them roughly over the sharp rocks in spite of their screams and groans. Before we had gone thirty yards from the knoll, the enemy rushed on to it, and began firing. Lieutenant Hughes, the adjutant of the regiment, and one of the most popular officers on the frontier, was killed. The bullets passed in the air with a curious sucking noise, like that produced by drawing the air between the lips. Several men also fell. Lieut.-Colonel Bradshaw ordered two Sepoys to carry the officer's body away. This they began to do. Suddenly a scattered crowd of tribesmen rushed over the crest of the hill and charged sword in hand, hurling great stones. It became impossible to remain an impassive spectator. Several of the wounded were dropped. The subadar major stuck to Lieutenant Cassells, and it is to him the lieutenant owes his life. The men carrying the other officer, dropped him and fled. The body sprawled upon the ground. A tall man in dirty white linen pounced down upon it with a curved sword. It was a horrible sight.

Had the swordsmen charged home, they would have cut everybody down. But they did not. These wild men of the mountains were afraid of closing. The retirement continued. Five or six times the two companies, now concentrated, endeavoured to stand. Each time the tribesmen pressed round both flanks. They had the whole advantage of ground, and commanded, as well as out-flanked the Sikhs. At length the bottom of the spur was reached, and the remainder of the two companies turned to bay in the nullah with fixed bayonets. The tribesmen came on impetuously, but stopped thirty yards away, howling, firing and waving their swords.

No other troops were in sight, except our cavalry, who could be seen retiring in loose squadron column—probably after their charge. They could give no assistance. The Buffs were nearly a mile away. Things looked grave. Colonel Goldney himself tried to re-form the men. The Sikhs, who now numbered perhaps sixty, were hard pressed, and fired without effect. Then some one—who it was is uncertain—ordered the bugler to sound the "charge." The shrill notes rang out not once but a dozen times. Every one began to shout. The officers waved their swords frantically. Then the Sikhs commenced to move slowly forward towards the enemy, cheering. It was a supreme moment. The tribesmen turned, and began to retreat. Instantly the soldiers opened a steady fire, shooting down their late persecutors with savage energy.

Then for the first time, I perceived that the repulse was general along the whole front. What I have described was only an incident. But the reader may learn from the account the explanation of many of our losses in the frontier war. The troops, brave and well-armed, but encumbered with wounded, exhausted by climbing and overpowered by superior force, had been ordered to retire. This is an operation too difficult for a weak force to accomplish. Unless supports are at hand, they must be punished severely, and the small covering parties, who remain to check the enemy, will very often be cut to pieces, or shot down. Afterwards in the Mamund Valley whole battalions were employed to do what these two Sikh companies had attempted. But Sikhs need no one to bear witness to their courage.

During the retirement down the spur, I was unable to observe the general aspect of the action, and now in describing it, I have dealt only with the misadventures of one insignificant unit. It is due to the personal perspective. While the two advanced companies were being driven down the hill, a general attack was made along the whole left front of the brigade, by at least 2000 tribesmen, most of whom were armed with rifles. To resist this attack there were the cavalry, the two supporting companies of the 35th Sikhs and five of the Guides Infantry, who were arriving. All became engaged. Displaying their standards, the enemy advanced with great courage in the face of a heavy fire. Many were killed and wounded, but they continued to advance, in a long skirmish line, on the troops. One company of the 35th became seriously involved. Seeing this, Captain Cole moved his squadron forward, and though the ground was broken, charged. The enemy took refuge in the nullah, tumbling into it standards and all, and opened a sharp fire on the cavalry at close range, hitting several horses and men. The squadron fell back. But the moral effect of their advance had been tremendous. The whole attack came to a standstill. The infantry fire continued. Then the tribesmen began to retire, and they were finally repulsed at about twelve o'clock.

An opportunity was now presented of breaking off the action. The brigade had started from camp divided, and in expectation that no serious resistance would be offered. It had advanced incautiously. The leading troops had been roughly handled. The enemy had delivered a vigorous counter attack. That attack had been repulsed with slaughter, and the brigade was concentrated. Considering the fatigues to which the infantry had been exposed, it would perhaps have been more prudent to return to camp and begin again next morning. But Brigadier-General Jeffries was determined to complete the destruction of Shahi-Tangi, and to recover the body of Lieutenant Hughes, which remained in the hands of the enemy. It was a bold course. But it was approved by every officer in the force.

A second attack was ordered. The Guides were to hold the enemy in check on the left. The Buffs, supported by the 35th Sikhs, were to take the village. Orders were signalled back to camp for all the available troops to reinforce the column in the field, and six fresh companies consequently started. At one o'clock the advance recommenced, the guns came into action on a ridge on the right of the brigade, and shelled the village continuously.

Again the enemy fell back "sniping," and very few of them were to be seen. But to climb the hill alone took two hours. The village was occupied at three o'clock, and completely destroyed by the Buffs. At 3.30 orders reached them to return to camp, and the second withdrawal began. Again the enemy pressed with vigour, but this time there were ten companies on the spur instead of two, and the Buffs, who became rear-guard, held everything at a distance with their Lee-Metford rifles. At a quarter to five the troops were clear of the hills and we looked about us.

While this second attack was being carried out, the afternoon had slipped away. At about two o'clock Major Campbell and Captain Cole, both officers of great experience on the frontier, had realised the fact, that the debate with the tribesmen could not be carried to a conclusion that day. At their suggestion a message was heliographed up to the General's staff officer on the spur near the guns, as follows: "It is now 2.30. Remember we shall have to fight our way home." But the brigadier had already foreseen this possibility, and had, as described, issued orders for the return march. These orders did not reach Captain Ryder's company on the extreme right until they had become hard pressed by the increasing attack of the enemy. Their wounded delayed their retirement. They had pushed far up the mountain side, apparently with the idea they were to crown the heights, and we now saw them two miles away on the sky line hotly engaged.

While I was taking advantage of a temporary halt, to feed and water my pony, Lieutenant MacNaghten of the 16th Lancers pointed them out to me, and we watched them through our glasses. It was a strange sight. Little figures running about confusedly, tiny puffs of smoke, a miniature officer silhouetted against the sky waving his sword. It seemed impossible to believe that they were fighting for their lives, or indeed in any danger. It all looked so small and unreal. They were, however, hard pressed, and had signalled that they were running out of cartridges. It was then five o'clock, and the approach of darkness was accelerated by the heavy thunderclouds which were gathering over the northern mountains.

At about 3.30 the brigadier had ordered the Guides to proceed to Ryder's assistance and endeavour to extricate his company. He directed Major Campbell to use his own discretion. It was a difficult problem, but the Guides and their leader were equal to it. They had begun the day on the extreme left. They had hurried to the centre. Now they were ordered to the extreme right. They had already marched sixteen miles, but they were still fresh. We watched them defiling across the front, with admiration. Meanwhile, the retirement of the brigade was delayed. It was necessary that all units should support each other, and the troops had to wait till the Guides had succeeded in extricating Ryder. The enemy now came on in great strength from the north-western end of the valley, which had been swarming with them all day, so that for the first time the action presented a fine spectacle.

Across the broad plain the whole of the brigade was in echelon. On the extreme right Ryder's company and the Guides Infantry were both severely engaged. Half a mile away to the left rear the battery, the sappers and two companies of the 35th Sikhs were slowly retiring. Still farther to the left were the remainder of the 35th, and, at an interval of half a mile, the Buffs. The cavalry protected the extreme left flank. This long line of troops, who were visible to each other but divided by the deep broad nullahs which intersected the whole plain, fell back slowly, halting frequently to keep touch. Seven hundred yards away were the enemy, coming on in a great half-moon nearly three miles long and firing continually. Their fire was effective, and among other casualties at this time Lieutenant Crawford, R.A., was killed. Their figures showed in rows of little white dots. The darkness fell swiftly. The smoke puffs became fire flashes. Great black clouds overspread the valley and thunder began to roll. The daylight died away. The picture became obscured, and presently it was pitch dark. All communication, all mutual support, all general control now ceased. Each body of troops closed up and made the best of their way to the camp, which was about seven miles off. A severe thunderstorm broke overhead. The vivid lightning displayed the marching columns and enabled the enemy to aim. Individual tribesmen ran up, shouting insults, to within fifty yards of the Buffs and discharged their rifles. They were answered with such taunts as the limited Pushtu of the British soldier allows and careful volleys. The troops displayed the greatest steadiness. The men were determined, the officers cheery, the shooting accurate. At half-past eight the enemy ceased to worry us. We thought we had driven them off, but they had found a better quarry.

The last two miles to camp were painful. After the cessation of the firing the fatigue of the soldiers asserted itself. The Buffs had been marching and fighting continuously for thirteen hours. They had had no food, except their early morning biscuit, since the preceding night. The older and more seasoned amongst them laughed at their troubles, declaring they would have breakfast, dinner and tea together when they got home. The younger ones collapsed in all directions.

The officers carried their rifles. Such ponies and mules as were available were laden with exhausted soldiers. Nor was this all. Other troops had passed before us, and more than a dozen Sepoys of different regiments were lying senseless by the roadside. All these were eventually carried in by the rear-guard, and the Buffs reached camp at nine o'clock.

Meanwhile, the Guides had performed a brilliant feat of arms, and had rescued the remnants of the isolated company from the clutches of the enemy. After a hurried march they arrived at the foot of the hill down which Ryder's men were retiring. The Sikhs, utterly exhausted by the exertions of the day, were in disorder, and in many cases unable from extreme fatigue even to use their weapons. The tribesmen hung in a crowd on the flanks and rear of the struggling company, firing incessantly and even dashing in and cutting down individual soldiers. Both officers were wounded. Lieutenant Gunning staggered down the hill unaided, struck in three places by bullets and with two deep sword cuts besides. Weary, outnumbered, surrounded on three sides, without unwounded officers or cartridges, the end was only a matter of moments. All must have been cut to pieces. But help was now at hand.

The Guides formed line, fixed bayonets and advanced at the double towards the hill. At a short distance from its foot they halted and opened a terrible and crushing fire upon the exulting enemy. The loud detonations of their company volleys were heard and the smoke seen all over the field, and on the left we wondered what was happening. The tribesmen, sharply checked, wavered. The company continued its retreat. Many brave deeds were done as the night closed in. Havildar Ali Gul, of the Afridi Company of the Guides, seized a canvas cartridge carrier, a sort of loose jacket with large pockets, filled it with ammunition from his men's pouches, and rushing across the fire-swept space, which separated the regiment from the Sikhs, distributed the precious packets to the struggling men. Returning he carried a wounded native officer on his back. Seeing this several Afridis in the Guides ran forward, shouting and cheering, to the rescue, and other wounded Sikhs were saved by their gallantry from a fearful fate. At last Ryder's company reached the bottom of the hill and the survivors re-formed under cover of the Guides.

These, thrown on their own resources, separated from the rest of the brigade by darkness and distance and assailed on three sides by the enemy, calmly proceeded to fight their way back to camp. Though encumbered with many wounded and amid broken ground, they repulsed every attack, and bore down all the efforts which the tribesmen made to intercept their line of retreat. They reached camp at 9.30 in safety, and not without honour. The skill and experience of their officers, the endurance and spirit of the men, had enabled them to accomplish a task which many had believed impossible, and their conduct in the action of the Mamund Valley fills a brilliant page in the history of the finest and most famous frontier regiment. [The gallantry of the two officers, Captain Hodson and Lieut. Codrington, who commanded the two most exposed companies, was the subject of a special mention in despatches, and the whole regiment were afterwards complimented by Brigadier-General Jeffreys on their fine performance.]

As the Buffs reached the camp the rain which had hitherto held off came down. It poured. The darkness was intense. The camp became a sea of mud. In expectation that the enemy would attack it, General Jeffreys had signalled in an order to reduce the perimeter. The camp was therefore closed up to half its original size.

Most of the tents had been struck and lay with the baggage piled in confused heaps on the ground. Many of the transport animals were loose and wandering about the crowded space. Dinner or shelter there was none. The soldiers, thoroughly exhausted, lay down supperless in the slush. The condition of the wounded was particularly painful. Among the tents which had been struck were several of the field hospitals. In the darkness and rain it was impossible to do more for the poor fellows than to improve the preliminary dressings and give morphia injections, nor was it till four o'clock on the next afternoon that the last were taken out of the doolies.

After about an hour the rain stopped, and while the officers were bustling about making their men get some food before they went to sleep, it was realised that all the troops were not in camp. The general, the battery, the sappers and four companies of infantry were still in the valley. Presently we heard the firing of guns. They were being attacked,—overwhelmed perhaps. To send them assistance was to risk more troops being cut off. The Buffs who were dead beat, the Sikhs who had suffered most severe losses, and the Guides who had been marching and fighting all day, were not to be thought of. The 38th Dogras were, however, tolerably fresh, and Colonel Goldney, who commanded in the absence of the General, at once ordered four companies to parade and march to the relief. Captain Cole volunteered to accompany them with a dozen sowars. The horses were saddled. But the order was countermanded, and no troops left the camp that night.

Whether this decision was justified or not the reader shall decide. In the darkness and the broken ground it was probable the relief would never have found the general. It was possible that getting involved among the nullahs they would have been destroyed. The defenders of the camp itself were none too many. The numbers of the enemy were unknown. These were weighty reasons. On the other hand it seemed unsoldierly to lie down to sleep while at intervals the booming of the guns reminded us, that comrades were fighting for their lives a few miles away in the valley.

CHAPTER XII:

AT INAYAT KILA

"Two thousand pounds of education
Drops to a ten-rupee jezail.

* * * * *

Strike hard who cares. Shoot straight who can.
The odds are on the cheaper man."

RUDYARD KIPLING.

Half an hour before dawn on the 17th, the cavalry were mounted, and as soon as the light was strong enough to find a way through the broken ground, the squadron started in search of the missing troops. We had heard no more of their guns since about two o'clock. We therefore concluded they had beaten off the enemy. There might, of course, be another reason for their silence. As we drew near Bilot, it was possible to distinguish the figures of men moving about the walls and houses. The advanced files rode cautiously forward. Suddenly they cantered up to the wall and we knew some at least were alive. Captain Cole, turning to his squadron, lifted his hand. The sowars, actuated by a common impulse, rose in their stirrups and began to cheer. But there was no response. Nor was this strange. The village was a shambles. In an angle of the outside wall, protected on the third side by a shallow trench, were the survivors of the fight. All around lay the corpses of men and mules. The bodies of five or six native soldiers were being buried in a hurriedly dug grave. It was thought that, as they were Mahommedans, their resting-place would be respected by the tribesmen. [These bodies were afterwards dug up and mutilated by the natives: a foul act which excited the fury and indignation of soldiers of every creed in the force. I draw the reader's attention to this unpleasant subject, only to justify what I have said in an earlier chapter of the degradation of mind in which the savages of the mountains are sunk.] Eighteen wounded men lay side by side in a roofless hut. Their faces, drawn by pain and anxiety, looked ghastly in the pale light of the early morning. Two officers, one with his left hand smashed, the other shot through both legs, were patiently waiting for the moment when the improvised tourniquets could be removed and some relief afforded to their sufferings. The brigadier, his khaki coat stained with the blood from a wound on his head, was talking to his only staff-officer, whose helmet displayed a bullet-hole. The most ardent lover of realism would have been satisfied. Food, doolies, and doctors soon arrived. The wounded were brought to the field hospitals to be attended to. The unwounded hurried back to camp to get breakfast and a bath. In half an hour, the ill-omened spot was occupied only by the few sowars engaged in shooting the wounded mules, and by the vultures who watched the proceedings with an expectant interest.

Gradually we learnt the story of the night. The battery, about thirty sappers and half the 35th Sikhs, were returning to camp. At about seven o'clock an order was sent for them to halt and remain out all night, to assist the Guides Infantry, whose firing could be heard and for whose safety the brigadier was above all things anxious. This order reached the battery, and with the sappers as an escort they turned back, recrossed a nullah and met the general with two companies of Sikhs outside the village of Bilot. The half-battalion of the 35th did not apparently receive the order, for they continued their march. Lieutenant Wynter, R.A., was sent back to look for them. He did not find them, but fell in with four fresh companies, two of the Guides and two of the 35th, who, under Major Worlledge, had been sent from camp in response to the general's demand for reinforcements. Lieutenant Wynter brought these back, as an escort to the guns. On arrival at the village, the brigadier at once sent them to the assistance of the Guides. He counted on his own two companies of Sikhs. But when Worlledge had moved off and had already vanished in the night, it was found that these two companies had disappeared. They had lost touch in the darkness, and, not perceiving that the general had halted, had gone on towards camp. Thus the battery was left with no other escort than thirty sappers.

A party of twelve men of the Buffs now arrived, and the circumstances which led them to the guns are worth recording. When the Buffs were retiring through the villages, they held a Mahommedan cemetery for a little while, in order to check the enemy's advance. Whilst there, Lieutenant Byron, Orderly Officer to General Jeffreys, rode up and told Major Moody, who commanded the rear companies, that a wounded officer was lying in a dooly a hundred yards up the road, without any escort. He asked for a few men. Moody issued an order, and a dozen soldiers under a corporal started to look for the dooly. They missed it, but while searching, found the general and the battery outside the village. The presence of these twelve brave men—for they fully maintained the honour of their regiment—with their magazine rifles, just turned the scale. Had not the luck of the British army led them to the village, it can hardly be doubted, and certainly was not doubted by any who were there, that the guns would have been captured and the general killed. Fortune, especially in war, uses tiny fulcra for her powerful lever.

The general now ordered the battery and sappers to go into the village, but it was so full of burning bhoosa, that this was found to be impossible, and they set to work to entrench themselves outside. The village was soon full of the enemy. From the walls and houses, which on two sides commanded the space occupied by the battery, they began to fire at about thirty yards' range. The troops were as much exposed as if they had been in a racket court, of which the enemy held the walls. They could not move, because they would have had to desert either the guns or the wounded. Fortunately, not many of the tribesmen at this point were armed with rifles. The others threw stones and burning bhoosa into the midst of the little garrison. By its light they took good aim. Everybody got under such cover as was available. There was not much. Gunner Nihala, a gallant native soldier, repeatedly extinguished the burning bhoosa with his cloak at the imminent peril of his life. Lieutenants Watson and Colvin, with their sappers and the twelve men of the Buffs, forced their way into the village, and tried to expel the enemy with the bayonet. The village was too large for so small a party to clear. The tribesmen moved from one part to another, repeatedly firing. They killed and wounded several of the soldiers, and a bullet smashed Lieutenant Watson's hand. He however continued his efforts and did not cease until again shot, this time so severely as to be unable to stand. His men carried him from the village, and it was felt that it would be useless to try again.

The attention of the reader is directed to the bravery of this officer. After a long day of marching, and fighting, in the dark, without food and with small numbers, the man who will go on, unshaken and unflinching, after he has received a severe and painful wound, has in respect of personal courage few equals and no superior in the world. It is perhaps as high a form of valour to endure as to dare. The combination of both is sublime. [Both officers have received the Victoria Cross for their conduct on this occasion.]

At nine o'clock the rain stopped the firing, as the tribesmen were afraid of wetting their powder, but at about ten they opened again. They now made a great hole in the wall of the village, through which about a dozen men fired with terrible effect. Others began loopholing the walls. The guns fired case shot at twenty yards' range at these fierce pioneers, smashing the walls to pieces and killing many. The enemy replied with bullets, burning bhoosa and showers of stones.

So the hours dragged away. The general and Captain Birch were both wounded, early in the night. Lieutenant Wynter, while behaving with distinguished gallantry, was shot through both legs at about 11.30. He was thus twice severely wounded within forty-five days. He now continued to command his guns, until he fainted from loss of blood. A native gunner then shielded him with his body, until he also was hit. The whole scene, the close, desperate fighting, the carcasses of the mules, the officers and men crouching behind them, the flaming stacks of bhoosa, the flashes of the rifles, and over all and around all, the darkness of the night—is worthy of the pencil of De Neuville.

At length, at about midnight, help arrived. Worlledge's two companies had gone in search of the Guides, but had not found them. They now returned and, hearing the firing at Bilot, sent an orderly of the 11th Bengal Lancers to ask if the general wanted assistance. This plucky boy—he was only a young recruit—rode coolly up to the village although the enemy were all around, and he stood an almost equal chance of being shot by our own men. He soon brought the two companies to the rescue, and the enemy, balked of their prey, presently drew off in the gloom. How much longer the battery and its defenders could have held out is uncertain. They were losing men steadily, and their numbers were so small that they might have been rushed at any moment. Such was the tale.

No operations took place on the 17th. The soldiers rested, casualties were counted, wounds were dressed, confidence was restored. The funerals of the British officers and men, killed the day before, took place at noon. Every one who could, attended; but all the pomp of military obsequies was omitted, and there were no Union Jacks to cover the bodies, nor were volleys fired over the graves, lest the wounded should be disturbed. Somewhere in the camp—exactly where, is now purposely forgotten—the remains of those who had lost, in fighting for their country, all that men can be sure of, were silently interred. No monument marked the spot. The only assurance that it should be undisturbed is, that it remains unknown. Nevertheless, the funerals were impressive. To some the game of war brings prizes, honour, advancement, or experience; to some the consciousness of duty well discharged; and to others—spectators, perhaps—the pleasure of the play and the knowledge of men and things. But here were those who had drawn the evil numbers—who had lost their all, to gain only a soldier's grave. Looking at these shapeless forms, coffined in a regulation blanket, the pride of race, the pomp of empire, the glory of war appeared but the faint and unsubstantial fabric of a dream; and I could not help realising with Burke: "What shadows we are and what shadows we pursue."

The actual casualties were, in proportion to the numbers engaged, greater than in any action of the British army in India for many years. Out of a force which at no time exceeded 1000 men, nine British officers, four native officers, and 136 soldiers were either killed or wounded. The following is the full return:—

BRITISH OFFICERS.

Killed—Lieutenant and Adjutant V. Hughes, 35th Sikhs.

"   "   A.T. Crawford, R.A.

Wounded severely—Captain W.I. Ryder, attd. 35th Sikhs.

"   "   Lieutenant O.G. Gunning, 35th Sikhs.

"   "   "   O.R. Cassells, 35th Sikhs.

"   "   "   T.C. Watson, R.E.

"   "   "   F.A. Wynter, R.A.

Wounded slightly—Brigadier-General Jeffreys, Commanding 2nd Bde.

M.F.F.

"   "   Captain Birch, R.A.

BRITISH SOLDIERS.

	Killed.	Wounded.
The Buffs	2	9

NATIVE RANKS.

	Killed.	Wounded.
11th Bengal Lancers	0	2
No.8 Mountain Battery	6	21
Guides Infantry	2	10
35th Sikhs	22	45
38th Dogras	0	2
Sappers	4	15

Total Casualties, 149; with 48 horses and mules.

The action of the 16th September is considered by some to have been a reverse. I do not think this view is justified by the facts. The troops accomplished every task they were set. They burned the village of Shahi-Tangi most completely, in spite of all opposition, and they inflicted on the tribesmen a loss of over 200 men. The enemy, though elated by the capture of twenty-two rifles from the bodies of the killed, were impressed by the bravery of the troops. "If," they are reported to have said, "they fight like this when they are divided, we can do nothing." Our losses were undoubtedly heavy and out of all proportion to the advantages gained. They were due to an ignorance, shared by all in the force, of the numbers and fighting power of the Mamunds. No one knew, though there were many who were wise after the event, that these tribesmen were as well armed as the troops, or that they were the brave and formidable adversaries they proved themselves. "Never despise your enemy" is an old lesson, but it has to be learnt afresh, year after year, by every nation that is warlike and brave. Our losses were also due to the isolation of Captain Ryder's company, to extricate which the whole force had to wait till overtaken by darkness. It has been said that war cannot be made without running risks, nor can operations be carried out in the face of an enemy armed with breech-loaders without loss. No tactics can altogether shield men from bullets. Those serene critics who note the errors, and forget the difficulties, who judge in safety of what was done in danger, and from the security of peace, pronounce upon the conduct of war, should remember that the spectacle of a General, wounded, his horse shot, remaining on the field with the last unit, anxious only for the safety of his soldiers, is a spectacle not unworthy of the pages of our military history.

The depression, caused by the loss of amiable and gallant comrades, was dispelled by the prospects of immediate action. Sir Bindon Blood, whose position at Nawagai was now one of danger, sent the brigadier, instead of reinforcements, orders to vigorously prosecute the operations against the tribesmen, and on the morning of the 18th the force moved to attack the village of Domodoloh, which the 38th Dogras had found so strongly occupied on the 16th. Again the enemy were numerous. Again they adopted their effective tactics; but this time no chances were given them. The whole brigade marched concentrated to the attack, and formed up on the level ground just out of shot. The general and his staff rode forward and reconnoitered.

The village lay in a re-entrant of the hills, from which two long spurs projected like the piers of a harbour. Behind, the mountains rose abruptly to a height of 5000 feet. The ground, embraced by the spurs, was filled with crops of maize and barley. A fort and watch-tower guarded the entrance. At 8.30 the advance was ordered. The enemy did not attempt to hold the fort, and it was promptly seized and blown up. The explosion was a strange, though, during the fighting in the Mamund Valley, not an uncommon sight. A great cloud of thick brown-red dust sprang suddenly into the air, bulging out in all directions. The tower broke in half and toppled over. A series of muffled bangs followed. The dust-cloud cleared away, and nothing but a few ruins remained.

The enemy now opened fire from the spurs, both of which became crowned with little circles of white smoke. The 35th Sikhs advancing cleared the right ridge: the 38th Dogras the left. The Guides moved on the village, and up the main re-entrant itself. The Buffs were in reserve. The battery came into action on the left, and began shelling the crests of the opposite hills. Taking the range with their instruments, they fired two shots in rapid succession, each time at slightly different ranges. The little guns exploded with a loud report. Then, far up the mountain side, two balls of smoke appeared, one above the other, and after a few seconds the noise of the bursting shells came faintly back. Usually one would be a little short of—and the other a little over—the point aimed at. The next shot, by dividing the error, would go home, and the dust of the splinters and bullets would show on the peak, from which the tribesmen were firing, and it would become silent and deserted—the scene of an unregarded tragedy. Gradually the spurs were cleared of the enemy and the Guides, passing through the village, climbed up the face of the mountain and established themselves among the great rocks of the steep water-course. Isolated sharpshooters maintained a dropping fire. The company whose operations I watched,—Lieutenant Lockhart's,—killed one of these with a volley, and we found him sitting by a little pool, propped against a stone. He had been an ugly man originally, but now that the bones of his jaw and face were broken in pieces by the bullet, he was hideous to look upon. His only garment was a ragged blue linen cloak fastened at the waist. There he sat—a typical tribesman, ignorant, degraded, and squalid, yet brave and warlike; his only property, his weapon, and that his countrymen had carried off. I could not help contrasting his intrinsic value as a social organism, with that of the officers who had been killed during the week, and those lines of Kipling which appear at the beginning of this chapter were recalled to mind with a strange significance. Indeed I often heard them quoted in the Watelai Valley.

The sappers had now entered the village, and were engaged in preparing the hovels of which it consisted for destruction. Their flat roofs are covered with earth, and will not burn properly, unless a hole is made first in each. This took time. Meanwhile the troops held on to the positions they had seized, and maintained a desultory fire with the enemy. At about noon the place was lighted up, and a dense cloud of smoke rose in a high column into the still air. Then the withdrawal of the troops was ordered. Immediately the enemy began their counter attack. But the Guides were handled with much skill. The retirement of each company was covered by the fire of others, judiciously posted farther down the hill. No opportunity was offered to the enemy. By one o'clock all the troops were clear of the broken ground. The Buffs assumed the duty of rear-guard, and were delighted to have a brisk little skirmish—fortunately unattended with loss of life—with the tribesmen, who soon reoccupied the burning village. This continued for, perhaps, half an hour, and meanwhile the rest of the brigade returned to camp.

The casualties in this highly successful affair were small. It was the first of six such enterprises, by which Brigadier-General Jeffreys, with stubborn perseverance, broke the spirit of the Mamund tribesmen.

	Killed.	Wounded.
35th Sikhs	2	3
Guides Infantry	0	1
38th Dogras	0	2

Total casualties, 8.

The enemy's losses were considerable, but no reliable details could be obtained.

On the 19th the troops rested, and only foraging parties left the camp. On the 20th, fighting was renewed. From the position at the entrance to the valley it was possible to see all the villages that lay in the hollows of the hills, and to distinguish not only the scenes of past but also of future actions. The particular village which was selected for chastisement was never mentioned by name, and it was not until the brigade had marched some miles from the camp, that the objective became evident. The tribesmen therefore continued in a state of "glorious uncertainty," and were unable to gather in really large numbers. At 5.30 A.M. the brigade started, and, preceded by the cavalry, marched up the valley—a long brown stream of men. Arrived nearly at the centre, the troops closed up into a more compact formation. Then suddenly the head wheeled to the left, and began marching on the village of Zagai. Immediately from high up on the face of the mountain a long column of smoke shot into the air. It was a signal fire. Other hills answered it. The affair now became a question of time. If the village could be captured and destroyed before the clans had time to gather, then there would be little fighting. But if the force were delayed or became involved, it was impossible to say on what scale the action would be.

The village of Zagai stands in a similar situation to that of Domodoloh. On either side long spurs advance into the valley, and the houses are built in terraces on the sides of the hollow so formed. Great chenar trees, growing in all their luxuriant beauty out of the rocky ground by the water-course, mark the hillside with a patch of green in contrast to the background of sombre brown. As the troops approached in fine array, the sound of incessant drumming was faintly heard, varied from time to time by the notes of a bugle. The cavalry reconnoitered and trotted off to watch the flank, after reporting the place strongly occupied. The enemy displayed standards on the crests of the spurs. The advance continued: the Guides on the left, the 38th Dogras in the centre, the Buffs on the right, and the 35th Sikhs in reserve. Firing began on the left at about nine o'clock, and a quarter of an hour later the guns came into action near the centre. The Guides and Buffs now climbed the ridges to the right and left. The enemy fell back according to their custom, "sniping." Then the 38th pushed forward and occupied the village, which was handed over to the sappers to destroy. This they did most thoroughly, and at eleven o'clock a dense white smoke was rising from the houses and the stacks of bhoosa. Then the troops were ordered to withdraw. "Facilis ascensus Averni sed . . . ;" without allowing the quotation to lead me into difficulties, I will explain that while it is usually easy to advance against an Asiatic, all retirements are matters of danger. While the village was being destroyed the enemy had been collecting. Their figures could be distinguished on the top of the mountain—a numerous line of dark dots against the sky; others had tried to come, from the adjoining valleys on the left and right. Those on the right succeeded, and the Buffs were soon sharply engaged. On the left the cavalry again demonstrated the power of their arm. A large force of tribesmen, numbering at least 600 men, endeavoured to reach the scene of action. To get there, however, they had to cross the open ground, and this, in face of the Lancers, they would not do. Many of these same tribesmen had joined in the attack on the Malakand,

and had been chased all across the plain of Khar by the fierce Indian horsemen. They were not ambitious to repeat the experience. Every time they tried to cross the space, which separated them from their friends, Captain Cole trotted forward with his squadron, which was only about fifty strong, and the tribesmen immediately scurried back to the hills. For a long time they were delayed, and contented themselves by howling out to the sowars, that they would soon "make mincemeat of them," to which the latter replied that they were welcome to try. At length, realising that they could not escape the cavalry, if they left the hills, they made a long circuit and arrived about half an hour after the village was destroyed and the troops had departed.

Nevertheless, as soon as the retirement was seen to be in progress, a general attack was made all along the line. On the left, the Guides were threatened by a force of about 500 men, who advanced displaying standards, and waving swords. They dispersed these and drove them away by a steady long-range fire, killing and wounding a large number. On the right, the Buffs were harassed by being commanded by another spur. Lieutenant Hasler's company, which I accompanied, was protected from this flanking fire by the ground. A great many bullets, however, hummed overhead, and being anxious to see whence these were coming, the lieutenant walked across the crest to the far side. The half-company here was briskly engaged. From a point high up the mountain an accurate fire was directed upon them. We tried to get the range of this point with the Lee-Metford rifles. It was, as nearly as could be determined, 1400 yards. The tribesmen were only armed with Martini-Henrys. They nevertheless made excellent practice. Lieutenant R.E. Power was shot through the arm and, almost immediately afterwards, Lieutenant Keene was severely wounded in the body. Luckily, the bullet struck his sword-hilt first or he would have been killed. Two or three men were also wounded here. Those who know the range and power of the Martini-Henry rifle will appreciate the skill and marksmanship which can inflict loss even at so great a range.

As the retirement proceeded, the tribesmen came to closer quarters. The Buffs, however, used their formidable weapon with great effect. I witnessed one striking demonstration of its power. Lieutenant F.S. Reeves remained behind with a dozen men to cover the withdrawal of his company, and in hopes of bringing effective fire to bear on the enemy, who at this time were pressing forward boldly. Three hundred yards away was a nullah, and along this they began running, in hopes of cutting off the small party. At one point, however, the line of their advance was commanded by our fire. Presently a man ran into the open. The section fired immediately. The great advantage of the rifle was that there was no difficulty about guessing the exact range, as the fixed sight could be used. The man dropped—a spot of white. Four others rushed forward. Again there was a volley. All four fell and remained motionless. After this we made good our retreat almost unmolested.

As soon as the troops were clear of the hills, the enemy occupied the rocks and ridges, and fired at the retreating soldiers. The Buffs' line of retirement lay over smooth, open ground. For ten minutes the fire was hot. Another officer and seven or eight men dropped. The ground was wet and deep, and the bullets cutting into the soft mud, made strange and curious noises. As soon as the troops got out of range, the firing ceased, as the tribesmen did not dare follow into the open.

On the extreme left, considerable bodies of the enemy appeared, and for a moment it seemed that they would leave the hills and come into the plain. The cavalry, however, trotted forward, and they ran back in confusion, bunching together as they did so. The battery immediately exploded two shrapnel shells in their midst with great effect. This ended the affair, and the troops returned to camp. The casualties were as follows:—

BRITISH OFFICERS.
Wounded severely—2nd Lieutenant G.N.S. Keene.
" slightly—Captain L.I.B. Hulke.
" " —Lieutenant R.E. Power.

BRITISH SOLDIERS.

	Killed.	Wounded.
Buffs 1		10

(Died of wounds).

Native Ranks.

	Wounded.
38th Dogras.................................... 2	

Total casualties, 16.

I shall make the reader no apology for having described at such length, what was after all only a skirmish. The picture of the war on the frontier is essentially one of detail, and it is by the study of the details alone that a true impression can be obtained.

On the 22nd and 23rd the villages of Dag and Tangi were respectively captured and destroyed, but as the resistance was slight and the operations were unmarked by any new features, I shall not weary the reader by further description. The casualties were:—

BRITISH OFFICER.
Wounded—Major S. Moody, the Buffs.

NATIVE RANKS.

	Killed.	Wounded.
Guides Infantry	1	2
38th Dogras	0	2

By these operations the tribesmen of the Mamund Valley had been severely punished. Any exultation which they might have felt over the action of the 16th was completely effaced. The brigade had demonstrated its power to take and burn any village that might be selected, and had inflicted severe loss on all who attempted to impede its action. The tribesmen were now thoroughly disheartened, and on the 21st began to sue for peace.

The situation was, however, complicated by the proximity of the Afghan frontier. The western side of the Mamund Valley is bounded by the mountains of the Hindu Raj range, along the summits of which is the Durand line of demarcation with the Amir. On the farther side of this range Gholam Hyder, the Afghan commander-in-chief, lay with a powerful force, which, at the time of the actions I have described, amounted to nine battalions, six squadrons and fourteen mountain guns. During the attack upon Zagai, numerous figures in khaki uniform had been observed on the higher slopes of the hills, and it was alleged that one particular group appeared to be directing the movements of the tribesmen. At any rate, I cannot doubt, nor did any one who was present during the fighting in the Mamund Valley, that the natives were aided by regular soldiers from the Afghan army, and to a greater extent by

Afghan tribesmen, not only by the supply of arms and ammunition but by actual intervention.

I am not in possession of sufficient evidence to pronounce on the question of the Amir's complicity in the frontier risings. It is certain, that for many years the Afghan policy has consistently been to collect and preserve agents, who might be used in raising a revolt among the Pathan tribes. But the advantages which the Amir would derive from a quarrel with the British are not apparent. It would seem more probable, that he has only tried throughout to make his friendship a matter of more importance to the Indian Government, with a view to the continuance or perhaps the increase of his subsidy. It is possible, that he has this year tested and displayed his power; and that he has desired to show us what a dangerous foe he might be, were he not so useful an ally. The question is a delicate and difficult one. Most of the evidence is contained in Secret State Papers. The inquiry would be profitless; the result possibly unwelcome. Patriotic discretion is a virtue which should at all times be zealously cultivated.

I do not see that the facts I have stated diminish or increase the probability of the Amir's complicity. As the American filibusters sympathise with the Cuban insurgents; as the Jameson raiders supported the outlanders of the Transvaal, so also the soldiers and tribesmen of Afghanistan sympathised with and aided their countrymen and coreligionists across the border. Probably the Afghan Colonial Office would have been vindicated by any inquiry.

It is no disparagement but rather to the honour of men, that they should be prepared to back with their lives causes which claim their sympathy. It is indeed to such men that human advancement has been due. I do not allude to this matter, to raise hostile feelings against the Afghan tribesmen or their ruler, but only to explain the difficulties encountered in the Mamund Valley by the 2nd Brigade of the Malakand Field Force: to explain how it was that defenders of obscure villages were numbered by thousands, and why the weapons of poverty-stricken agriculturists were excellent Martini-Henry rifles.

The Mamunds themselves were now genuinely anxious for peace. Their valley was in our hands; their villages and crops were at our mercy; but their allies, who suffered none of these things, were eager to continue the struggle. They had captured most of the rifles of the dead soldiers on the 16th, and they had no intention of giving them up. On the other hand, it was obvious that the British Raj could not afford to be defied in this matter. We had insisted on the rifles being surrendered, and that expensive factor, Imperial prestige, demanded that we should prosecute operations till we got them, no matter what the cost might be. The rifles were worth little. The men and officers we lost were worth a great deal. It was unsound economics, but Imperialism and economics clash as often as honesty and self-interest. We were therefore committed to the policy of throwing good money after bad in order to keep up our credit; as a man who cannot pay his tradesmen, sends them fresh orders in lieu of settlement. Under these unsatisfactory conditions, the negotiations opened. They did not, however, interfere with the military situation, and the troops continued to forage daily in the valley, and the tribesmen to fire nightly into the camp.

At the end of the week a message from the Queen, expressing sympathy with the sufferings of the wounded, and satisfaction at the conduct of the troops, was published in Brigade orders. It caused the most lively pleasure to all, but particularly to the native soldiers, who heard with pride and exultation that their deeds and dangers were not unnoticed by that august Sovereign before whom they know all their princes bow, and to whom the Sirkar itself is but a servant. The cynic and the socialist may sneer after their kind; yet the patriot, who examines with anxious care those forces which tend to the cohesion or disruption of great communities, will observe how much the influence of a loyal sentiment promotes the solidarity of the Empire.

The reader must now accompany me to the camp of the 3rd Brigade, twelve miles away, at Nawagai. We shall return to the Mamund Valley and have a further opportunity of studying its people and natural features.

CHAPTER XIII:

NAWAGAI

"When the wild Bajaur mountain men lay choking with
    their blood,
And the Kafirs held their footing . . ."

"A Sermon in Lower Bengal," SIR A. LYALL.

Few spectacles in nature are so mournful and so sinister as
the implacable cruelty with which a wounded animal is pursued by
its fellows. Perhaps it is due to a cold and bracing climate, perhaps
to a Christian civilisation, that the Western peoples of the world
have to a great extent risen above this low original instinct. Among
Europeans power provokes antagonism, and weakness excites pity.
All is different in the East. Beyond Suez the bent of men's minds
is such, that safety lies only in success, and peace in prosperity. All
desert the falling. All turn upon the fallen.

The reader may have been struck, in the account of the
fighting in the Mamund Valley, with the vigour with which the
tribesmen follow up a retreating enemy and press an isolated party.
In war this is sound, practical policy. But the hillmen adopt it rather
from a natural propensity, than from military knowledge. Their
tactics are the outcome of their natures. All their actions, moral,
political, strategic, are guided by the same principle. The powerful
tribes, who had watched the passage of the troops in sullen fear,
only waited for a sign of weakness to rise behind them. As long
as the brigades dominated the country, and appeared confident
and successful, their communications would be respected, and

the risings localised; but a check, a reverse, a retreat would raise tremendous combinations on every side.

If the reader will bear this in mind, it will enable him to appreciate the position with which this chapter deals, and may explain many other matters which are beyond the scope of these pages. For it might be well also to remember, that the great drama of frontier war is played before a vast, silent but attentive audience, who fill a theatre, that reaches from Peshawar to Colombo, and from Kurrachee to Rangoon.

The strategic and political situation, with which Sir Bindon Blood was confronted at Nawagai on the 17th of September, was one of difficulty and danger. He had advanced into a hostile country. In his front the Mohmands had gathered at the Hadda Mullah's call to oppose his further progress. The single brigade he had with him was not strong enough to force the Bedmanai Pass, which the enemy held. The 2nd Brigade, on which he had counted, was fully employed twelve miles away in the Mamund Valley. The 1st Brigade, nearly four marches distant on the Panjkora River, had not sufficient transport to move. Meanwhile General Elles's division was toiling painfully through the difficult country north-east of Shabkadr, and could not arrive for several days. He was therefore isolated, and behind him was the "network of ravines," through which a retirement would be a matter of the greatest danger and difficulty.

Besides this, his line of communications, stretching away through sixty miles of hostile country, or country that at any moment might become hostile, was seriously threatened by the unexpected outbreak in the Mamund Valley. He was between two fires. Nor was this all. The Khan of Nawagai, a chief of great power and influence, was only kept loyal by the presence of Sir Bindon Blood's brigade. Had that brigade marched, as was advocated by the Government of India, back to join Brigadier-General Jeffreys in the Mamund Valley, this powerful chief would have thrown his whole weight against the British. The flame in the Mamund Valley, joining the flame in the Bedmanai Pass, would have produced a mighty conflagration, and have spread far and wide among the inflammable tribesmen. Bajaur would have risen to a man. Swat, in spite of its recent punishment, would have stirred ominously. Dir would have repudiated its ruler and joined the combination. The whole mountain region would have been ablaze. Every valley would have poured forth armed men. General Elles, arriving at Lakarai, would have found, instead of a supporting brigade, a hostile gathering, and might even have had to return to Shabkadr without accomplishing anything.

Sir Bindon Blood decided to remain at Nawagai; to cut the Hadda Mullah's gathering from the tribesmen in the Mamund Valley; to hold out a hand to General Elles; to keep the pass open and the khan loyal. Nawagai was the key of the situation. But that key could not be held without much danger. It was a bold course to take, but it succeeded, as bold courses, soundly conceived, usually do. He therefore sent orders to Jeffreys to press operations against the Mamund tribesmen; assured the Khan of Nawagai of the confidence of the Government, and of their determination to "protect" him from all enemies; heliographed to General Elles that he would meet him at Nawagai; entrenched his camp and waited.

He did not wait long in peace. The tribesmen, whose tactical instincts have been evolved by centuries of ceaseless war, were not slow to realise that the presence of the 3rd Brigade at Nawagai was fatal to their hopes. They accordingly resolved to attack it. The Suffi and Hadda Mullahs exerted the whole of their influence upon their credulous followers. The former appealed to the hopes of future happiness. Every Ghazi who fell fighting should sit above the Caaba at the very footstool of the throne, and in that exalted situation and august presence should be solaced for his sufferings by the charms of a double allowance of celestial beauty. Mullah Hadda used even more concrete inducements. The muzzles of the guns should be stopped for those who charged home. No bullet should harm them. They should be invulnerable. They should not go to Paradise yet. They should continue to live honoured and respected upon earth. This promise appears to have carried more weight, as the Hadda Mullah's followers had three times as many

killed and wounded as the candidates for the pleasures of the world to come. It would almost seem, that in the undeveloped minds of these wild and superstitious sons of the mountains, there lie the embryonic germs of economics and practical philosophy, pledges of latent possibilities of progress.

Some for the pleasures of this world, and some
Sigh for the prophet's paradise to come.
    Ah! take the cash and let the credit go,
Nor heed the rumble of a distant drum.

OMAR KHAYYAM

It is the practice of wise commanders in all warfare, to push their cavalry out every evening along the lines of possible attack, to make sure that no enemy has concentrated near the camp in the hopes of attacking at nightfall. On the 18th, Captain Delamain's squadron of the 11th Bengal Lancers came in contact with scattered parties of the enemy coming from the direction of the Bedmanai Pass. Desultory skirmishing ensued, and the cavalry retired to camp. Some firing took place that night, and a soldier of the Queen's Regiment who strayed about fifty yards from his picket, was pulled down and murdered by the savage enemies, who were lurking all around. The next evening the cavalry reconnoitered as usual. The squadron pushed forward protected by its line of advanced scouts across the plain towards the Bedmanai Pass. Suddenly from a nullah a long line of tribesmen rose and fired a volley. A horse was shot. The squadron wheeled about and cantered off, having succeeded in what is technically called "establishing contact."

A great gathering of the enemy, some 3000 strong, now appeared in the plain. For about half an hour before sunset they danced, shouted and discharged their rifles. The mountain battery fired a few shells, but the distance was too great to do much good, or shall I say harm? Then it became dark. The whole brigade remained that night in the expectation of an attack, but only a very half-hearted attempt was made. This was easily repulsed, one man in the Queen's Regiment being killed among the troops.

On the 20th, however, definite information was received from the Khan of Nawagai, that a determined assault would be made on the camp that night. The cavalry reconnaissance again came in touch with the enemy at nightfall. The officers had dinner an hour earlier, and had just finished, when, at about 8.30, firing began. The position of the camp was commanded, though at long ranges, by the surrounding heights. From these a searching rifle fire was now opened. All the tents were struck. The officers and men not employed in the trenches were directed to lie down. The majority of the bullets, clearing the parapets of the entrenchment on one side, whizzed across without doing any harm to the prostrate figures; but all walking about was perilous, and besides this the plunging fire from the heights was galling to every one.

Determined and vigorous sword charges were now delivered on all sides of the camp. The enemy, who numbered about 4000, displayed the greatest valour. They rushed right up to the trenches and fell dead and dying, under the very bayonets of the troops. The brunt of the attack fell upon the British Infantry Regiment, the Queen's. This was fortunate, as many who were in camp that night say, that such was the determination of the enemy in their charges, that had they not been confronted with magazine rifles, they might have got into the entrenchments.

The fire of the British was, however, crushing. Their discipline was admirable, and the terrible weapon with which they were armed, with its more terrible bullet, stopped every rush. The soldiers, confident in their power, were under perfect control. When the enemy charged, the order to employ magazine fire was passed along the ranks. The guns fired star shell. These great rockets, bursting into stars in the air, slowly fell to the ground shedding a pale and ghastly light on the swarming figures of the tribesmen as they ran swiftly forward. Then the popping of the musketry became one intense roar as the ten cartridges, which the magazine of the rifle holds, were discharged almost instantaneously. Nothing could live in front of such a fire. Valour, ferocity, fanaticism, availed nothing. All were swept away. The whistles sounded. The independent firing stopped, with machine-like precision, and the steady section volleys were resumed. This happened not once, but a dozen times during the six hours that the attack was maintained. The 20th Punjaub Infantry, and the cavalry also, sustained and repulsed the attacks delivered against their fronts with steadiness. At length the tribesmen sickened of the slaughter, and retired to their hills in gloom and disorder.

The experience of all in the camp that night was most unpleasant. Those who were in the trenches were the best off. The others, with nothing to do and nothing to look at, remained for six hours lying down wondering whether the next bullet would hit them or not. Some idea of the severity of the fire may be obtained from the fact that a single tent showed sixteen bullet holes.

Brigadier-General Wodehouse was wounded at about eleven o'clock. He had walked round the trenches and conferred with his commanding officers as to the progress of the attack and the expenditure of ammunition, and had just left Sir Bindon Blood's side, after reporting, when a bullet struck him in the leg, inflicting a severe and painful, though fortunately not a dangerous, wound.

Considering the great number of bullets that had fallen in the camp, the British loss was surprisingly small. The full return is as follows:—

BRITISH OFFICERS.

Wounded severely—Brigadier-General Wodehouse.
    "   slightly—Veterinary-Captain Mann.

BRITISH SOLDIERS.

	Killed.	Wounded.
Queen's Regiment	1	3

NATIVE RANKS—Wounded, 20.
FOLLOWERS—   "   6.
Total, 32 of all ranks.

The casualties among the cavalry horses and transport animals were most severe. Over 120 were killed and wounded.

The enemy drew off, carrying their dead with them, for the most part, but numerous bodies lying outside the shelter trench attested the valour and vigour of their attack. One man was found the next morning, whose head had been half blown off, by a discharge of case shot from one of the mountain guns. He lay within a yard of the muzzle, the muzzle he had believed would be stopped, a victim to that blind credulity and fanaticism, now happily passing away from the earth, under the combined influences of Rationalism and machine guns.

It was of course very difficult to obtain any accurate estimate of the enemy's losses. It was proved, however, that 200 corpses were buried on the following day in the neighbourhood, and large numbers of wounded men were reported to have been carried through the various villages. A rough estimate should place their loss at about 700.

The situation was now cleared. The back of the Hadda Mullah's gathering was broken, and it dispersed rapidly. The Khan of Nawagai feverishly protested his unswerving loyalty to the Government. The Mamunds were disheartened. The next day General Elles's leading brigade appeared in the valley. Sir Bindon Blood rode out with his cavalry. The two generals met at Lakarai. It was decided that General Elles should be reinforced by the 3rd Brigade of the Malakand Field Force, and should clear the Bedmanai Pass and complete the discomfiture of the Hadda Mullah. Sir Bindon Blood with the cavalry would join Jeffreys' force in the Mamund Valley, and deal with the situation there. The original plan of taking two brigades from the Malakand to Peshawar was thus discarded; and such troops of Sir Bindon Blood's force as were required for the Tirah expedition would, with the exception of the 3rd Brigade, reach their points of concentration via Nowshera. As will be seen, this plan was still further modified to meet the progress of events.

I had rejoined the 3rd Brigade on the morning of the 21st, and in the evening availed myself of an escort, which was proceeding across the valley, to ride over and see General Elles's brigade. The mobilisation of the Mohmand Field Force was marked by the employment, for the first time, of the Imperial Service Troops. The Maharaja of Patiala, and Sir Pertab Singh, were both with the force. The latter was sitting outside his tent, ill with fever, but cheery and brave as ever. The spectacle of this splendid Indian prince, whose magnificent uniform in the Jubilee procession had attracted the attention of all beholders, now clothed in business-like khaki, and on service at the head of his regiment, aroused the most pleasing reflections. With all its cost in men and money, and all its military and political mistakes, the great Frontier War of 1897 has at least shown on what foundations the British rule in India rests, and made clear who are our friends and who our enemies.

I could not help thinking, that polo has had a good deal to do with strengthening the good relations of the Indian princes and the British officers. It may seem strange to speak of polo as an Imperial factor, but it would not be the first time in history that national games have played a part in high politics. Polo has been the common ground on which English and Indian gentlemen have met on equal terms, and it is to that meeting that much mutual esteem and respect is due. Besides this, polo has been the salvation of the subaltern in India, and the young officer no longer, as heretofore, has a "centre piece" of brandy on his table night and day. The pony and polo stick have drawn him from his bungalow and mess-room, to play a game which must improve his nerve, his judgment and his temper. The author of the Indian Polity asserts that the day will come when British and native officers will serve together in ordinary seniority, and on the same footing. From what I know of the British officer, I do not myself believe that this is possible; but if it should ever came to pass, the way will have been prepared on the polo ground.

The camp of the 3rd Brigade was not attacked again. The tribesmen had learnt a bitter lesson from their experiences of the night before. The trenches were, however, lined at dark, and as small parties of the enemy were said to be moving about across the front, occupied by the Queen's, there was some very excellent volley firing at intervals throughout the night. A few dropping shots came back out of the darkness, but no one was the worse, and the majority of the force made up for the sleep they had lost the night before.

The next morning Sir Bindon Blood, his staff and three squadrons of the 11th Bengal Lancers, rode back through the pass of Nawagai, and joined General Jeffreys at Inayat Kila. The 3rd Brigade now left the Malakand Field Force, and passed under the command of General Elles and beyond the proper limits of this chronicle; but for the sake of completeness, and as the reader may be anxious to hear more of the fine regiment, whose astonishing fire relieved the strategic situation at Nawagai, and inflicted such terrible losses on the Hadda Mullah's adherents, I shall briefly trace their further fortunes.

After General Wodehouse was wounded the command of the 3rd Brigade devolved upon Colonel Graves. They were present at the forcing of the Bedmanai Pass on the 29th of September, and on the two following days they were employed in destroying the fortified villages in the Mitai and Suran valleys; but as these operations were unattended by much loss of life, the whole brigade reached Shabkadr with only three casualties. Thence the Queen's were despatched to Peshawar to take part in the Tirah expedition, in which they have added to the high reputation they had acquired in the Malakand and Mohmand Field Forces.

CHAPTER XIV:

BACK TO THE MAMUND VALLEY

"Again I revisit the hills where we sported,
The streams where we swam, and the fields where we
    fought."

"On a Distant View of Harrow," BYRON.

It is with a vague and undefined feeling of satisfaction that I conduct the reader back to the entrenched camp of Inayat Kila at the entrance of the Mamund Valley, where so much happened, and with which so many memories and experiences are associated. Now that the troops are gone, the scene of life and activity has become solitary and silent. The graves of the officers and men who fell there are lost in the level of the plain. Yet the name is still remembered in not a few English homes, nor will the tribesmen, looking at the deserted entrenchment, easily forget the visit of the 2nd Brigade.

When, on the afternoon of the 15th, the camp had first been pitched, only a small and hasty shelter-trench surrounded it. But as the weeks passed, the parapets grew higher, the ditches deeper, and the pits more numerous, until the whole place became a redoubt. Traverses were built along the perimeter to protect the defenders from flanking fire. Great walls of earth and stone sheltered the horses and mules. Fifty yards out, round the whole camp, a wire trip was carefully laid, to break a rush, and the paths and tracks leading to the entrances had become beaten, level roads. The aspect of permanency was comforting.

Since the action of the 16th September, the 2nd Brigade had been unable to move. Transport—the life and soul of an army—is an even more vital factor here than in less undeveloped countries. The mobility of a brigade depends entirely on its pack animals. On the 14th many mules were killed. On the 16th the field hospitals were filled with wounded. It now became impossible for the camp to move, because the wounded could not be carried. It was impossible to leave them behind, because, deducting an adequate guard, the rest of the brigade would have been too few for fighting. The 2nd Brigade was therefore a fixture. Its striking power was limited to out and home marches. The first step taken by Sir Bindon Blood was to restore its mobility by getting the wounded sent down to the base. Some changes in the constitution of the force were also made. The 11th Bengal Lancers, who now joined the Mohmand Field Force, were succeeded by the Guides Cavalry. The 35th Sikhs, who had suffered such severe losses, were replaced by the 31st Punjaub Infantry from Panjkora. The Buffs, who were full of fever, were exchanged for the Royal West Kent from the Malakand. No.7 British Mountain Battery took the place of No.8, which was now reduced to four guns, having lost in the week's fighting half its officers, a third of its mules, and a quarter of its men.

Camels to carry the wounded were sent up from Panjkora. The Buffs escorted the long convoy down the line of communications. Every one in camp was sorry to see the last of them. In the fighting of the week they had made it clear that the British Infantry battalion is the backbone of every mixed brigade, and they shared with the Guides Infantry one of those enviable reputations for steadiness which are so hard to gain and so easy to lose on active service.

On the 24th of September Sir Bindon Blood received despatches appointing him to the command of the First Division of the Tirah Expeditionary Force, and as the negotiations with the Mamund Jirgahs were then in progress, and it seemed that a settlement might be reached, he proceeded with his staff to Panjkora. Here he was on the telegraph wire, and could communicate easily and quickly with India, and at the same time watch the progress of events at Inayat Kila. Mr. Davis conducted the diplomatic relations with the Mamunds. On the 26th a Jirgah from the tribe came into camp. They deposited 4000 rupees as a token of submission, and brought in fifty firearms. These, however, were of the oldest and most antiquated types, and were obviously not the weapons with which so many soldiers had been killed and wounded. This was pointed out to the tribal representatives. They protested that they had no others. They were poor men, they said, and their property was at the mercy of the Government. But they had no other arms.

The political officer was firm, and his terms were explicit. Either they must give up the twenty-two rifles captured from the 35th Sikhs, on the 16th, or their villages would be destroyed. No other terms would he accept. To this they replied, that they had not got the rifles. They had all been taken, they said, and I think with truth, by the Afghan tribesmen from the Kunar Valley. These would not give them up. Besides—this also with truth—they had been taken in "fair war."

One man, who had lived some years in Calcutta, was especially eloquent on the subject, and argued the case with much skill. He was however, crushed by Mr. Davies asking whether there were "no greybeards in the tribe," and why they were "led by a babu" [a native clerk—the Oriental embodiment of Red Tape]. The discussion was extended to the whole question of their quarrel with the British power. They admitted having sent their young men to attack the Malakand and Chakdara. "All the world was going ghaza," they said. They could not stay behind. They also owned to having gone five miles from their valley to attack the camp at Markhanai. Why had the Sirkar burnt their village? they asked. They had only tried to get even—for the sake of their honour. All this showed a most unsatisfactory spirit from the Government point of view, and it was evident that the brigade could not leave the valley until the tribesmen adopted a more submissive attitude. The matter reverted to the crucial point. Would they give up their rifles or not? To this they replied evasively, that they would consult their fellow-tribesmen and return an answer on the next day. This practically amounted to a refusal, and as no reply was received on the 27th, the negotiations ceased.

In consequence of this and of the threatening attitude of the tribesmen throughout Dir and Bajaur, Sir Bindon Blood telegraphed to the Government of India and recommended the retention of a large force in these territories. By so doing he virtually resigned the command which awaited him in the Tirah expedition. This disinterested decision caused the liveliest satisfaction throughout the force. The Government accepted the advice of their general. The Tirah force was reconstituted, and Major-General W.P. Symons received the command of its first division. A force of eleven battalions, seven squadrons and three batteries was placed at Sir Bindon Blood's disposal, and he was directed to deal with the local situation as he should see fit. He immediately ordered General Jeffreys to resume the punitive operations against the Mamunds.

In pursuance of these orders, the 2nd Brigade, on the 29th, destroyed all the villages in the centre of the valley, some twelve or fourteen in number, and blew up with dynamite upwards of thirty towers and forts. The whole valley was filled with the smoke, which curled upwards in dense and numerous columns, and hung like a cloud over the scene of destruction. The continued explosions of the demolitions resembled a bombardment. The tribesmen, unable to contend with the troops in the open, remained sullenly on the hillsides, and contented themselves with firing from long range at the cavalry patrols.

I feel that this is a fitting moment to discuss the questions which village-burning raises. I have described with independent impartiality the progress of the quarrel between the British and the tribesmen. In a similar spirit I approach the examination of the methods of offence employed. Many misconceptions, some of which are caused by an extraordinary ignorance, exist on this subject in England. One member of the House of Commons asked the Secretary of State whether, in the punishment of villages, care was taken that only the houses of the guilty parties should be destroyed. He was gravely told that great care was taken. The spectacle of troops, who have perhaps carried a village with the bayonet and are holding it against a vigorous counter-attack, when every moment means loss of life and increase of danger, going round and carefully discriminating which houses are occupied by "guilty parties," and which by unoffending people, is sufficiently ridiculous. Another member asked, "Whether the villages were destroyed or only the fortifications." "Only the fortifications," replied the minister guilelessly. What is the actual fact? All along the Afghan border every man's house is his castle. The villages are the fortifications, the fortifications are the villages. Every house is loopholed, and whether it has a tower or not depends only on its owner's wealth. A third legislator, in the columns of his amusing weekly journal, discussed the question at some length, and commented on the barbarity of such tactics. They were not only barbarous, he affirmed, but senseless. Where did the inhabitants of the villages go? To the enemy of course! This reveals, perhaps, the most remarkable misconception of the actual facts. The writer seemed to imagine that the tribesmen consisted of a regular army, who fought, and a peaceful, law-abiding population, who remained at their business, and perhaps protested against the excessive military expenditure from time to time. Whereas in reality, throughout these regions, every inhabitant is a soldier from the first day he is old enough to hurl a stone, till the last day he has strength to pull a trigger, after which he is probably murdered as an encumbrance to the community.

Equipped with these corrected facts, I invite the reader to examine the question of the legitimacy of village-burning for himself. A camp of a British brigade, moving at the order of the Indian Government and under the acquiescence of the people of the United Kingdom, is attacked at night. Several valuable and expensive officers, soldiers and transport animals are killed and wounded. The assailants retire to the hills. Thither it is impossible to follow them. They cannot be caught. They cannot be punished. Only one remedy remains—their property must be destroyed. [It may be of interest, to consider for a moment the contrast between the effects of village-burning on the Indian Frontier and in Cuba. In Cuba a small section of the population are in revolt; the remainder are sympathisers. To screw these lukewarm partisans up to the fighting-point, the insurgents destroy their villages and burn the sugar-came. This, by placing the alternative of "fight or starve" before the inhabitants, has the effect of driving them to take up arms against the Spaniards, whom they all hate, and join the rebels in the field. Thus in Cuba it is the endeavour of the Government to protect property, and of the rebels to destroy it. It was with the aim of keeping the wavering population loyal, that General Weyler collected them all into the towns, with such painful results. His policy was cruel but sound, and, had it been accompanied by vigorous military operations, might have been successful.] Their villages are made hostages for their good behavior. They are fully aware of this, and when they make an attack on a camp or convoy, they do it because they have considered the cost and think it worth while. Of course, it is cruel and barbarous, as is everything else in war, but it is only an unphilosophic mind that will hold it legitimate to take a man's life, and illegitimate to destroy his property. The burning of mud hovels cannot at any rate be condemned by nations whose customs of war justify the bombardment of the dwelling-houses of a city like Paris, to induce the garrison to surrender by the sufferings of the non-combatants.

In official parlance the burning of villages is usually expressed euphemistically as "So many villages were visited and punished," or, again, "The fortifications were demolished." I do not believe in all this circumlocution. The lack of confidence in the good sense of the British democracy, which the Indian Government displays, is one of its least admirable characteristics. Exeter Hall is not all England; and the people of our islands only require to have the matter put fairly before them to arrive at sound, practical conclusions. If this were not so, we should not occupy our present position in the world.

To return to the Mamund Valley. The difference between villages in the plains and those in the hills was forcibly demonstrated. On the 29th over a dozen villages in the plains were destroyed without the loss of a single life. On the 30th the tale ran somewhat differently. The village of Agrah adjoins the village of Zagai, the capture of which has already been recorded. It stood in a broad re-entrant of the mountains, and amid ground so tangled and broken, that to move over it is difficult, and to describe it impossible. On the steep face of the mountain great rocks, sometimes thirty feet high, lay tossed about: interspersed with these were huts or narrow terraces, covered with crops, and rising one above the other by great steps of ten or twelve feet each. The attack on such a place was further complicated by the fact that the same re-entrant contained another village called Gat, which had to be occupied at the same time. This compelled the brigade to attack on a broader front than their numbers allowed. It was evident, as the Guides Cavalry approached the hills, that resistance was contemplated. Several red standards were visible to the naked eye, and the field-glasses disclosed numerous figures lining the ridges and spurs. The squadrons, advancing as far as the scrub would allow them, soon drew the fire of isolated skirmishers. Several troops dismounted, and returned the salute with their carbines, and at 8.45 a dropping fire began. The brigade now came into action in the following formation. The cavalry, on the extreme left, covered the head of a considerable valley, from which the flank was threatened; the Guides Infantry and the Royal West Kent Regiment prolonged the line to the centre of the attack; the 31st Punjaub Infantry moved against the spurs to the right of the village, and the 38th Dogras were in reserve. The action was begun by the Guides Infantry storming the ridges to the left of the enemy's position. These were strongly held and fortified by sungars, behind which the defenders were sheltered. The Guides advanced at a brisk pace, and without much firing, across the open ground to the foot of the hills. The tribesmen, shooting from excellent cover, maintained a hot fire. The bullets kicked up the dust in all directions, or whistled viciously through the air; but the distance was short, and it was soon apparent that the enemy did not mean to abide the assault. When the troops got within 100 yards and fixed bayonets, a dozen determined men were still firing from the sungars. The Afridi and Pathan companies of the Guides, uttering shrill cries of exultation, culminating in an extraordinary yell, dashed forward, climbed the hill as only hillmen can climb, and cleared the crest. On the side of the next hill the figures of the retreating tribesmen were visible, and many were shot down before they could find shelter.

It was a strange thing, to watch these conspicuous forms toiling up the hillside, dodging this way and that way, as the bullets cut into the earth around them; but with the experience of the previous ten minutes fresh in the memory, pity was not one of the emotions it aroused. A good many fell, subsiding peacefully, and lying quite still. Their fall was greeted by strange little yells of pleasure from the native soldiers. These Afridi and Pathan companies of the Guides Infantry suggest nothing so much as a well-trained pack of hounds. Their cries, their movements, and their natures are similar.

The West Kents had now come into line on the Guides' right, and while the latter held the long ridge they had taken, the British regiment moved upon the village. Here the resistance became very severe. The tangled and broken ground, rising in terraces, sometimes ten feet high, and covered with high crops, led to fighting at close quarters with loss on both sides. Loud and continuous grew the musketry fire. The 31st Punjaub Infantry, who had ascended the spur on the right, soon joined hands with the West Kents, and both regiments became hotly engaged. Meantime the Mountain Battery, which had come into action near the centre, began to throw its shells over the heads of the infantry on to the higher slopes, from which the enemy were firing. It soon became evident that the troops were too few for the work. On the left the Guides Infantry were unable to leave the ridge they had captured, lest it should be reoccupied by the enemy, who were showing in great strength. A gap opened in consequence, between the Guides and Royal West Kents, and this enabled the tribesmen to get round the left flank of the British regiment, while the 31st Punjaub Infantry, on the right, were also turned by the enveloping enemy. It is to these circumstances that most of the losses were due.

The British regiment forced its way through the village, and encountered the enemy strongly posted in sungars among the rocks above it. Here they were sharply checked. The leading company had stormed one of these fortifications, and the enemy at once retired higher up the hill. About fifteen men were inside the work, and perhaps thirty more just below it. The whole place was commanded by the higher ground. The enemy's fire was accurate and intense.

Of those inside, four or five were instantly killed or wounded. The sungar was a regular trap, and the company were ordered to retire. Lieutenant Browne-Clayton remained till the last, to watch the withdrawal, and in so doing was shot dead, the bullet severing the blood-vessels near the heart. The two or three men who remained were handing down his body over the rock wall, when they were charged by about thirty Ghazis and driven down the hill. A hundred and fifty yards away, Major Western had three companies of the West Kents in support. He immediately ordered Captain Styles to retake the sungar, and recover the body. The company charged. Captain Styles was the first to reach the stone wall, and with Lieutenant Jackson cleared it of such of the enemy as remained. Five or six men were wounded in the charge, and others fell in the sungar. The advanced position of this company was soon seen to be untenable, and they were ordered to fall back to the edge of the village, where the whole regiment was hotly engaged.

Meanwhile the 31st Punjaub Infantry, who had advanced under Colonel O'Bryen on the right, were exposed to a severe fire from a rocky ridge on their flank. Their attack was directed against a great mass of boulders, some of them of enormous size, which were tenaciously held by the enemy. The fighting soon became close. The two advanced companies were engaged at a distance of under 100 yards. Besides this the cross fire from their right flank added to their difficulties. In such a position the presence of Colonel O'Bryen was invaluable. Moving swiftly from point to point, he directed the fire and animated the spirit of the men, who were devoted to him. It was not long before the enemy's marksmen began to take aim at this prominent figure. But for a considerable period, although bullets struck the ground everywhere around him, he remained unhurt. At last, however, he was shot through the body, and carried mortally wounded from the action.

I pause to consider for a moment the conditions, and circumstances, by which the pursuit of a military career differs from all others. In political life, in art, in engineering, the man with talents who behaves with wisdom may steadily improve his position in the world. If he makes no mistakes he will probably achieve success. But the soldier is more dependent upon external influences. The only way he can hope to rise above the others, is by risking his life in frequent campaigns. All his fortunes, whatever they may be, all his position and weight in the world, all his accumulated capital, as it were, must be staked afresh each time he goes into action. He may have seen twenty engagements, and be covered with decorations and medals. He may be marked as a rising soldier. And yet each time he comes under fire his chances of being killed are as great as, and perhaps greater than, those of the youngest subaltern, whose luck is fresh. The statesman, who has put his power to the test, and made a great miscalculation, may yet retrieve his fortunes. But the indiscriminating bullet settles everything. As the poet somewhat grimly has it:—

Stone-dead hath no better.

Colonel O'Bryen had been specially selected, while still a young man, for the command of a battalion. He had made several campaigns. Already he had passed through the drudgery of the lower ranks of the service, and all the bigger prizes of the military profession appeared in view: and though the death in action of a colonel at the head of his regiment is as fine an end as a soldier can desire, it is mournful to record the abrupt termination of an honourable career at a point when it might have been of much value to the State.

The pressure now became so strong along the whole line that the brigadier, fearing that the troops might get seriously involved, ordered the withdrawal to commence. The village was however burning, and the enemy, who had also suffered severely from the close fighting, did not follow up with their usual vigour. The battery advanced to within 600 yards of the enemy's line, and opened a rapid fire of shrapnel to clear those spurs that commanded the line of retirement. The shells screamed over the heads of the West Kent Regiment, who were now clear of the hills and in front of the guns, and burst in little white puffs of smoke along the crest of the ridge, tearing up the ground into a thick cloud of dust by the hundreds of bullets they contained.

A continuous stream of doolies and stretchers commenced to flow from the fighting line. Soon all available conveyances were exhausted, and the bodies of the wounded had to be carried over the rough ground in the arms of their comrades—a very painful process, which extorted many a groan from the suffering men. At length the withdrawal was completed, and the brigade returned to camp. The presence of the cavalry, who covered the rear, deterred the enemy from leaving the hills.

Riding back, I observed a gruesome sight. At the head of the column of doolies and stretchers were the bodies of the killed, each tied with cords upon a mule. Their heads dangled on one side and their legs on the other. The long black hair of the Sikhs, which streamed down to the ground, and was draggled with dust and blood, imparted a hideous aspect to these figures. There was no other way, however, and it was better than leaving their remains to be insulted and defiled by the savages with whom we were fighting. At the entrance to the camp a large group of surgeons—their sleeves rolled up—awaited the wounded. Two operating tables, made of medical boxes, and covered with water-proof sheets, were also prepared. There is a side to warfare browner than khaki.

The casualties in the attack upon Agrah were as follows:—

BRITISH OFFICERS.

Killed—Lieut.-Col. J.L. O'Bryen, 31st Punjaub Infantry.

"   2nd Lieut. W.C. Brown-Clayton, Royal West Kent.

Wounded severely—Lieutenant H. Isacke, Royal West Kent.

"   "   "   E.B. Peacock, 31st Punjaub Infantry.

Wounded slightly—Major W.G.B. Western, Royal West Kent.

"   "   Captain R.C. Styles, Royal West Kent.

"   "   "   N.H.S. Lowe, Royal West Kent.

"   "   2nd Lieut. F.A. Jackson, Royal West Kent.

BRITISH SOLDIERS.

	Killed.	Wounded.
Royal West Kent	3	20

NATIVE RANKS.

	Killed.	Wounded.
Guides Cavalry	0	4
31st Punjaub Infantry	7	15
38th Dogras	0	4

Total casualties, 61.

As soon as Sir Bindon Blood, at his camp on the Panjkora, received the news of the sharp fighting of the 30th, [After the action of the 30th of September, Lieut.-Colonel McRae, of the 45th Sikhs, was sent up to command the 31st Punjaub Infantry in the place of Lieut.-Colonel O'Bryen, and I was myself attached as a temporary measure to fill another of the vacancies. This is, I believe, the first time a British Cavalry officer has been attached to a native infantry regiment. After the kindness and courtesy with which I was treated, I can only hope it will not be the last.] he decided to proceed himself to Inayat Kila with reinforcements. He arrived on the 2nd October, bringing No.8 Mountain Battery; a wing of the 24th Punjaub Infantry; and two troops of the Guides Cavalry; and having also sent orders for the Highland Light Infantry and four guns of the 10th Field Battery to follow him at once. He was determined to make a fresh attack on Agrah, and burn the village of Gat, which had only been partially destroyed. And this attack was fixed for the 5th. By that date the big 12-pounder guns of the Field Battery were to have arrived, and the fire of fourteen pieces would have been concentrated on the enemy's position. Every one was anxious to carry matters to a conclusion with the tribesmen at all costs.

On the 3rd, the force was ordered to take and burn the village of Badelai, against which, it may be remembered, the Buffs had advanced on the 16th, and from which they had been recalled in a hurry to support the 35th Sikhs. The attack and destruction of the village presented no new features; the tribesmen offered little resistance, and retired before the troops. But as soon as the brigade began its homeward march, they appeared in much larger numbers than had hitherto been seen. As the cavalry could not work among the nullahs and the broken ground, the enemy advanced boldly into the plain. In a great crescent, nearly four miles long, they followed the retiring troops. A brisk skirmish began at about 800 yards. Both batteries came into action, each firing about 90 shells. The Royal West Kent Regiment made good shooting with their Lee-Metford rifles. All the battalions of the brigade were engaged. The enemy, whose strength was estimated to be over 3000, lost heavily, and drew off at 2.30, when the force returned to camp. Sir Bindon Blood and his staff watched the operations and reconnoitered the valley. The casualties were as follows:—

Royal West Kent—dangerously wounded, 1.
Guides Cavalry—wounded, 2.
31st Punjaub Infantry—killed, 1; wounded, 5.
Guides Infantry—wounded, 3.
38th Dogras—killed, 1; wounded, 3.
    Total casualties, 16.

The next day the Highland Light Infantry and the field guns arrived. The former marched in over 700 strong, and made a fine appearance. They were nearly equal in numbers to any two battalions in the brigade. Sickness and war soon reduce the fighting strength. The guns had accomplished a great feat in getting over the difficult and roadless country. They had had to make their own track, and in many places the guns had been drawn by hand. The 10th Field Battery had thus gone sixty miles further into the hill country than any other wheeled traffic. They had quite a reception when they arrived. The whole camp turned out to look with satisfaction on the long polished tubes, which could throw twelve pounds a thousand yards further than the mountain guns could throw seven. They were, however, not destined to display their power. The Mamunds had again sued for peace. They were weary of the struggle. Their valley was desolate. The season of sowing the autumn crops approached. The arrival of reinforcements convinced them that the Government were determined to get their terms. Major Deane came up himself to conduct the negotiations. Meanwhile all important operations were suspended, though the foraging and "sniping" continued as usual.

The force was now large enough for two brigades to be formed, and on the arrival of Brigadier-General Meiklejohn it was reconstituted as follows:—

1st Brigade.
Commanding—Brigadier-General Meiklejohn, C.B., C.M.G.
Highland Light Infantry.
31st Punjaub Infantry.
4 Cos. 24th Punjaub Infantry.
10th Field Battery.
No.7 British Mountain Battery.

2nd Brigade.
Commanding—Brigadier-General Jeffries, C.B.
The Royal West Kent.
38th Dogras.
Guides Infantry.
No.8 Mountain Battery.
The Guides Cavalry.

The camp was greatly extended and covered a large area of ground. In the evenings, the main street presented an animated appearance. Before the sun went down, the officers of the different regiments, distinguished by their brightly-coloured field caps, would assemble to listen to the pipes of the Scottish Infantry, or stroll up and down discussing the events of the day and speculating on the chances of the morrow. As the clear atmosphere of the valley became darkened by the shadows of the night, and the colours of the hills faded into an uniform black, the groups would gather round the various mess tents, and with vermuth, cigarettes and conversation pass away the pleasant half-hour before dinner and "sniping" began.

I would that it were in my power to convey to the reader, who has not had the fortune to live with troops on service, some just appreciation of the compensations of war. The healthy, open-air life, the vivid incidents, the excitement, not only of realisation, but of anticipation, the generous and cheery friendships, the chances of distinction which are open to all, invest life with keener interests and rarer pleasures. The uncertainty and importance of the present, reduce the past and future to comparative insignificance, and clear the mind of minor worries. And when all is over, memories remain, which few men do not hold precious. As to the hardships, these though severe may be endured. Ascetics and recluses have in their endeavours to look beyond the grave suffered worse things. Nor will the soldier in the pursuit of fame and the enjoyment of the pleasures of war, be exposed to greater discomforts than Diogenes in his tub, or the Trappists in their monastery. Besides all this, his chances of learning about the next world are infinitely greater. And yet, when all has been said, we are confronted with a mournful but stubborn fact. In this contrary life, so prosaic is the mind of man, so material his soul, so poor his spirit, that there is no one who has been six months on active duty who is not delighted to get safe home again, to the comfortable monotonies of peace.

CHAPTER XV:

THE WORK OF THE CAVALRY

The negotiations of the Mamunds had this time opened under more propitious circumstances. The tribesmen were convinced by the arrival of the large reinforcements that the Government were in earnest. The return of "the big general," as they called Sir Bindon Blood, to distinguish him from the brigadiers, impressed them with the fact that the operations would be at once renewed, if they continued recalcitrant. They had still a few villages unburned, and these they were anxious to save. Besides, they disliked the look of the long topes, or field guns, of whose powers they were uncertain. They therefore displayed a much more humble spirit.

On the other hand, every one in the force had realised that there were "more kicks than ha'pence" to be got out of the Mamund Valley. All the villages in the plain had been destroyed. Only a few of those in the hollows of the hills remained. To these the enemy had retired. In Arrian's History of Alexander's Conquests we read the following passage: "The men in Bazira [Bazira is the same as Bajaur], despairing of their own affairs, abandoned the city . . . and fled to the rock, as the other barbarians were doing. For all the inhabitants deserted the cities, and began to fly to the rock which is in their land." Then it was that Alexander's difficulties began. Nor need we wonder, when the historian gravely asserts that "so stupendous is the rock in this land . . . that it was found impregnable even by Heracles, the son of Zeus." Thus history repeats itself, and the people of Bajaur their tactics. There was, however, no doubt as to the ability of the brigades to take and burn any village they might select. At the same time it was certain that they would encounter relays of Afghan tribesmen, and regular soldiers from the Amir's army, and that they would lose officers and men in the operation. The matter had to be carried to a conclusion at whatever cost, but the sooner the end was reached, the better.

But in spite of the auguries of peace, the foraging parties were usually fired upon, and this furnished several opportunities for the display of the value of the cavalry. I shall avail myself of the occasion to review the performances of the mounted arm during the operations. As soon as the brigades entered Bajaur, the 11th Bengal Lancers were employed more and more in that legitimate duty of cavalry—reconnaissance. Major Beatson made daily expeditions towards the various valleys and passes about which information was needed. This use of cavalry is an entirely new one on the frontier—it having been thought that it was dangerous to employ them in this way. Though horsemen need good ground to fight on to advantage, they can easily move over any country, however broken, and where they are boldly used, can collect as much information as is necessary.

Reconnaissance is by no means the only opportunity for cavalry employment on the frontier. They are as formidable in offensive tactics as they are useful in collecting intelligence.

The task which is usually confided to them in these mountain actions is to protect one of the flanks. The ground hardly ever admits of charging in any formation, and it is necessary for the men to use their carbines. On 30th September the cavalry were so employed. On the left of the hostile position was a wide valley full of scrubby trees, and stone walls, and occupied by large numbers of the enemy. Had these tribesmen been able to debouch from this valley, they would have fallen on the flank of the brigade, and the situation would have become one of danger. For five hours two weak squadrons of the Guides Cavalry were sufficient to hold them in check.

The methods they employed are worth noticing. Little groups of six or seven men were dismounted, and these with their carbines replied to the enemy's fire. Other little groups of mounted men remained concealed in nullahs or hollows, or behind obstacles. Whenever the enemy tried to rush one of the dismounted parties, and to do so advanced from the bad ground, the mounted patrols galloped forward and chased them back to cover. The terror that these tribesmen have of cavalry contrasts with their general character.

It was a beautiful display of cavalry tactics in this kind of warfare, and, considering the enormous numbers of the enemy, who were thus kept from participating in the main action, it demonstrated the power and value of the mounted arm with convincing force.

On the 6th of October, I witnessed some very similar work, though on a smaller scale. A squadron was engaged in covering the operations of a foraging party. A line of patrols, moving rapidly about, presented difficult targets to the enemy's sharpshooters. I found the remainder of the squadron dismounted in rear of a large bank of stones. Twenty sowars with their carbines were engaged in firing at the enemy, who had occupied a morcha—a small stone fort—some 300 yards away. Desultory skirmishing continued for some time, shots being fired from the hills, half a mile away, as well as from the morcha. Bullets kept falling near the bank, but the cover it afforded was good and no one was hurt. At length word was brought that the foraging was finished and that the squadron was to retire under cover of the infantry. Now came a moment of some excitement. The officer in command knew well that the instant his men were mounted they would be fired at from every point which the enemy held. He ordered the first troop to mount, and the second to cover the retirement. The men scrambled into their saddles, and spreading out into an extended line cantered away towards a hollow about 300 yards distant. Immediately there was an outburst of firing. The dust rose in spurts near the horsemen, and the bullets whistled about their ears. No one was however hit. Meanwhile, the remaining troop had been keeping up a rapid fire on the enemy to cover their retirement. It now became their turn to go. Firing a parting volley the men ran to their horses, mounted, and followed the first troop at a hand-gallop, extending into a long line as they did so. Again the enemy opened fire, and again the dusty ground showed that the bullets were well directed. Again, however, nobody was hurt, and the sowars reached the hollow, laughing and talking in high glee. The morning's skirmish had, nevertheless, cost the squadron a man and a horse, both severely wounded.

Such affairs as these were of almost daily occurrence during the time that the 2nd Brigade occupied the camp at Inayat Kila. They were of the greatest value in training the soldiers. The Guides Cavalry know all there is to know of frontier war, but there are many other regiments who would be made infinitely more powerful fighting organisations if they were afforded the opportunity for such experience.

The great feature which the war of 1897 on the Indian Frontier has displayed is the extraordinary value of cavalry. At Shabkadr a charge of the 13th Bengal Lancers was more than successful. In the Swat Valley, during the relief of Chakdara, the Guides Cavalry and 11th Bengal Lancers inflicted the most terrible loss on the enemy. To quote the words of Sir Bindon Blood's official report to the Adjutant-General, these regiments, "eager for vengeance, pursued, cut up and speared them in every direction, leaving their bodies thickly strewn over the fields." Again, after the action of Landakai, the cavalry made a most vigorous pursuit and killed large numbers of the enemy. While I was with the Malakand Field Force, I was a witness of the constant employment of the cavalry, and was several times informed by general officers that they would gladly have a larger number at their disposal. The reader may recall some of the numerous instances which these pages have recorded of cavalry work. On the morning of the 15th September, it was the cavalry who were able to catch up the enemy before they could reach the hills, and take some revenge for the losses of the night. In the action of the 16th, the charge of Captain Cole's squadron brought the whole attack of the enemy to a standstill, and enabled the infantry by their fire to convert the hesitation of the tribesmen into a retreat. Indeed, in every fight in the Mamund Valley, the cavalry were the first in, and the last out. In the official despatches Sir Bindon Blood thus alludes to the work of the cavalry:—"I would now wish to invite attention to the invaluable nature of the services rendered by the cavalry. At Nawagai, three squadrons of the 11th Bengal Lancers swept the country everywhere that cavalry could go, carrying out reconnaissances, protecting signalling parties and watching every movement of the enemy. In the Mamund Valley a squadron of the same regiment, under Captain E.H. Cole, took part in every engagement that occurred while they were there, establishing such a reputation that the enemy, even when in greatly superior numbers, never dared to face them in the open. Afterwards, when Captain Cole and his men left the Mamund Valley, the Guides Cavalry, under Lieut.-Col. Adams, being in greater strength, acted still more effectually in the same manner, showing tactical skill of a high order, combined with conspicuous gallantry."—Official Despatches. From Gazette of India, 3rd December, 1897.

There has been a boom in cavalry. But one section, and that the most important, has been deprived of its share in the good fortune. The authorities have steadily refused to allow any British cavalry to cross the frontier. Of course this is defended on the ground of expense. "British cavalry costs so much," it is said, "and natives do the work just as well." "Better," say some. But it is a poor kind of economy thus to discourage a most expensive and important branch of the service. The ambition that a young officer entering the army ought to set before him, is to lead his own men in action. This ought to inspire his life, and animate his effort. "Stables" will no longer be dull, when he realises that on the fitness of his horses, his life and honour may one day depend. If he thinks that his men may soon be asked to stand beside him at a pinch, he will no longer be bored by their interests and affairs. But when he realises that all is empty display, and that his regiment is a sword too costly to be drawn, he naturally loses keenness and betakes himself to polo as a consolation. It is a good one.

It was my fortune to meet many young men in frontier regiments, both cavalry and infantry, who had already served in three, and even four, campaigns. Daring, intelligent and capable, they are proofs of the value of their training, and are fit to lead their men under any conditions, and in any country. Subalterns in British cavalry regiments do occasionally manage to see a little active service as transport officers, signalling officers, war correspondents, or on the staff; but to lead in the field the men they have trained in peace, is a possibility which is never worth contemplating. To the young man who wants to enjoy himself, to spend a few years agreeably in a military companionship, to have an occupation—the British cavalry will be suited. But to the youth who means to make himself a professional soldier, an expert in war, a specialist in practical tactics, who desires a hard life of adventure and a true comradeship in arms, I would recommend the choice of some regiment on the frontier, like those fine ones I have seen, the Guides and the 11th Bengal Lancers.

I am aware that those who criticise an existing state of things ought to be prepared with some constructive legislation which would remedy the evils they denounce. Though it is unlikely that the Government of India will take my advice, either wholly or in good part, I hereby exhort them to quit the folly of a "penny wise" policy, and to adhere consistently to the principles of employing British and native troops in India in a regular proportion. That is to say, that when two native cavalry regiments have been sent on service across the frontier, the third cavalry regiment so sent shall be British.

Besides this, in order to give cavalry officers as many opportunities of seeing active service as possible, subalterns should be allowed to volunteer for emergency employment with native cavalry. I have talked to several officers who command native cavalry regiments, and they tell me that such an arrangement would work excellently, and that, as they are always short of officers, it would supply a want. I would suggest that subalterns should, with the approval of their colonels, be attached to the native regiment, and after passing in Hindustani and being reported as qualified to serve with the native troops, be considered available for employment as described. I shall be told there are financial difficulties. I do not believe this. There are plenty of cavalry subalterns whose eagerness to see service is so strong, that they would submit to any arrangement that the rapacity of Government might impose. Indeed there is no reason that an actual economy should not be effected. The sums of money that the Indian Government offer, as rewards for officers who can speak Hindustani, have not hitherto tempted many cavalry officers to make a study of the language. Here is an incentive, more powerful and costing nothing.

To be technical is, I am aware, a serious offence, and I realise that if this book ever obtained so evil a reputation it would be shunned, as the House of Commons is shunned on a Service night. I have strayed far away from the Malakand Field Force into the tangled paths of military controversy, and I must beg the reader to forgive, as he will surely forget, what has been written.

The fighting described in the last chapter, and the continual drain of disease, had again filled the field hospitals, and in order to preserve the mobility of the force, it was decided to send all sick and wounded down to the base at once. The journey—over 100 miles by road—would take nearly a fortnight, and the jolting and heat made such an experience a painful and weary one to injured men. But the stern necessities of war render these things inevitable, and the desire of the men to get nearer home soothes much of their suffering. The convoy of sick and wounded was to be escorted as far as the Panjkora River by the Royal West Kent, who were themselves in need of some recuperation. To campaign in India without tents is always a trial to a British regiment; and when it is moved to the front from some unhealthy station like Peshawar, Delhi, or Mian Mir, and the men are saturated with fever and weakened by the summer heats, the sick list becomes long and serious. Typhoid from drinking surface water, and the other various kinds of fever which follow exposure to the heats of the day or the chills of the night, soon take a hundred men from the fighting strength, and the general of an Indian frontier force has to watch with equal care the movements of the enemy and the fluctuations of the hospital returns. As soon, therefore, as Sir Bindon Blood saw that the Mamunds were desirous of peace, and that no further operations against them were probable, he sent one of his British regiments to their tents near the Panjkora.

About sixty wounded men from the actions of 30th September and 3rd October, and the same number of sick, formed the bulk of the convoy. The slight cases are carried on camels, in cradles made by cutting a native bedstead in two, and called "Kajawas." The more serious cases are carried in doolies or litters, protected from the sun by white curtains, and borne by four natives. Those who are well enough ride on mules. The infantry escort is disposed along the line with every precaution that can be suggested, but the danger of an attack upon the long straggling string of doolies and animals in difficult and broken ground is a very real and terrible one.

The cheeriness and patience of the wounded men exceeds belief. Perhaps it is due to a realisation of the proximity in which they have stood to death; perhaps partly to that feeling of relief with which a man turns for a spell from war to peace. In any case it is remarkable. A poor fellow—a private in the Buffs—was hit at Zagai, and had his arm amputated at the shoulder. I expressed my sympathy, and he replied, philosophically: "You can't make omelettes without breaking eggs," and after a pause added, with much satisfaction, "The regiment did well that day." He came of a fighting stock, but I could not help speculating on the possible future which awaited him. Discharge from the service as medically unfit, some miserable pension insufficient to command any pleasures but those of drink, a loafer's life, and a pauper's grave. Perhaps the regiment—the officers, that is to say—would succeed in getting him work, and would from their own resources supplement his pension. But what a wretched and discreditable system is that, by which the richest nation in the world neglects the soldiers who have served it well, and which leaves to newspaper philanthropy, to local institutions, and to private charity, a burden which ought to be proudly borne by the State.

Starting at six, the column reached Jar, a march of eight miles, at about ten o'clock. Here we were joined by a wing of the 24th Punjaub Infantry, who were coming up to relieve the Royal West Kents. The camp at Jar has the disadvantage of being commanded by a hill to the north, and the Salarzais, another pestilent tribe, whose name alone is an infliction, delight to show their valour by firing at the troops during the night. Of course this could be prevented by moving the camp out of range of this hill. But then, unfortunately, it would be commanded by another hill to the south, from which the Shamozai section of the Utman Khels—to whom my former remarks also apply—would be able to amuse themselves. The inconvenience of the situation had therefore to be faced.

We had not been long in camp before the eldest son of the Khan of Jar, who had been comparatively loyal during the operations, came to inform the colonel in command that there would be "sniping" that night. Certain evil men, he said, had declared their intention of destroying the force, but he, the heir-apparent to the Khanate of Jar, and the ally of the Empress, would protect us. Four pickets of his own regular army should watch the camp, that our slumbers might not be disturbed, and when challenged by the sentries, they would reply, "chokidar" (watchman). This all seemed very satisfactory, but we entrenched ourselves as usual, not, as we explained, because we doubted our protector's powers or inclinations, buy merely as a matter of form.

At midnight precisely, the camp was awakened by a dozen shots in rapid succession. The khan's pickets could be heard expostulating with the enemy, who replied by jeers and bitter remarks.

The firing continued for an hour, when the "snipers," having satisfied their honour, relieved their feelings and expended their cartridges, went away rejoicing. The troops throughout remained silent, and vouchsafed no reply.

It may seem difficult to believe that fifty bullets could fall in a camp, only 100 yards square—crowded with animals and men—without any other result than to hit a single mule in the tail. Such was, however, the fact. This shows of what value, a little active service is to the soldier. The first time he is under fire, he imagines himself to be in great danger. He thinks that every bullet is going to hit him, and that every shot is aimed at him. Assuredly he will be killed in a moment. If he goes through this ordeal once or twice, he begins to get some idea of the odds in his favour. He has heard lots of bullets and they have not hurt him. He will get home safely to his tea this evening, just as he did the last time. He becomes a very much more effective fighting machine.

From a military point of view, the perpetual frontier wars in one corner or other of the Empire are of the greatest value. This fact may one day be proved, should our soldiers ever be brought into contact with some peace-trained, conscript army, in anything like equal numbers.

Though the firing produced very little effect on the troops—most of whom had been through the experience several times before—it was a severe trial to the wounded, whose nerves, shattered by pain and weakness, were unable to bear the strain. The surgeon in charge—Major Tyrell—told me that the poor fellows quivered at every shot as if in anticipation of a blow. A bullet in the leg will made a brave man a coward. A blow on the head will make a wise man a fool. Indeed I have read that a sufficiency of absinthe can make a good man a knave. The triumph of mind over matter does not seem to be quite complete as yet.

I saw a strange thing happen, while the firing was going on, which may amuse those who take an interest in the habits and development of animals. Just in front of my tent, which was open, was a clear space, occupied by a flock of goats and sheep. The brilliant moonlight made everything plainly visible. Every time a bullet whistled over them or struck the ground near, they ducked and bobbed in evident terror. An officer, who also noticed this, told me it was the first time they had been under fire; and I have been wondering ever since, whether this explains their fear, or makes it more inexplicable.

I have devoted a good deal in this chapter to the account of the "sniping" at Jar on the night of the 9th of October, and, perhaps, a critic may inquire, why so much should be written about so common an incident. It is, however, because this night firing is so common a feature, that I feel no picture of the war on the Indian frontier would be complete without some account of it.

The next day we crossed the Panjkora River, and I started to ride down the line of communications to the base at Nowshera. At each stage some of the comforts of civilisation and peace reappeared. At Panjkora we touched the telegraph wire; at Sarai were fresh potatoes; ice was to be had at Chakdara; a comfortable bed at the Malakand; and at length, at Nowshera, the railway. But how little these things matter after all. When they are at hand, they seem indispensable, but when they cannot be obtained, they are hardly missed. A little plain food, and a philosophic temperament, are the only necessities of life.

I shall not take the reader farther from the scene of action. He is free and his imagination may lead him back to the highland valleys, where he may continue for a space among camps and men, and observe the conclusion of the drama.

CHAPTER XVI:

SUBMISSION

"Their eyes were sunken and weary
    With a sort of listless woe,
And they looked from their desolate eyrie
    Over the plains below.

"Two had wounds from a sabre,
    And one from an Enfield Ball."

"Rajpoot Rebels," LYALL.

At last the negotiations with the Mamunds began to reach a conclusion. The tribe were really desirous of peace, and prepared to make any sacrifices to induce the brigades to leave the valley. The Khan of Khar now proved of valuable assistance. He consistently urged them to make peace with the Sirkar, and assured them that the troops would not go away until they had their rifles back. Finally the Mamunds said they would get the rifles. But the path of repentance was a stony one. On the very night that the tribesmen decided for peace at any price, a thousand warlike Afghans, spoiling for a fight, arrived from the Kunar Valley, on the other side of the mountains, and announced their intention of attacking the camp at once. The Mamunds expostulated with them. The retainers of the Khan of Khar implored them not to be so rash. In the end these unwelcome allies were persuaded to depart. But that night the camp was warned that an attack was probable. The inlying pickets were accordingly doubled, and every man slept in his clothes, so as to be ready. The pathos of the situation was provided by the fact, that the Mamunds were guarding us from our enemies. The wretched tribe, rather than face a renewal of hostilities, had posted pickets all round the camp to drive away "snipers" and other assailants. Their sincerity was beyond suspicion.

The next day the first instalment of rifles was surrendered. Fifteen Martini-Henrys taken on the 16th from the 35th Sikhs were brought into camp, by the Khan of Khar's men, and deposited in front of the general's tent. Nearly all were hacked and marked by sword cuts, showing that their owners, the Sikhs, had perished fighting to the last. Perhaps, these firearms had cost more in blood and treasure than any others ever made. The remainder of the twenty-one were promised later, and have since all been surrendered. But the rifles as they lay on the ground were a bitter comment on the economic aspect of the "Forward Policy." These tribes have nothing to surrender but their arms. To extort these few, had taken a month, had cost many lives, and thousands of pounds. It had been as bad a bargain as was ever made. People talk glibly of "the total disarmament of the frontier tribes" as being the obvious policy. No doubt such a result would be most desirable. But to obtain it would be as painful and as tedious an undertaking, as to extract the stings of a swarm of hornets, with naked fingers.

After the surrender of the rifles, the discussion of terms proceeded with smoothness. Full jirgahs were sent to the camp from the tribe, and gradually a definite understanding was reached. The tribesmen bewailed the losses they had sustained. Why, they asked, had the Sirkar visited them so heavily? Why, replied Major Deane, had they broken the peace and attacked the camp? The elders of the tribe, following the practice of all communities, threw the blame on their "young men." These had done the evil, they declared. All had paid the penalty. At length definite terms were agreed to, and a full durbar was arranged for the 11th of the month for their ratification.

Accordingly on that date, at about one o'clock in the afternoon, a large and representative jirgah of Mamunds, accompanied by the Khans of Khar, Jar and Nawagai, arrived at the village of Nawa Kila, about half a mile from the camp. At three o'clock Sir Bindon Blood, with Major Deane, Chief Political Officer; Mr. Davis, Assistant Political Officer; most of the Headquarters staff, and a few other officers, started, escorted by a troop of the Guides

Cavalry, for the durbar. The general on arrival shook hands with the friendly khans, much to their satisfaction, and took a seat which had been provided. The tribesmen formed three sides of a square. The friendly khans were on the left with their retainers. The Mamund jirgahs filled two other sides. Sir Bindon Blood, with Major Deane on his left and his officers around him, occupied the fourth side.

Then the Mamunds solemnly tendered their submission. They expressed their deep regret at their action, and deplored the disasters that had befallen them. They declared, they had only fought because they feared annexation. They agreed to expel the followers of Umra Khan from the valley. They gave security for the rifles that had not yet been surrendered. They were then informed that as they had suffered severe punishment and had submitted, the Sirkar would exact no fine or further penalty from them. At this they showed signs of gratification. The durbar, which had lasted fifteen minutes, was ended by the whole of the tribesmen swearing with uplifted hands to adhere to the terms and keep the peace. They were then dismissed.

The losses sustained by the Mamunds in the fighting were ascertained to be 350 killed, besides the wounded, with whom the hill villages were all crowded, and who probably amounted to 700 or 800. This estimate takes no account of the casualties among the transfrontier tribesmen, which were presumably considerable, but regarding which no reliable information could be obtained. Sir Bindon Blood offered them medical aid for their wounded, but this they declined. They could not understand the motive, and feared a stratagem. What the sufferings of these wretched men must have been, without antiseptics or anaesthetics, is terrible to think of. Perhaps, however, vigorous constitutions and the keen air of the mountains were Nature's substitutes.

Thus the episode of the Mamund Valley came to an end. On the morning of the 12th, the troops moved out of the camp at Inayat Kila for the last time, and the long line of men, guns and transport animals, trailed slowly away across the plain of Khar. The tribesmen gathered on the hills to watch the departure of their enemies, but whatever feelings of satisfaction they may have felt at the spectacle, were dissipated when they turned their eyes towards their valley. Not a tower, not a fort was to be seen. The villages were destroyed. The crops had been trampled down. They had lost heavily in killed and wounded, and the winter was at hand. No defiant shots pursued the retiring column. The ferocious Mamunds were weary of war.

And as the soldiers marched away, their reflections could not have been wholly triumphant. For a month they had held Inayat Kila, and during that month they had been constantly fighting. The Mamunds were crushed. The Imperial power had been asserted, but the cost was heavy. Thirty-one officers and 251 men had been killed and wounded out of a fighting force that had on no occasion exceeded 1200 men.

The casualties of General Jeffrey's brigade in the Mamund Valley were as follows:—

British Officers............	Killed or died of wounds....	7
" "	Wounded..............................	17
" Soldiers	Killed	7
" "	Wounded..............................	41
Native Officers............	Killed	0
" "	Wounded..............................	7
" Soldiers	Killed	48
" "	Wounded............................	147
Followers		8
		—
	Total.....................................	282
Horses and mules		150

The main cause of this long list of casualties was, as I have already written, the proximity of the Afghan border. But it would be unjust and ungenerous to deny to the people of the Mamund Valley that reputation for courage, tactical skill and marksmanship, which they have so well deserved. During an indefinite period they had brawled and fought in the unpenetrated gloom of barbarism. At length they struck a blow at civilisation, and civilisation, though compelled to record the odious vices that the fierce light of scientific war exposed, will yet ungrudgingly admit that they are a brave and warlike race. Their name will live in the minds of men for some years, even in this busy century, and there are families in England who will never forget it. But perhaps the tribesmen, sitting sullenly on the hillsides and contemplating the ruin of their habitations, did not realise all this, or if they did, still felt regret at having tried conclusions with the British Raj. Their fame had cost them dear. Indeed, as we have been told, "nothing is so expensive as glory."

The troops camped on the night of the 12th at Jar, and on the following day moved up the Salarzai Valley to Matashah. Here they remained for nearly a week. This tribe, terrified by the punishment of the Mamunds, made no regular opposition, though the camp was fired into regularly every night by a few hot-blooded "snipers." Several horses and mules were hit, and a sowar in the Guides Cavalry was wounded. The reconnaissances in force, which were sent out daily to the farther end of the valley, were not resisted in any way, and the tribal jirgahs used every effort to collect the rifles which they had been ordered to surrender. By the 19th all were given up, and on the 20th the troops moved back to Jar. There Sir Bindon Blood received the submission of the Utman Khels, who brought in the weapons demanded from them, and paid a fine as an indemnity for attacking the Malakand and Chakdara.

The soldiers, who were still in a fighting mood, watched with impatience the political negotiations which produced so peaceful a triumph.

All Indian military commanders, from Lord Clive and Lord Clive's times downwards, have inveighed against the practice of attaching civil officers to field forces. It has been said, frequently with truth, that they hamper the military operations, and by interfering with the generals, infuse a spirit of vacillation into the plans. Although the political officers of the Malakand Field Force were always personally popular with their military comrades, there were many who criticised their official actions, and disapproved of their presence. The duties of the civil officers, in a campaign, are twofold: firstly, to negotiate, and secondly, to collect information. It would seem that for the first of these duties they are indispensable. The difficult language and peculiar characters of the tribesmen are the study of a lifetime. A knowledge of the local conditions, of the power and influence of the khans, or other rulers of the people; of the general history and traditions of the country, is a task which must be entirely specialised. Rough and ready methods are excellent while the tribes resist, but something more is required when they are anxious to submit. Men are needed who understand the whole question, and all the details of the quarrel, between the natives and the Government, and who can in some measure appreciate both points of view. I do not believe that such are to be found in the army. The military profession is alone sufficient to engross the attention of the most able and accomplished man.

Besides this I cannot forget how many quiet nights the 2nd Brigade enjoyed at Inayat Kila when the "snipers" were driven away by the friendly pickets; how many fresh eggs and water melons were procured, and how easily letters and messages were carried about the country [As correspondent of the Pioneer, I invariably availed myself of this method of sending the press telegrams to the telegraph office at Panjkora, and though the route lay through twenty miles of the enemy's country, these messages not only never miscarried, but on several occasions arrived before the official despatches or any heliographed news. By similar agency the bodies of Lieutenant-Colonel O'Bryen and Lieutenant Browne-Clayton, killed in the attack upon Agrah on the 30th of September, were safely and swiftly conveyed to Malakand for burial.] through the relations which the political officers, Mr. Davis and Mr. Gunter, maintained, under very difficult circumstances, with these tribesmen, who were not actually fighting us.

Respecting the second duty, it is difficult to believe that the collection of information as to the numbers and intentions of the enemy would not be better and more appropriately carried out by the Intelligence Department and the cavalry. Civil officers should not be expected to understand what kind of military information a general requires. It is not their business. I am aware that Mr. Davis procured the most correct intelligence about the great night attack at Nawagai, and thus gave ample warning to Sir Bindon Blood. But on the other hand the scanty information available about the Mamunds, previous to the action of the 16th, was the main cause of the severe loss sustained on that day. Besides, the incessant rumours of a night attack on Inayat Kila, kept the whole force in their boots about three nights each week. Civil officers should discharge diplomatic duties, and military officers the conduct of war. And the collection of information is one of the most important of military duties. Our Pathan Sepoys, the Intelligence Branch, and an enterprising cavalry, should obtain all the facts that a general requires to use in his plans. At least the responsibility can thus be definitely assigned.

On one point, however, I have no doubts. The political officers must be under the control of the General directing the operations. There must be no "Imperium in imperio." In a Field Force one man only can command—and all in it must be under his authority. Differences, creating difficulties and leading to disasters, will arise whenever the political officers are empowered to make arrangements with the tribesmen, without consulting and sometimes without even informing the man on whose decisions the success of the war and the lives of the soldiers directly depend.

The subject is a difficult one to discuss, without wounding the feelings of those gallant men, who take all the risks of war, while the campaign lasts, and, when it is over, live in equal peril of their lives among the savage populations, whose dispositions they study, and whose tempers they watch. I am glad to have done with it.

During the stay of the brigades in Bajaur, there had been several cases of desertion among the Afridi Sepoys. On one occasion five men of the 24th Punjaub Infantry, who were out on picket, departed in a body, and taking their arms with them set off towards Tirah and the Khyber Pass. As I have recorded several instances of gallantry and conduct among the Afridis and Pathans in our ranks, it is only fitting that the reverse of the medal should be shown. The reader, who may be interested in the characters of the subject races of the Empire, and of the native soldiers, on whom so much depends, will perhaps pardon a somewhat long digression on the subject of Pathans and Sikhs.

It should not be forgotten by those who make wholesale assertions of treachery and untrustworthiness against the Afridi and Pathan soldiers, that these men are placed in a very strange and false position. They are asked to fight against their countrymen and co-religionists. On the one side are accumulated all the forces of fanaticism, patriotism and natural ties. On the other military associations stand alone. It is no doubt a grievous thing to be false to an oath of allegiance, but there are other obligations not less sacred. To respect an oath is a duty which the individual owes to society. Yet, who would by his evidence send a brother to the gallows? The ties of nature are older and take precedence of all other human laws. When the Pathan is invited to suppress his fellow-countrymen, or even to remain a spectator of their suppression, he finds himself in a situation at which, in the words of Burke, "Morality is perplexed, reason staggered, and from which affrighted nature recoils."

There are many on the frontier who realise these things, and who sympathise with the Afridi soldier in his dilemma. An officer of the Guides Infantry, of long experience and considerable distinction, who commands both Sikhs and Afridis, and has led both many times in action, writes as follows: "Personally, I don't blame any Afridis who desert to go and defend their own country, now that we have invaded it, and I think it is only natural and proper that they should want to do so."

Such an opinion may be taken as typical of the views of a great number of officers, who have some title to speak on the subject, as it is one on which their lives might at any moment depend.

The Sikh is the guardian of the Marches. He was originally invented to combat the Pathan. His religion was designed to be diametrically opposed to Mahommedanism. It was a shrewd act of policy. Fanaticism was met by fanaticism. Religious abhorrence was added to racial hatred. The Pathan invaders were rolled back to the mountains, and the Sikhs established themselves at Lahore and Peshawar. The strong contrast, and much of the animosity, remain to-day. The Sikh wears his hair down to his waist; the Pathan shaves his head. The Sikh drinks what he will; the Pathan is an abstainer. The Sikh is burnt after death; the Pathan would be thus deprived of Paradise. As a soldier the Pathan is a finer shot, a hardier man, a better marcher, especially on the hillside, and possibly an even more brilliant fighter. He relies more on instinct than education: war is in his blood; he is a born marksman, but he is dirty, lazy and a spendthrift.

In the Sikh the more civilised man appears. He does not shoot naturally, but he learns by patient practice. He is not so tough as the Pathan, but he delights in feats of strength—wrestling, running, or swimming. He is a much cleaner soldier and more careful. He is frequently parsimonious, and always thrifty, and does not generally feed himself as well as the Pathan. [Indeed in some regiments the pay of very thin Sikhs is given them in the form of food, and they have to be carefully watched by their officers till they get fat and strong.]

There are some who say that the Sikh will go on under circumstances which will dishearten and discourage his rival, and that if the latter has more dash he has less stamina. The assertion is not supported by facts. In 1895, when Lieut.-Colonel Battye was killed near the Panjkora River and the Guides were hard pressed, the subadar of the Afridi company, turning to his countrymen, shouted: "Now, then, Afridi folk of the Corps of Guides, the Commanding Officer's killed, now's the time to charge!" and the British officers had the greatest difficulty in restraining these impetuous soldiers from leaving their position, and rushing to certain death. The story recalls the speech of the famous cavalry colonel at the action of Tamai, when the squares were seen to be broken, and an excited and demoralised correspondent galloped wildly up to the squadrons, declaring that all was lost. "How do you mean, 'all's lost'? Don't you see the 10th Hussars are here?" There are men in the world who derive as stern an exultation from the proximity of disaster and ruin as others from success, and who are more magnificent in defeat than others are in victory. Such spirits are undoubtedly to be found among the Afridis and Pathans.

I will quote, in concluding this discussion, the opinion of an old Gurkha subadar who had seen much fighting. He said that he liked the Sikhs better, but would sooner have Afridis with him at a pinch than any other breed of men in India. It is comfortable to reflect, that both are among the soldiers of the Queen.

Although there were no Gurkhas in the Malakand Field Force, it is impossible to consider Indian fighting races without alluding to these wicked little men. In appearance they resemble a bronze Japanese. Small, active and fierce, ever with a cheery grin on their broad faces, they combine the dash of the Pathan with the discipline of the Sikh. They spend all their money on food, and, unhampered by religion, drink, smoke and swear like the British soldier, in whose eyes they find more favour than any other—as he regards them—breed of "niggers." They are pure mercenaries, and, while they welcome the dangers, they dislike the prolongation of a campaign, being equally eager to get back to their wives and to the big meat meals of peace time.

After the Utman Khels had been induced to comply with the terms, the brigades recrossed the Panjkora River, and then marching by easy stages down the line of communications, returned to the Malakand. The Guides, moving back to Mardan, went into cantonments again, and turned in a moment from war to peace.

The Buffs, bitterly disappointed at having lost their chance of joining in the Tirah expedition, remained at Malakand in garrison. A considerable force was retained near Jalala, to await the issue of the operations against the Afridis, and to be ready to move against the Bunerwals, should an expedition be necessary.

Here we leave the Malakand Field Force. It may be that there is yet another chapter of its history which remains to be written, and that the fine regiments of which it is composed will, under their trusted commander, have other opportunities of playing the great game of war. If that be so, the reader shall decide whether the account shall prolong the tale I have told, or whether the task shall fall to another hand. [It is an excellent instance of the capricious and haphazard manner in which honours and rewards are bestowed in the army, that the operations in the Mamund Valley and throughout Bajaur are commemorated by no distinctive clasp. The losses sustained by the Brigade were indisputably most severe. The result was successful. The conduct of the troops has been officially commended. Yet the soldiers who were engaged in all the rough fighting I have described in the last eight chapters have been excluded from any of the special clasps which have been struck. They share the general clasp with every man who crossed the frontier and with some thousands who never saw a shot fired.]

CHAPTER XVII:

MILITARY OBSERVATIONS

" . . . And thou hast talk'd
Of sallies and retires, of trenches, tents,
Of palisadoes, frontiers, parapets,
Of basilisks, of cannon, culverin."

"Henry IV.," Part I., Act ii., Sc.3.

It may at first seem that a chapter wholly devoted to military considerations is inappropriate to a book which, if it is to enjoy any measure of success, must be read by many unconnected with the army. But I remember that in these days it is necessary for every one, who means to be well informed, to have a superficial knowledge of every one else's business. Encouraged also by what Mr. Gladstone has called "the growing militarism of the times," I hope that, avoiding technicalities, it may be of some general interest to glance for a moment at the frontier war from a purely professional point of view. My observations must be taken as applying to the theatre of the war I have described, but I do not doubt that many of them will be applicable to the whole frontier.

The first and most important consideration is transport. Nobody who has not seen for himself can realise what a great matter this is. I well recall my amazement, when watching a camel convoy more than a mile and a half long, escorted by half a battalion of infantry. I was informed that it contained only two days' supplies for one brigade. People talk lightly of moving columns hither and thither, as if they were mobile groups of men, who had only to march about the country and fight the enemy wherever found, and very few understand that an army is a ponderous mass which drags painfully after it a long chain of advanced depots, stages, rest camps, and communications, by which it is securely fastened to a stationary base. In these valleys, where wheeled traffic is impossible, the difficulties and cost of moving supplies are enormous; and as none, or very few, are to be obtained within the country, the consideration is paramount. Mule transport is for many reasons superior to camel transport. The mule moves faster and can traverse more difficult ground. He is also more hardy and keeps in better condition. When Sir Bindon Blood began his advance against the Mohmands he equipped his 2nd Brigade entirely with mules. It was thus far more mobile, and was available for any rapid movement that might become necessary. To mix the two—camels and mules—appears to combine the disadvantages of both, and destroy the superiority of either.

I have already described the Indian service camp and the "sniping" without which no night across the frontier could be complete. I shall therefore only notice two points, which were previously omitted, as they looked suspiciously technical. As the night firing is sometimes varied by more serious attacks, and even actual assaults and sword rushes, it is thought advisable to have the ditch of the entrenchment towards the enemy. Modern weapons notwithstanding, the ultimate appeal is to the bayonet, and the advantage of being on the higher ground is then considerable.

When a battery forms part of the line round a camp, infantry soldiers should be placed between the guns. Artillery officers do not like this; but, though they are very good fellows, there are some things in which it is not well to give way to them. Every one is prone to over-estimate the power of his arm.

In the Mamund Valley all the fighting occurred in capturing villages, which lay in rocky and broken ground in the hollows of the mountains, and were defended by a swarm of active riflemen. Against the quickly moving figures of the enemy it proved almost useless to fire volleys. The tribesmen would dart from rock to rock, exposing themselves only for an instant, and before the attention of a section could be directed to them and the rifles aimed, the chance and the target would have vanished together. Better results were obtained by picking out good shots and giving them permission to fire when they saw their opportunity, without waiting for the word of command. But speaking generally, infantry should push on to the attack with the bayonet without wasting much time in firing, which can only result in their being delayed under the fire of a well-posted enemy.

After the capture and destruction of the village, the troops had always to return to camp, and a retirement became necessary. The difficulty of executing such an operation in the face of an active and numerous enemy, armed with modern rifles, was great. I had the opportunity of witnessing six of these retirements from the rear companies. Five were fortunate and one was disastrous, but all were attended with loss, and as experienced officers have informed me, with danger. As long as no one is hit everything is successful, but as soon as a few men are wounded, the difficulties begin. No sooner has a point been left—a knoll, a patch of corn, some rocks, or any other incident of ground—than it is seized by the enemy. With their excellent rifles, they kill or wound two or three of the retiring company, whose somewhat close formation makes them a good mark. Now, in civilised war these wounded would be left on the ground, and matters arranged next day by parley. But on the frontier, where no quarter is asked or given, to carry away the wounded is a sacred duty. It is also the strenuous endeavour of every regiment to carry away their dead. The vile and horrid mutilations which the tribesmen inflict on all bodies that fall into their hands, and the insults to which they expose them, add, to unphilosophic minds, another terror to death. Now, it takes at least four men, and very often more, to carry away a body. Observe the result. Every man hit, means five rifles withdrawn from the firing line. Ten men hit, puts a company out of action, as far as fighting power is concerned. The watchful enemy press. The groups of men bearing the injured are excellent targets. Presently the rear-guard is encumbered with wounded. Then a vigorous charge with swords is pushed home. Thus, a disaster occurs.

Watching the progress of events, sometimes from one regiment, sometimes from another, I observed several ways by which these difficulties could be avoided. The Guides, long skilled in frontier war, were the most valuable instructors. As the enemy seize every point as soon as it is left, all retirements should be masked by leaving two or three men behind from each company. These keep up a brisk fire, and after the whole company have taken up a new position, or have nearly done so, they run back and join them. Besides this, the fire of one company in retiring should always be arranged to cover another, and at no moment in a withdrawal should the firing ever cease. The covering company should be actually in position before the rear company begins to move, and should open fire at once. I was particularly struck on 18th September by the retirement of the Guides Infantry. These principles were carried out with such skill and thoroughness that, though the enemy pressed severely, only one man was wounded. The way in which Major Campbell, the commanding officer, availed himself of the advantages of retiring down two spurs and bringing a cross fire to bear to cover the alternate retirements, resembled some intricate chess problem, rather than a military evolution.

The power of the new Lee-Metford rifle with the new Dum-Dum bullet—it is now called, though not officially, the "ek-dum" [Hindustani for "at once."] bullet—is tremendous. The soldiers who have used it have the utmost confidence in their weapon. Up to 500 yards there is no difficulty about judging the range, as it shoots quite straight, or, technically speaking, has a flat trajectory. This is of the greatest value. Of the bullet it may be said, that its stopping power is all that could be desired. The Dum-Dum bullet, though not explosive, is expansive. The original Lee-Metford bullet was a pellet of lead covered by a nickel case with an opening at the base. In the improved bullet this outer case has been drawn backward, making the hole in the base a little smaller and leaving the lead at the tip exposed. The result is a wonderful and from the technical point of view a beautiful machine. On striking a bone this causes the bullet to "set up" or spread out, and it then tears and splinters everything before it, causing wounds which in the body must be generally mortal and in any limb necessitate amputation. Continental critics have asked whether such a bullet is not a violation of the Geneva or St. Petersburg Conventions; but no clause of these international agreements forbids expansive bullets, and the only provision on the subject is that shells less than a certain size shall not be employed. I would observe that bullets are primarily intended to kill, and that these bullets do their duty most effectually, without causing any more pain to those struck by them, than the ordinary lead variety. As the enemy obtained some Lee-Metford rifles and Dum-Dum ammunition during the progress of the fighting, information on this latter point is forthcoming. The sensation is described as similar to that produced by any bullet—a violent numbing blow, followed by a sense of injury and weakness, but little actual pain at the time. Indeed, now-a-days, very few people are so unfortunate as to suffer much pain from wounds, except during the period of recovery. A man is hit. In a quarter of an hour, that is to say, before the shock has passed away and the pain begins, he is usually at the dressing station. Here he is given morphia injections, which reduce all sensations to a uniform dullness. In this state he remains until he is placed under chloroform and operated on.

The necessity for having the officers in the same dress as the men, was apparent to all who watched the operations. The conspicuous figure which a British officer in his helmet presented in contrast to the native soldiers in their turbans, drew a well-aimed fire in his direction. Of course, in British regiments, the difference is not nearly so marked. Nevertheless, at close quarters the keen-eyed tribesmen always made an especial mark of the officers, distinguishing them chiefly, I think, by the fact that they do not carry rifles. The following story may show how evident this was:—

When the Buffs were marching down to Panjkora, they passed the Royal West Kent coming up to relieve them at Inayat Kila. A private in the up-going regiment asked a friend in the Buffs what it was like at the front. "Oh," replied the latter, "you'll be all right so long as you don't go near no officers, nor no white stones." Whether the advice was taken is not recorded, but it was certainly sound, for three days later—on 30th September—in those companies of the Royal West Kent regiment that were engaged in the village of Agrah, eight out of eleven officers were hit or grazed by bullets.

The fatigues experienced by troops in mountain warfare are so great, that every effort has to be made to lighten the soldier's load. At the same time the more ammunition he carries on his person the better. Mules laden with cartridge-boxes are very likely to be shot, and fall into the hands of the enemy. In this manner over 6000 rounds were lost on the 16th of September by the two companies of Sikhs whose retirement I have described.

The thick leather belts, pouches, and valise equipment of British infantry are unnecessarily heavy. I have heard many officers suggest having them made of web. The argument against this is that the web wears out. That objection could be met by having a large supply of these equipments at the base and issuing fresh ones as soon as the old were unfit for use. It is cheaper to wear out belts than soldiers.

Great efforts should be made to give the soldier a piece of chocolate, a small sausage, or something portable and nutritious to carry with him to the field. In a war of long marches, of uncertain fortunes, of retirements often delayed and always pressed, there have been many occasions when regiments and companies have unexpectedly had to stop out all night without food. It is well to remember that the stomach governs the world.

The principle of concentrating artillery has long been admitted in Europe. Sir Bindon Blood is the first general who has applied it to mountain warfare in India. It had formerly been the custom to use the guns by twos and threes. As we have seen, at the action of Landakai, the Malakand Field Force had eighteen guns in action, of which twelve were in one line. The fire of this artillery drove the enemy, who were in great strength and an excellent position, from the ground. The infantry attack was accomplished with hardly any loss, and a success was obtained at a cost of a dozen lives which would have been cheap at a hundred.

After this, it may seem strange if I say that the artillery fire in the Mamund Valley did very little execution. It is nevertheless a fact. The Mamunds are a puny tribe, but they build their houses in the rocks; and against sharpshooters in broken ground, guns can do little. Through field-glasses it was possible to see the enemy dodging behind their rocks, whenever the puffs of smoke from the guns told them that a shell was on its way. Perhaps smokeless powder would have put a stop to this. But in any case, the targets presented to the artillery were extremely bad.

Where they really were of great service, was not so much in killing the enemy, but in keeping them from occupying certain spurs and knolls. On 30th September, when the Royal West Kent and the 31st Punjaub Infantry were retiring under considerable pressure, the British Mountain Battery moved to within 700 yards of the enemy, and opened a rapid fire of shrapnel on the high ground which commanded the line of retreat, killing such of the tribesmen as were there, and absolutely forbidding the hill to their companions.

In all rearguard actions among the mountains the employment of artillery is imperative. Even two guns may materially assist the extrication of the infantry from the peaks and crags of the hillside, and prevent by timely shells the tribesmen from seizing each point as soon as it is evacuated. But there is no reason why the artillery should be stinted, and at least two batteries, if available, should accompany a brigade to the attack.

Signalling by heliograph was throughout the operations of the greatest value. I had always realised the advantages of a semi-permanent line of signal stations along the communications to the telegraph, but I had doubted the practicability of using such complicated arrangements in action. In this torrid country, where the sun is always shining, the heliograph is always useful. As soon as any hill was taken, communication was established with the brigadier, and no difficulty seemed to be met with, even while the attack was in progress, in sending messages quickly and clearly. In a country intersected by frequent ravines, over which a horse can move but slowly and painfully, it is the surest, the quickest, and indeed the only means of intercommunication. I am delighted to testify to these things, because I had formerly been a scoffer.

I have touched on infantry and artillery, and, though a previous chapter has been almost wholly devoted to the cavalry, I cannot resist the desire to get back to the horses and the lances again. The question of sword or lance as the cavalryman's weapon has long been argued, and it may be of interest to consider what are the views of those whose experience is the most recent. Though I have had no opportunity of witnessing the use of the lance, I have heard the opinions of many officers both of the Guides and the 11th Bengal Lancers. All admit or assert that the lance is in this warfare the better weapon. It kills with more certainty and convenience, and there is less danger of the horseman being cut down. As to length, the general opinion seems to be in favour of a shorter spear. This, with a counter poise at the butt, gives as good a reach and is much more useful for close quarters. Major Beatson, one of the most distinguished cavalry officers on the frontier, is a strong advocate of this. Either the pennon should be knotted, or a boss of some sort affixed about eighteen inches below the point. Unless this be done there is a danger of the lance penetrating too far, when it either gets broken or allows the enemy to wriggle up and strike the lancer. This last actually happened on several occasions.

Now, in considering the question to what extent a squadron should be armed with lances, the system adopted by the Guides may be of interest. In this warfare it is very often necessary for the cavalryman to dismount and use his carbine. The lance then gets in the way and has to be tied to the saddle. This takes time, and there is usually not much time to spare in cavalry skirmishing. The Guides compromise matters by giving one man in every four a lance. This man, when the others dismount, stays in the saddle and holds their horses. They also give the outer sections of each squadron lances, and these, too, remain mounted, as the drill-book enjoins. But I become too technical.

I pass for a moment to combined tactics. In frontier warfare Providence is on the side of the good band-o-bust [arrangements]. There are no scenic effects or great opportunities, and the Brigadier who leaves the mountains with as good a reputation as he entered them has proved himself an able, sensible man. The general who avoids all "dash," who never starts in the morning looking for a fight and without any definite intention, who does not attempt heroic achievements, and who keeps his eye on his watch, will have few casualties and little glory. For the enemy do not become formidable until a mistake has been made. The public who do not believe in military operations without bloodshed may be unattentive. His subordinate officers may complain that they have had no fighting. But in the consciousness of duty skillfully performed and of human life preserved he will find a high reward.

A general review of the frontier war will, I think, show the great disadvantages to which regular troops are exposed in fighting an active enterprising enemy that can move faster and shoot better, who knows the country and who knows the ranges. The terrible losses inflicted on the tribesmen in the Swat Valley show how easily disciplined troops can brush away the bravest savages in the open. But on the hillside all is changed, and the observer will be struck by the weakness rather than the strength of modern weapons. Daring riflemen, individually superior to the soldiers, and able to support the greatest fatigues, can always inflict loss, although they cannot bar their path.

The military problem with which the Spaniards are confronted in Cuba is in many points similar to that presented in the Afghan valleys; a roadless, broken and undeveloped country; an absence of any strategic points; a well-armed enemy with great mobility and modern rifles, who adopts guerilla tactics. The results in either case are, that the troops can march anywhere, and do anything, except catch the enemy; and that all their movements must be attended with loss.

If the question of subduing the tribes be regarded from a purely military standpoint, if time were no object, and there was no danger of a lengthy operation being interrupted by a change of policy at home, it would appear that the efforts of commanders should be, to induce the tribesmen to assume the offensive. On this point I must limit my remarks to the flat-bottomed valleys of Swat and Bajaur. To coerce a tribe like the Mamunds, a mixed brigade might camp at the entrance to the valley, and as at Inayat Kila, entrench itself very strongly. The squadron of cavalry could patrol the valley daily in complete security, as the tribesmen would not dare to leave the hills. All sowing of crops and agricultural work would be stopped. The natives would retaliate by firing into the camp at night. This would cause loss; but if every one were to dig a good hole to sleep in, and if the officers were made to have dinner before sundown, and forbidden to walk about except on duty after dark, there is no reason why the loss should be severe. At length the tribesmen, infuriated by the occupation of their valley, and perhaps rendered desperate by the approach of famine and winter, would make a tremendous attempt to storm the camp. With a strong entrenchment, a wire trip to break a rush, and modern rifles, they would be driven off with great slaughter, and once severely punished would probably beg for terms. If not, the process would be continued until they did so.

Such a military policy would cost about the same in money as the vigorous methods I have described, as though smaller numbers of troops might be employed, they would have to remain mobilised and in the field for a longer period. But the loss in personnel would be much less. As good an example of the success of this method as can be found, is provided by Sir Bindon Blood's tactics at Nawagai, when, being too weak to attack the enemy himself, he encouraged them to attack him, and then beat them off with great loss.

From the point which we have now reached, it is possible, and perhaps not undesirable, to take a rapid yet sweeping glance of the larger military problems of the day. We have for some years adopted the "short service" system. It is a continental system. It has many disadvantages. Troops raised under it suffer from youth, want of training and lack of regimental associations. But on the Continent it has this one, paramount recommendation: it provides enormous numbers. The active army is merely a machine for manufacturing soldiers quickly, and passing them into the reserves, to be stored until they are wanted. European nations deal with soldiers only in masses. Great armies of men, not necessarily of a high standard of courage and training, but armed with deadly weapons, are directed against one another, under varying strategical conditions. Before they can rebound, thousands are slaughtered and a great battle has been won or lost. The average courage of the two nations may perhaps have been decided. The essence of the continental system is its gigantic scale.

We have adopted this system in all respects but one, and that the vital one. We have got the poor quality, without the great quantity. We have, by the short service system, increased our numbers a little, and decreased our standard a good deal. The reason that this system, which is so well adapted to continental requirements, confers no advantages upon us is obvious. Our army is recruited by a voluntary system. Short service and conscription are inseparable. For this reason, several stern soldiers advocate conscription. But many words will have to be spoken, many votes voted, and perhaps many blows struck before the British people would submit to such an abridgment of their liberties, or such a drag upon their commerce. It will be time to make such sacrifices when the English Channel runs dry.

Without conscription we cannot have great numbers. It should therefore be our endeavour to have those we possess of the best quality; and our situation and needs enforce this view. Our soldiers are not required to operate in great masses, but very often to fight hand to hand. Their campaigns are not fought in temperate climates and civilised countries. They are sent beyond the seas to Africa or the Indian frontier, and there, under a hot sun and in a pestilential land, they are engaged in individual combat with athletic savages. They are not old enough for the work.

Young as they are, their superior weapons and the prestige of the dominant race enable them to maintain their superiority over the native troops. But in the present war several incidents have occurred, unimportant, insignificant, it is true, but which, in the interests of Imperial expediency, are better forgotten. The native regiments are ten years older than the British regiments. Many of their men have seen service and have been under fire. Some of them have several medals. All, of course, are habituated to the natural conditions. It is evident how many advantages they enjoy. It is also apparent how very serious the consequences would be if they imagined they possessed any superiority. That such an assumption should even be possible is a menace to our very existence in India. Intrinsic merit is the only title of a dominant race to its possessions. If we fail in this it is not because our spirit is old and grown weak, but because our soldiers are young, and not yet grown strong.

Boys of twenty-one and twenty-two are expected to compete on equal terms with Sikhs and Gurkhas of thirty, fully developed and in the prime of life. It is an unfair test. That they should have held their own is a splendid tribute to the vigour of our race. The experiment is dangerous, and it is also expensive. We continue to make it because the idea is still cherished that British armies will one day again play a part in continental war. When the people of the United Kingdom are foolish enough to allow their little army to be ground to fragments between continental myriads, they will deserve all the misfortunes that will inevitably come upon them.

I am aware that these arguments are neither original nor new. I have merely arranged them. I am also aware that there are able, brilliant men who have spent their lives in the service of the State, who do not take the views I have quoted. The question has been regarded from an Indian point of view. There is probably no colonel in India, who commands a British regiment, who would not like to see his men five years older. It may be that the Indian opinion on the subject is based only on partial information, and warped by local circumstances. Still I have thought it right to submit it to the consideration of the public, at a time when the army has been filling such a prominent position, not only in the Jubilee procession and the frontier war, but also in the estimates presented to the House of Commons.

Passing from the concrete to the abstract, it may not be unfitting that these pages, which have recorded so many valiant deeds, should contain some brief inquiry into the nature of those motives which induce men to expose themselves to great hazards, and to remain in situations of danger. The circumstances of war contain every element that can shake the nerves. The whizzing of the projectiles; the shouts and yells of a numerous and savage enemy; the piteous aspect of the wounded, covered with blood and sometimes crying out in pain; the spurts of dust which on all sides show where Fate is stepping—these are the sights and sounds which assail soldiers, whose development and education enable them to fully appreciate their significance. And yet the courage of the soldier is the commonest of virtues. Thousands of men, drawn at random from the population, are found to control the instinct of self-preservation. Nor is this courage peculiar to any particular nation. Courage is not only common, but cosmopolitan. But such are the apparent contradictions of life, that this virtue, which so many seem to possess, all hold the highest. There is probably no man, however miserable, who would not writhe at being exposed a coward. Why should the common be precious? What is the explanation?

It appears to be this. The courage of the soldier is not really contempt for physical evils and indifference to danger. It is a more or less successful attempt to simulate these habits of mind. Most men aspire to be good actors in the play. There are a few who are so perfect that they do not seem to be actors at all. This is the ideal after which the rest are striving. It is one very rarely attained.

Three principal influences combine to assist men in their attempts: preparation, vanity and sentiment. The first includes all the force of discipline and training. The soldier has for years contemplated the possibility of being under fire. He has wondered vaguely what kind of an experience it would be. He has seen many who have gone through it and returned safely. His curiosity is excited. Presently comes the occasion. By road and railway he approaches daily nearer to the scene. His mind becomes familiar with the prospect. His comrades are in the same situation. Habit, behind which force of circumstances is concealed, makes him conform. At length the hour arrives. He observes the darting puffs of smoke in the distance. He listens to the sounds that are in the air. Perhaps he hears something strike with a thud and sees a soldier near him collapse like a shot pheasant. He realises that it may be his turn next. Fear grips him by the throat.

Then vanity, the vice which promotes so many virtues, asserts itself. He looks at his comrades and they at him. So far he has shown no sign of weakness. He thinks, they are thinking him brave. The dearly longed-for reputation glitters before his eyes. He executes the orders he receives.

But something else is needed to made a hero. Some other influence must help him through the harder trials and more severe ordeals which may befall him. It is sentiment which makes the difference in the end. Those who doubt should stroll to the camp fire one night and listen to the soldiers' songs. Every one clings to something that he thinks is high and noble, or that raises him above the rest of the world in the hour of need. Perhaps he remembers that he is sprung from an ancient stock, and of a race that has always known how to die; or more probably it is something smaller and more intimate; the regiment, whatever it is called—"The Gordons," "The Buffs," "The Queen's,"—and so nursing the name—only the unofficial name of an infantry battalion after all—he accomplishes great things and maintains the honour and the Empire of the British people.

It may be worth while, in the matter of names, to observe the advantages to a regiment of a monosyllabic appellation. Every one will remember Lieut.-Colonel Mathias' speech to the Gordons. Imagine for a moment that speech addressed to some regiment saddled with a fantastic title on the territorial system, as, for instance, Mr. Kipling's famous regiment, "The Princess Hohenzollern-Sigmaringen-Anspach's Merthyr Tydvilshire Own Royal Loyal Light Infantry." With the old numbers all started on equal terms.

This has been perhaps a cold-blooded chapter. We have considered men as targets; tribesmen, fighting for their homes and hills, have been regarded only as the objective of an attack; killed and wounded human beings, merely as the waste of war. We have even attempted to analyse the high and noble virtue of courage, in the hopes of learning how it may be manufactured.

The philosopher may observe with pity, and the philanthropist deplore with pain, that the attention of so many minds should be directed to the scientific destruction of the human species; but practical people in a business-like age will remember that they live in a world of men—not angels—and regulate their conduct accordingly.

CHAPTER XVIII. AND LAST. :

THE RIDDLE OF THE FRONTIER

"Myself when young did eagerly frequent
    Doctor and saint, and heard great argument
About it and about, but evermore
    Came out by the same door wherein I went."

OMAR KHAYYAM.

These pages, which have chronicled a variety of small incidents, have hitherto concerned themselves little with the great matters out of which those incidents have arisen. As an opening chapter should lead the reader to expect the considerations that the book contains, so the conclusion should express the opinion he might form from the perusal. When, at an earlier period, I refrained from discussing the question of frontier policy, I declared that its consideration was only postponed until a more propitious moment. That moment now presents itself. There will not be wanting those who will remind me, that in this matter my opinion is not supported by age or experience. To such I shall reply, that if what is written is false or foolish, neither age nor experience should fortify it; and if it is true, it needs no such support. The propositions of Euclid would be no less indisputable were they propounded by an infant or an idiot.

The inquirer sees the vast question unfold itself with feelings like those with which the fisherman in the old story watched the genius he had unwittingly released, rise from the bottle in clouds of smoke, which overspread the whole sky. Every moment the subject appears not only wider but deeper. When I reflect on the great number of diverse and often conflicting facts which may be assembled under every head—military, economic, political or moral—and consider the accumulations of specialised and technical knowledge necessary for their proper appreciation, I am convinced that to compass the whole is beyond the mind and memory of man. Of such a question it is difficult to take broad views, and dangerous to generalise. Still less is it possible, as many people appear to imagine, to settle it with a phrase or an epigram. A point is reached where all relation between detail and proportion is lost. It is a picture of such great size that to see it all, it is necessary to stand so far off that neither colours nor figures are distinguishable. By constantly changing the point of view, some true perspective is possible, and even then the conception must be twisted and distorted, by the imperfections of the mental mirror.

Sensible of the magnitude of the task, and conscious of my own weakness, I propose to examine in a spirit of cautious inquiry and of tolerance the present "Forward Policy," and thence to approach the main question, to the answer of which that policy is only a guess.

I must revert to a period when the British power, having conquered the plains of India and subdued its sovereigns, paused at the foot of the Himalayas and turned its tireless energy to internal progress and development. The "line of the mountains" formed a frontier as plain and intelligible as that which defines the limits of the sea. To the south lay the British Empire in India; to the north were warlike tribes, barbarous, unapproachable, irreclaimable; and far beyond these, lay the other great Power of Asia.

It was long the wisdom of Anglo-Indian statesmen to preserve a situation which contained so many elements of finality, and so many guarantees of peace. When the northern savages, impelled by fanaticism or allured by plunder, descended from the mountains and invaded the plains, they were met by equal courage and superior discipline, and driven in disorder to their confines. But this was found to be an inadequate deterrent, and the purely defensive principle had to be modified in favor of that system of punitive expeditions which has been derided as the policy of "Butcher and Bolt."

Gradually, as the circumstances altered, the methods of dealing with them changed. The punitive expeditions had awakened an intense hostility among the tribesmen. The intrigues of Russia had for some time been watched with alarm by the Indian Government. As long as the border could remain a "No-man's land"—as it were a "great gulf fixed"—all was well; but if any power was to be supreme, that power must neither be Russia nor Afghanistan. ["We shall consider it from the first incumbent upon the Government of India to prevent, at any cost, the establishment within this outlying country of the political preponderance of any other power."—Letter from Government of India to the Secretary of State, No.49, 28th February, 1879.] The predominance of Russian influence in these territories would give them the power to invade India at their discretion, with what chances of success need not be here discussed. The predominance of Afghan influence would make the Amir master of the situation, and enable him to blackmail the Indian Government indefinitely. A change of policy, a departure from the old frontier line, presented itself with increasing force to responsible men. To-day we see the evils that have resulted from that change. The dangers that inspired it have been modified.

For some years the opinion in favour of an advance grew steadily among those in power in India. In 1876 a decisive step was taken. Roused by the efforts of the Amir to obtain the suzerainty of the Pathan tribes, Lord Lytton's Government stretched a hand through Cashmere towards Chitral, and the Mehtar of that State became the vassal, nominally of the Maharaja of Cashmere, but practically of the Imperial Government. The avowed object was to ultimately secure the effectual command of the passes of the Hindu Kush. [Despatch No.17, 11th June, 1877.] The British Ministry, the famous ministry of Lord Beaconsfield, approved the action and endorsed the policy. Again, in 1879, the Vice-regal Government, in an official despatch, declared their intention of acquiring, "through the ruler of Cashmere, the power of making such political and military arrangements as will effectually command the passes of the Hindu Kush." [Despatch No.49, 28th February, 1879.] "If," so runs the despatch, "we *extend and by degrees consolidate our influence* [The italics are mine] over this country, and if we resolve that no foreign interference can be permitted on this side of the mountains or within the drainage system of the Indus, we shall have laid down a natural line of frontier, which is distinct, intelligible and likely to be respected." [Despatch No.49, 28th February, 1879.]

No declaration of policy or intention could have been more explicit. The words to "extend and consolidate our influence" can, when applied to barbarous peoples, have no other meaning than ultimate annexation. Thus the scheme of an advance from the plains of India into the mountain region, which had long been maturing in men's minds and which was shaped and outlined by many small emergencies and expedients, was clearly proclaimed. The forward movement had begun. A fresh and powerful impulse was imparted after the termination of Lord Ripon's viceroyalty. The open aggression which characterised the Russian frontier policy of '84 and '85 had been met by a supine apathy and indifference to the interests of the State, which deserved, and which, had the issues been less important, might have received actual punishment. It was natural that his immediate successors should strive to dissociate themselves from the follies and the blunders of those years. The spirit of reaction led to the final abandonment of the venerable policy of non-intervention. Instead of the "line of the mountains," it was now maintained that the passes through them must be held. This is the so-called "Forward Policy." It is a policy which aims at obtaining the frontier—Gilgit, Chitral, Jelalabad, Kandahar.

In pursuance of that policy we have been led to build many frontier forts, to construct roads, to annex territories, and to enter upon more intimate relations with the border tribes. The most marked incident in that policy has been the retention of Chitral. This act was regarded by the tribesmen as a menace to their independence, and by the priesthood as the prelude to a general annexation. Nor were they wrong, for such is the avowed aim of the "Forward Policy." The result of the retention of Chitral has been, as I have already described, that the priesthood, knowing that their authority would be weakened by civilisation, have used their religious influence on the people to foment a general rising.

It is useless to discuss the Chitral question independently. If the "Forward Policy" be justified, then the annexation of Chitral, its logical outcome, is also justified. The bye and the main plots stand or fall together.

So far then we have advanced and have been resisted. The "Forward Policy" has brought an increase of territory, a nearer approach to what is presumably a better frontier line and—war. All this was to have been expected. It may be said of the present system that it precludes the possibility of peace. Isolated posts have been formed in the midst of races notoriously passionate, reckless and warlike. They are challenges. When they are assailed by the tribesmen, relieving and punitive expeditions become necessary. All this is the outcome of a recognised policy, and was doubtless foreseen by those who initiated it. What may be called strange is that the forts should be badly constructed—cramped, as the Malakand positions; commanded, like Chakdara; without flank defences, as at Saraghari; without proper garrisons, as in the Khyber. This is a side issue and accidental. The rest of the situation has been deliberately created.

The possibility of a great combination among the border tribes was indeed not contemplated. Separated by distance, and divided by faction, it was anticipated they could be dealt with in detail. On this point we have been undeceived.

That period of war and disturbance which was the inevitable first consequence of the "Forward Policy" must in any case have been disturbed and expensive. Regarded from an economic standpoint, the trade of the frontier valleys will never pay a shilling in the pound on the military expenditure necessary to preserve order. Morally, it is unfortunate for the tribesmen that our spheres of influence clash with their spheres of existence. Even on the military question, a purely technical question, as to whether an advanced frontier line is desirable or not, opinion is divided. Lord Roberts says one thing; Mr. Morley another.

There is no lack of arguments against the "Forward Policy." There are many who opposed its initiation. There are many who oppose it now; who think that nothing should have lured the Government of India beyond their natural frontier line, and who maintain that it would have been both practical and philosophic had they said: "Over all the plains of India will we cast our rule. There we will place our governors and magistrates; our words shall be respected and our laws obeyed. But that region, where the land rises like the waves of a sea, shall serve us as a channel of stormy waters to divide us from our foes and rivals."

But it is futile to engage in the controversies of the past. There are sufficient in the present, and it is with the present we are concerned.

We have crossed the Rubicon. In the opinion of all those who know most about the case, the forward movement is now beyond recall. Indeed, when the intense hostility of the Border tribes, the uncertain attitude of the Amir, the possibilities of further Russian aggression and the state of feeling in India are considered, it is difficult to dispute this judgment. Successive Indian Administrations have urged, successive English Cabinets have admitted, the necessity of finding a definite and a defensible frontier. The old line has been left, and between that line and an advanced line continuous with Afghan territory, and south of which all shall be reduced to law and order, there does not appear to be any prospect of a peaceful and permanent settlement.

The responsibility of placing us in this position rests with those who first forsook the old frontier policy of holding the "line of the mountains." The historian of the future, with impartial pen and a more complete knowledge, must pronounce on the wisdom of their act. In the meantime it should be remembered of these great men, that they left their public offices amid the applause and admiration of their contemporaries, and, "in the full tide of successful experiment." Nor can so much be said of all those who have assailed them. Those who decided, have accepted the responsibility, and have defended their action. But I am inclined to think that the rulers of India, ten years ago or a hundred years ago, were as much the sport of circumstances as their successors are to-day.

Let us return to the present and our own affairs. We have embarked on stormy and perilous waters. The strong current of events forbids return. The sooner the farther shore is reached, the sooner will the dangers and discomforts of the voyage be over. All are anxious to make the land. The suggestions as to the course are numerous. There are some, bad and nervous sailors perhaps, who insist upon returning, although they are told it is impossible, and who would sink the ship sooner than go on, were they not outnumbered by their shipmates. While they are delaying, the current bears us towards more disturbed waters and more rocky landing places.

There are others who call out for "Full steam ahead," and would accomplish the passage at once, whatever the risks. But alas! The ship is run out of coal and can only spread its sails to the varying breezes, take advantage of favorable tides, and must needs lie to when the waves are high.

But the sensible passenger may, though he knows the difficulties of the voyage and the dangers of the sea, fairly ask the man at the wheel to keep a true and constant course. He may with reason and justice insist that, whatever the delays which the storms or accidents may cause, the head of the vessel shall be consistently pointed towards the distant port, and that come what will she shall not be allowed to drift aimlessly hither and thither on the chance of fetching up somewhere some day.

The "Full steam ahead" method would be undoubtedly the most desirable. This is the military view. Mobilise, it is urged, a nice field force, and operate at leisure in the frontier valleys, until they are as safe and civilised as Hyde Park. Nor need this course necessarily involve the extermination of the inhabitants. Military rule is the rule best suited to the character and comprehension of the tribesmen. They will soon recognise the futility of resistance, and will gradually welcome the increase of wealth and comfort that will follow a stable government. Besides this, we shall obtain a definite frontier almost immediately. Only one real objection has been advanced against this plan. But it is a crushing one, and it constitutes the most serious argument against the whole "Forward Policy." It is this: we have neither the troops nor the money to carry it out.

The inevitable alternative is the present system, a system which the war has interrupted, but to which we must return at its close; a system of gradual advance, of political intrigue among the tribes, of subsidies and small expeditions.

Though this policy is slow, painful and somewhat undignified, there is no reason that it should not be sure and strong. But it must be consistently pursued. Dynamite in the hands of a child is not more dangerous than a strong policy weakly carried out. The reproach which may be justly laid upon the rulers of India, whether at home or abroad, is that while they recognise the facts, they shrink from the legitimate conclusions.

They know they cannot turn back. They fully intend to go on. Yet they fear to admit the situation, to frankly lay their case before the country, and trust to the good sense and courage of an ancient democracy. The result is, that they tie their hands by ridiculous and unnecessary proclamations, such as that which preceded the Chitral expedition of 1895. The political officers who watch the frontier tribes are expected to obtain authority by force of personal character, yet strictly according to regulations, and to combine individuality with uniformity. And sometimes this timidity leads to such dismal acts of folly as the desertion of the Khyber forts.

But in spite of all obstacles and errors there is a steady advance, which may be accelerated, and made easier, by many small reforms. These questions of detail approach so near the province of the specialist, that I shall not attempt to enumerate or discuss them. It is suggested among other things that wider powers should be given to the political officers, in their ordinary duties of peace. Others advocate occasional demonstrations of troops, to impress the tribesmen with the fact that those they see are not the full strength of the Sirkar. Bolder minds have hinted at transplanting young Pathans, and educating them in India after the custom of the Romans. But this last appears to be suitable to a classic rather than a Christian age.

From a general survey of the people and the country, it would seem that silver makes a better weapon than steel. A system of subsidies must tend to improve our relations with the tribes, enlist their interests on the side of law and order, and by increasing their wealth, lessen their barbarism. In the matter of the supply of arms the Government would find it cheaper to enter the market as a purchaser, and have agents to outbid the tribesmen, rather than to employ soldiers. As water finds its own level, so the laws of economics will infallibly bring commodities to the highest bidder. Doubtless there are many other lessons which the present war will have taught. These may lighten a task which, though long and heavy, is not beyond the powers or pluck of the British people.

We are at present in a transition stage, nor is the manner nor occasion of the end in sight. Still this is no time to despair. I have often noticed in these Afghan valleys, that they seem to be entirely surrounded by the hills, and to have no exit. But as the column has advanced, a gap gradually becomes visible and a pass appears. Sometimes it is steep and difficult, sometimes it is held by the enemy and must be forced, but I have never seen a valley that had not a way out. That way we shall ultimately find, if we march with the firm but prudent step of men who know the dangers; but, conscious of their skill and discipline, do not doubt their ability to deal with them as they shall arise. In such a spirit I would leave the subject, with one farewell glance.

Looking on the story of the great frontier war; at all that has been told, and all that others may tell, there must be many who to-day will only deplore the losses of brave soldiers and hard-earned money. But those who from some future age shall, by steady light of history, dispassionately review the whole situation, its causes, results and occasion, may find other reflections, as serious perhaps, but less mournful. The year 1897, in the annals of the British people, was marked by a declaration to the whole world of their faith in the higher destinies of their race. If a strong man, when the wine sparkles at the feast and the lights are bright, boasts of his prowess, it is well he should have an opportunity of showing in the cold and grey of the morning that he is no idle braggart. And unborn arbiters, with a wider knowledge, and more developed brains, may trace in recent events the influence of that mysterious Power which, directing the progress of our species, and regulating the rise and fall of Empires, has afforded that opportunity to a people, of whom at least it may be said, that they have added to the happiness, the learning and the liberties of mankind.

APPENDIX.

THE ATTACK ON THE MALAKAND.
26th July—1st August, 1897.

FROM THE DESPATCH OF BRIGADIER-GENERAL W.H. MEIKLEJOHN, C.B., C.M.G.

FORWARDED TO THE ADJUTANT-GENERAL IN INDIA BY SIR BINDON BLOOD.

43. All have done well, but I should like to bring before His Excellency for favorable consideration the following names of officers and men:—

24th Punjaub Infantry.

Lieut.-Colonel J. Lamb, who, on the first alarm being sounded on the night of the 26th July, had taken prompt action in reinforcing the outpost line held by his regiment, and later was of great assistance in directing the defence of the central enclosure, till he was severely wounded.

Captain H.F. Holland showed great courage in assisting to drive a number of the enemy out of the central enclosure, and was severely wounded in doing so.

I would especially wish to mention Lieutenant S.H. Climo, who commanded the 24th Punjaub Infantry after Lieut.-Colonel Lamb and Captain Holland had been wounded. This officer has shown soldierly qualities and ability of the highest order. He has commanded the regiment with dash and enterprise, and shown a spirit and example which has been followed by all ranks. I trust His Excellency will be pleased to favourably notice Lieutenant Climo, who has proved himself an officer who will do well in any position, and is well worthy of promotion.

Lieutenant A.K. Rawlins has behaved well all through. I would recommend him to His Excellency for the plucky way in which he went to the fort on the 26th July to bring reinforcements, and again for the dash he showed in leading his men on the 27th and 28th, of which Lieutenant Climo speaks most highly.

Lieutenant E.W. Costello, 22nd Punjaub Infantry, temporarily attached to the 24th Punjaub Infantry, has behaved exceedingly well, and is the subject of a separate recommendation.

31st Punjaub Infantry.

Major M.I. Gibbs, who commanded the regiment in the absence of Major O'Bryen, with skill and in every way to my satisfaction.

Lieutenant H.B. Ford, Acting-Adjutant, 31st Punjaub Infantry, rendered valuable assistance in helping to bring in a wounded Sepoy during the withdrawal from north camp. He also behaved with courage in resisting an attack of the enemy on the night of the 28th, when he was severely wounded.

Surgeon-Lieutenant J.H. Hugo, attached to 31st Punjaub Infantry, rendered valuable service on the night of the 28th in saving Lieutenant H.B. Ford from bleeding to death. Lieutenant Ford was wounded and a branch of an artery was cut. There were no means of securing the artery, and Surgeon-Lieutenant Hugo for two hours stopped the bleeding by compressing the artery with his fingers. Had be not had the strength to do so, Lieutenant Ford must have died. Early in the morning, thinking that the enemy had effected an entrance into camp, Surgeon-Lieutenant Hugo picked up Lieutenant Ford with one arm, and, still holding the artery with the fingers of the other hand, carried him to a place of safety.

45th (Rattray's) Sikhs.

Colonel H.A. Sawyer was away on leave when hostilities broke out, but he returned on the 29th and took over command of the regiment from Lieut.-Colonel McRae, and from that time rendered me every assistance.

I would specially bring to the notice of His Excellency the Commander-in-chief the name of Lieut.-Colonel H.N. McRae, who commanded the regiment on the 26th, 27th and 28th. His prompt action in seizing the gorge at the top of the Buddhist road on the night of the 26th, and the gallant way in which he held it, undoubtedly saved the camp from being rushed on that side. For this, and for the able way in which he commanded the regiment during the first three days of the fighting, I would commend him to His Excellency's favorable consideration.

Also Lieutenant R.M. Barff, Officiating-Adjutant of the regiment, who, Lieut.-Colonel McRae reports, behaved with great courage and rendered him valuable assistance.

The Guides.

I also wish to bring the name of Lieut.-Colonel R.B. Adams of the Guides to His Excellency's notice. The prompt way in which the corps mobilised, and their grand march, reflect great credit on him and the corps. Since arrival at the Malakand on the 27th July and till the morning of the 1st August, Lieut.-Colonel Adams was in command of the lower camp, i.e., that occupied by central and left position, and in the execution of this command, and the arrangements he made for improving the defenses, he gave me every satisfaction. I have also to express my appreciation of the way in which he conducted the cavalry reconnaissance on the 1st August, on which occasion his horse was shot under him.

Great credit is due to Lieutenant P.C. Eliott-Lockhart, who was in command of the Guides Infantry, for bringing up the regiment from Mardan to Malakand in such good condition after their trying march.

Captain G.M. Baldwin, D.S.O., behaved with great courage and coolness during the reconnaissance of the 1st August, and though severely wounded by a sword cut on the head, he remained on the ground and continued to lead his men.

Lieutenant H.L.S. Maclean also behaved with courage, and displayed an excellent example on the night of the 28th July, when he was severely wounded.

11th Bengal Lancers.

Major S. Beatson commanded the squadron, 11th Bengal Lancers, which arrived at Malakand on the 29th, and led them with great skill and dash on the occasion of the reconnaissance on the 1st August.

No.8 Bengal Mountain Battery.

Lieutenant F.A. Wynter was the only officer with No.8 Bengal Mountain Battery from the 26th till the 30th July, and he commanded it during that time, when all the severest of the fighting was going on, with great ability, and has proved himself a good soldier. I should like especially to mention him for His Excellency's consideration. The battery did excellent work all through.

No.5 Company Queen's Own Madras Sappers and Miners.

Lieutenant A.R. Winsloe, R.E., commanded the company from the 27th July till the 1st August to my entire satisfaction. His services in strengthening the defences were invaluable.

Lieutenant F.W. Watling, R.E., was in command of the company in the absence of Captain Johnson on the 26th, and commanded it well until he was wounded in gallantly trying to resist a charge of the enemy. After Lieutenant Watling was wounded the command of the company for the remainder of the night of the 26th, and till Lieutenant Winsloe returned on the 27th, devolved on Lieutenant E.N. Manley, R.E. He performed his duties with great credit, and afterwards was of great assistance, by his zeal and his exertions, to Lieutenant Winsloe.

Medical Staff.

Brigade-Surgeon-Lieut.-Colonel F.A. Smyth was most zealous, and performed his duties to my satisfaction. He volunteered to perform the duties of Provost Marshal, and did so for a short time during the illness of Lieutenant H.E. Cotterill.

The arrangements made by Surgeon-Major S. Hassand, Senior Medical Officer, 38th Native Field Hospital, and the indefatigable attention and care with which he devoted himself to the wounded, deserve great praise. The list of casualties is large, and Surgeon-Major Hassand has been untiring in his exertions for their relief.

I hope His Excellency will think fit to consider his services favourably.

Surgeon-Captain T.A.O. Langston, 38th Native Field Hospital, rendered valuable assistance in attending to the wounded under a heavy fire on the night of the 26th and each following night, and behaved with courage and devotion in carrying out his duties under very exceptional circumstances. Surgeon-Lieutenant W. Carr has worked night and day in the hospitals, in trying to alleviate the sufferings of the wounded, and has most ably and efficiently aided Surgeon-Major Hassand.

Brigade Staff.

Major L. Herbert, my Deputy Assistant Adjutant and Quartermaster-General, was of the greatest assistance to me by the zeal and energy with which he performed his duties from the moment the news of the approach of the enemy was received till he was severely wounded while standing next to me in the enclosure of the Sappers and Miners' camp on the night of the 26th. Since being wounded, he has carried on all his office duties on his bed. I would wish to commend his gallant conduct for the favorable consideration of the Commander-in-Chief.

Although Major H.A. Deane is in no way under my authority, I feel I am under a great obligation to him for the valuable assistance he rendered me with his advice and for volunteering to put himself at my disposal with the object of carrying on the active duties of Deputy Assistant Adjutant-General, when Major Herbert was wounded. He was indefatigable in assisting me in every way he could, and I am anxious to put on record my grateful appreciation of the services he rendered me.

44. The above list of names may appear to be somewhat long; but I would point out that the fighting was almost constant for a week, and was of such a close nature as to demand incessant exertion from every officer in the force, and to elicit constant acts of courage and gallant example which cannot be overlooked.

45. I would not like to close this despatch without paying a tribute to the memory of a fine soldier, and charming companion whose death the whole force deplores.

Major W.W. Taylor had behaved with the greatest gallantry and dash in meeting the enemy's first charge with Lieut.-Colonel McRae, and, had he lived, he would undoubtedly distinguished himself in his career. His loss in a heavy one to his regiment, and to the Service, and there is no one in the brigade who does not mourn him as a friend.

I have also to deplore the death of Honorary-Lieutenant L. Manley, who as my Commissariat Officer had rendered me great assistance, and who died fighting manfully. His loss is a very serious one to the brigade.

46. I attach separately, for favorable consideration, a list of native officers, non-commissioned officers and men, who have done especially good service; some of whom I have therein recommended for the order of merit.

I trust these recommendations will meet with the favorable consideration of His Excellency the Commander-in-Chief.

THE RELIEF OF CHAKDARA
2ND AUGUST, 1897

FROM THE DESPATCH OF MAJOR-GENERAL
SIR BINDON BLOOD, K.C.B.

19. I have the honour to invite the special attention of His Excellency the Commander-in-Chief in India to the good services of the following officers during the operations described above, namely:—

Brigadier-General W.H. Meiklejohn, C.B., C.M.G., carried out his duties in command of the force which relieved Chakdara Fort with great gallantry and judgment.

Colonel A.J.F. Reid, Officiating Colonel on the Staff, Malakand Brigade, afforded me valuable assistance by carrying out the rearrangement of the defensive posts at the Malakand on the 1st August, after the Relieving Force had been drawn from them, and in making the preparations for Colonel T.H. Goldney's attack on the 2nd.

Colonel T.H. Goldney, 35th Sikhs, disposed and led the troops on the morning of the 2nd in the successful attack on the hill, since named after him, in a most judicious and satisfactory manner.

Major E.A.P. Hobday, R.A., was most energetic and indefatigable in assisting Colonel A.J.F. Reid and me in carrying out the multifarious work which had to be done at the Malakand, and in the Swat Valley on the 1st, 2nd and 3rd.

Brigadier-General Meiklejohn reports favourably on the following officers who were under his command during the operations above detailed, viz:—

Captain G.F.H. Dillon, 40th Pathans, who acted as Staff Officer to the Relieving Force, showed great readiness and resource, and his assistance was of the utmost value.

Lieutenants C.R. Gaunt, 4th Dragoon Guards, Orderly Officer, and E. Christian, Royal Scots Fusiliers, Signalling Officer, carried out their duties most satisfactorily.

Lieut.-Colonel R.B. Adams, Queen's Own Corps of Guides, commanded the cavalry (four squadrons) with the Relieving Force in the most gallant and judicious manner.

The following officers commanding units and detachments of the Reliving Force are stated by Brigidier-General Meiklejohn to have carried out their duties in a thoroughly capable and satisfactory manner, viz.:—

Colonel H.A. Sawyer, 45th Sikhs.

Major Stuart Beatson, 11th Bengal Lancers.

Captain A.H.C. Birch, R.A. (8th Bengal Mountain Battery).

Lieutenant G. de H. Smith, 2nd Regiment, Central India Horse, attached to Queen's Own Corps of Guides (cavalry).

Lieutenant A.R. Winsloe, R.E. (No.5 Company Queen's Own Sapper's and Miners).

Lieutenant P.C. Eliott-Lockhart, Queen's Own Corps of Guides (infantry).

Surgeon-General H.F. Whitchurch, V.C., attended to the wounded under fire throughout the fighting.

The following officers under Colonel T.H. Goldney's command led their detachments under my own observation with gallantry and judgment, viz.:—

Lieut.-Colonel L.J.E. Bradshaw, 35th Sikhs.
Captain L.C.H. Stainforth, 38th Dogras.

Jemader Nawab, who commanded two guns of No.8 Bengal Mountain Battery in support of Colonel Goldney's attack, attracted my favorable notice by his smartness, quickness and thorough knowledge of his work.

I would also wish to bring to His Excellency's notice the good work done by Major H. Burney, Gordon Highlanders, Assistant Adjutant-General; Major H. Burney, Gordon Highlanders, Assistant Adjutant-General; Major H. Wharry, D.S.O., Chief Commissariat Officer, and Captain A.B. Dunsterville, 1st Battalion East Surrey Regiment, my Aide-de-Camp; the only officers of the Divisional Staff of my force who had arrived at the Malakand on the 2nd August. These officers worked very hard and were of great use to me.

20. Major H.A. Deane, C.S.I., Political Agent, Dir and Swat, was not in any way under my orders during the operations above described, but notwithstanding, I hope I may be permitted to express the obligations under which I lie to him for valuable information and general assistance which he gave me.

THE DEFENCE OF CHAKDARA.
26TH JULY—2ND AUGUST, 1897.

FROM THE DESPATCH OF MAJOR-GENERAL
SIR BINDON BLOOD, K.C.B.

15. During the fighting above described, the conduct of the whole of the garrison, whether fighting men, departmental details, or followers, is reported to have been most gallant. Not the least marked display of courage and constancy was that made by the small detachment in the signal tower, who were without water for the last eighteen hours of the siege. The signallers, under No.2729, Lance-

Naik Vir Singh, 45th Sikhs, who set a brilliant example, behaved throughout in a most courageous manner; one of them, No.2829, Sepoy Prem Singh, climbing several times out of a window in the tower with a heliograph, and signaling outside to the Malakand under a hot fire from sungars in every direction.

16. I would beg to recommend all the British and native officers who took part in the defence I have described for the favorable consideration of His Excellency the Commander-in-Chief as under, viz.:—

Captain H. Wright, 11th Bengal Lancers, who, with his detachment of forty sabres of his regiment, made the gallant ride through the enemy from the Malakand to Chakdara Fort, on the morning of the 27th July, and commanded the garrison from that morning till its relief on the 2nd August.

Captain D. Baker, 2nd Bombay Infantry, who rode to Chakdara Fort with Captain Wright, and made himself most useful. Lieutenant H.B. Rattray, 45th Sikhs, who commanded the garrison from the commencement of the attack on the 26th July till the arrival of Captain Wright the next day, and is reported by that officer to have been the life and soul of the defence. 2nd Lieutenant J.L. Wheatley, 45th Sikhs, had charge of the gun and Maxim detachments, and it was largely owing to his care and judgment that these weapons were so effective in the defence.

Lieutenant A.B. Minchin, 25th Punjaub Infantry, Assistant Political Agent, was in the fort throughout the siege, and was most useful.

Ressaidar Tilok Singh, 11th Bengal Lancers, accompanied Captain Wright in his ride of the 27th July, and is very favorably mentioned by that officer.

Jemadar Sudama commanded the detachment of the 21st Bengal Lancers who were at Chakdara Fort on the 26th July, and was present throughout the siege, and is also very favorably reported on.

Subadar Jwala Singh, 45th Sikhs, was present throughout the siege, and showed great intelligence and readiness of resource, as well as courage and coolness, under fire.

Jemadar Ala Singh, 45th Sikhs, had command of the sections on the parapet of the river fort, and showed conspicuous courage and coolness under heavy fire.

Lieutenant Rattray reports that No.522 Hospital Assistant Piara Singh, 11th Bengal Lancers, rendered valuable assistance, not only in the sortie on the 2nd, and at other times in bringing up ammunition, etc., to the men on the parapets under fire.

17. I shall further have the honor, in a separate communication, to submit, for the favorable consideration of His Excellency the Commander-in-Chief, the names of several non-commissioned officers and men who distinguished themselves during the siege of Chakdara Fort, in view of their being granted the order of merit, should His Excellency think them deserving of that distinction.

From Major-General Sir B. Blood, K.C.B., Commanding the Malakand
Field Force, to the Adjutant-General in India,—No.5, "Despatches, Malakand Field Force,"—Dated 27th October, 1897.

I regret to find that in my report, "Despatches, Malakand Field Force," No.3, of the 20th August, 1897, I omitted to include the name of Surgeon-Captain E.V. Hugo, Indian Medical Service, amongst those of the officers recommended to the favorable consideration of His Excellency the Commander-in-Chief for their services during the recent defence of Chakdara Fort. I now have great pleasure in stating that Surgeon-General Hugo served with distinction throughout the defence in question, and in recommending him for favorable consideration accordingly.

ACTION OF LANDAKAI AND EXPEDITION INTO UPPER SWAT.
AUGUST, 1987.

FROM THE DESPATCHES OF MAJOR-GENERAL SIR BINDON BLOOD, K.C.B.

32. In concluding this part of my report, I would wish to express my admiration of the fine soldierly qualities exhibited by all ranks of the special force which I led into Upper Swat. They fought the action at Landakai in a brilliant manner, working over high hills, under a burning sun, with the greatest alacrity, and showing everywhere the greatest keenness to close with the enemy. They carried out admirably the trying duties necessitated by marching in hot weather with a transport train of more than 2000 mules, and they endured with perfect cheerfulness the discomforts of several nights' bivouac in heavy rain. The officers of the Divisional Staff and of by personal staff who were with me, [Major H.H. Burney, Assistant Adjutant-General (Gordon Highlanders); Lieut.-Colonel A. Masters, Assistant Quartermaster-General (2nd Regiment Central India Horse); Captain H.E. Stanton, Deputy Assistant Quartermaster-General, Intelligence Branch (Royal Artillery); Colonel W. Aitken, Colonel on the Staff, Royal Artillery; Captain H.D. Grier, Adjutant, R.A.; Major E. Blunt, Senior Officer of Royal Engineers; Captain E.W.M. Norie, Superintendent, Army Signalling (Middlesex Regiment); Captain C.G.F. Edwards, Provost Marshal (5th Punjaub Cavalry); Captain A.B. Dunsterville, A.D.C. (1st Battalion East Surrey Regiment); Captain A.R. Dick, Orderly Officer. BRIGADE STAFF.—Major E.A.P. Hobday, Deputy Assistant Adjutant-General (Royal Artillery); Captain G.F.H. Dillon, Deputy Assistant Quartermaster-General (40th Bengal Infantry); Captain C.H. Beville, Commissariat Transport Department; Captain J.M. Camilleri, in charge of Transport (13th Bengal Infantry); Surgeon-Lieut.-Colonel J.T.B. Bookey, I.M.S.; Lieutenant C.R. Gaunt, Orderly officer, 4th Dragoon Guards. COMMANDING OFFICERS OF DIVISIONAL TROOPS.—Lieut.-Colonel R.B. Adams, Queen's Own Corps of Guides; Major C.A. Anderson, 10th Field Battery, Royal Artillery; Major M.F. Fegan, No.7 Mountain Battery, Royal Artillery; Captain A.H.C. Birch, No.8 Bengal Mountain Battery; Captain E.P. Johnson, No.5 Company Queen's Own Sappers and Miners.] Brigadier-General W.H. Meiklejohn, C.B., C.M.G., and his staff, and the several heads of departments and commanding officers of Divisional Troops, all carried out their duties in an entirely satisfactory manner.

Major H.A. Deane, Political Agent, and his assistant, Lieutenant A.B. Minchin, gave valuable assistance in collecting intelligence and supplies.

33. While the operations above described were in progress, a diversion was made towards the southern border of the Buner country from Mardan by the 1st Reserve Brigade, which, on its headquarters leaving Mardan, came under my command as the 3rd Brigade, Malakand Field Force.

34. A force [1st Battalion Highland Light Infantry, under Lieut.-Colonel R.D.B. Rutherford; 39th Garhwal Rifles, under Lieut.-Colonel B.C. Greaves; No.3 Company Bombay Sappers and Miners, under Captain C.E. Baddeley, R.E.; one squadron 10th Bengal Lancers, under Captain W.L. Maxwell; two guns No.1 Mountain Battery, Royal Artillery, under Lieutenant H.L.N. Beynon, R.A.] under Brigadier-General J. Wodehouse, C.B., C.M.G., was concentrated on the 17th August at Rustum, eighteen miles north-east of Mardan, and about four miles from the Buner border, with the object of acting as a containing force, and so preventing the sections of the Bunerwhals who had not already committed themselves against us from joining in opposition to our advance into Upper Swat.

35. The presence of this force had the desired effect, and Brigadier-General Wodehouse and his staff made good use of the time they spent at Rustum in acquiring valuable information about several of the passes in the neighborhood.

36. Brigadier-General Wodehouse states that throughout the operations of his force, which involved considerable fatigue and exposure to heat and rain, the spirit of his troops left nothing to be desired. He makes special mention of the work of No.3 Company Bombay Sappers and Miners, under Captain C.E. Baddeley, R.E. He also reports very favourably on the assistance given him by Lieutenant C.P. Down, Assistant Commissioner, and has expressed to me a high opinion of that officer's abilities and acquirements, particularly of his proficiency in the local vernacular.

THE ACTION OF 16TH SEPTEMBER.

FROM SIR BINDON BLOOD'S DESPATCH CONTAINING THE SUMMARY OF BRIGADIER-GENERAL JEFFREY'S REPORT OF THE ACTION

27. The behavior of the troops throughout this trying day was very good. The steadiness and discipline shown by the 1st Battalion of the Buffs, under Lieu.-Colonel Ommnanney, were admirable, while Brigadier-General Jeffreys has specially commended the gallantry with which the Guides Infantry, under Major Campbell, brought off Captain Ryder's detachment of the 35th Sikhs, carrying the wounded on their backs under a heavy fire. He has further strongly endorsed Major Campbell's favourable mention of the courage and judgment shown by Captain G.B. Hodson, and Lieutenant H.W. Codrington, of the Guides, who commanded the companies of the battalion which were chiefly in contact with the enemy; the gallantry of Surgeon-Captain J. Fisher, Indian Medical Service, who made a most determined, though unsuccessful, attempt to take medical aid to the wounded of Captain Ryder's detachment through a hot fire; of Surgeon-Lieutenant E.L. Perry, Indian Medical Service; of Jemadar Sikander Khan of the Guides, and of several non-commissioned officers and Sepoys of the same corps, regarding whom I have had the honour to make a separate communication.

28. Brigadier-General Jeffreys has also described in very favorable terms the gallant and valuable work done on this day by Captain Cole and his squadron of the 11th Bengal Lancers. He has commended the conduct of Captain W.I. Ryder and Lieutenant O.G. Gunning, 35th Sikhs, who were both wounded, and of Jemadar Narayan Singh, Havildar Ram Singh and Sepoy Karram Singh [This man's case has formed the subject of a separate communication.] of the same regiment. He has also brought to notice a gallant act of Captain A.H.C. Birch, R.A., commanding No.8 Bengal Mountain Battery, and his trumpeter, Jiwan, in rescuing a wounded Sepoy of the 35th Sikhs, as well as the distinguished gallantry of Jemadars Nawab and Ishar Singh and several non-commissioned officers and

men of the same battery, in regard to which I have made separate communications to you.

29. Brigadier-General Jeffreys further refers in the strongest terms of commendation to the gallant conduct of Lieutenants T.C. Watson [twice wounded in attempting to clear the village] and J.M.C. Colvin, R.E., and of the handful of men of the Buffs and No.4 Company Bengal Sappers and Miners, who spent the night of the 16th-17th with him in the village of Bilot. The conduct of these officers and men [of whom six were killed and eighteen wounded on this occasion, out of a total of fifty-four] in entering the village several times in the dark in face of a heavy fire directed upon them at close quarters, seems deserving of the highest recognition, and I have consequently made a special communication to you on the subject. Brigadier-General Jeffreys has also commended the gallant conduct of his Deputy Assistant Adjutant-General, [The remainder of Brigadier-General Jeffrey's staff was with the main body when it got separated from them.] Major E.O.F. Hamilton, 1st Battalion the Queen's Royal West Surrey Regiment; and finally, he has praised the courage and resolution of Lieutenant W.L.S. Churchill, 4th Hussars, the correspondent of the Pioneer Newspaper with the force, who made himself useful at a critical moment.

OPERATIONS OF THE MALAKAND FIELD FORCE

FROM THE CONCLUDING DESPATCH OF MAJOR-GENERAL SIR BINDON BLOOD, K.C.B.

58. The commissariat arrangements under Major H. Wharry, D.S.O., were most successful. The rations were always abundant, and of uniformly good quality; and I may here observe that in five previous campaigns I have never seen the supply of bread anything like so continuously good, as it has been throughout the operations of the Malakand Field Force. No doubt the excellence of the commissariat arrangements has had a great deal to do with the good state of health of the troops, which I have remarked upon.

59. The transport was most efficient throughout the operations under reference, and its management, under the direction of Captain C.G.R. Thackwell, Divisional Transport Officer, who

was most ably and energetically assisted by Veterinary-Captain H.T.W. Mann, Senior Veterinary Officer, was most successful. In proof of this I will cite a report just made to me by Brigadier-General Jeffreys, commanding the 2nd Brigade of my force, that this morning, on inspecting 1265 mules attached his brigade, which have just returned from seven weeks in the field, he found fourteen sore backs, and four animals otherwise unfit for work, or a total of only eighteen disabled animals in all.

60. The medical service was carried out in a very satisfactory manner. Some difficulties arose on the transfer of officers and material to the Tirah Expeditionary Force on its formation, especially as large convoys of sick and wounded were on the line of this force at the time, but these difficulties were successfully overcome by Colonel A.J.F. Reid, commanding the Malakand Brigade, who was in charge of the Line, and matters were ultimately restored to smooth working on the arrival of Surgeon-Colonel J.C.G. Carmichael, Indian Medical Service, who is now Principal Medical Officer of the Force.

61. The telegraph arrangements were well carried out by Lieutenant W. Robertson, R.E., under the direction of Mr. C.E. Pitman, C.I.E. The postal service under Mr. H.C. Sheridan was also satisfactory.

62. The working of the several departments of the Headquarters' staff was most satisfactory and successful. The heads of departments were:—

Major H.H. Burney, Gordon Highlanders, Assistant Adjutant-General.

Lieutenant-Colonel A. Masters, 2nd Regiment Central India Horse, Assistant Quartermaster-General.

Captain H.E. Stanton, D.S.O., R.A., Deputy Assistant Quartermaster-General (Intelligence).

Captain E.W.M. Norie, Middlesex Regiment, Superintendent, Army Signalling.

Surgeon-Colonel J.C.G. Carmichael, Indian Medical Service, Principal Medical Officer.

Lieutenant-Colonel W. Aitken, C.B., R.A., Commanding Royal Artillery.

Colonel J.E. Broadbent, R.E., Commanding Royal Engineers—relieved early in October by Lieutenant-Colonel W. Peacocke, C.M.G., R.E.

Captain W.E. Banbury, 25th Madras Infantry, Field Treasure Chest Officer.

Captain W.W. Cookson, R.A., Ordnance Officer.

Major H. Wharry, D.S.O., Staff Corps, Chief Commissariat Officer.

Veterinary-Captain H.T.W. Mann, [Wounded in action, 20th September, 1897.] Army Veterinary Department, Senior Veterinary Officer.

Captain C.L. Robertson, R.E., Survey officer.

Captain C.G.F. Edwards, 5th Punjaub Cavalry, Provost Marshal.

The Rev. L. Klogh, Chaplain.

Lieutenant W. Robertson, R.E., in charge of Telegraphs.

63. I am under great obligations to my personal staff—Captain A.B. Dunsterville, 1st Battalion East Suttey Regiment, Aide-de-Camp; Captain A.R. Dick, 2nd Punjaub Cavalry, and Lieutenant Viscount Fincastle, 16th (The Queen's) Lancers.

64. It will have been gathered from the foregoing narrative that the three brigades of the force were ably commanded by Brigadier-Generals W.H. Meiklejohn, C.B., C.M.G., 1st Brigade; P.D. Jeffreys, [Wounded in action, 16th September, 1897.] C.B., 2nd Brigade, and J.H. Wodehouse, C.B., C.M.G., [Wounded in action, 20th September, 1897.] 3rd Brigade, who were efficiently seconded by their staffs. The Line of Communications and the Base were also most efficiently managed by Colonel A.J.F. Reid, Commanding the Malakand Brigade, and by Lieut.-Colonel A.V. Schalch, 11th Bengal Infantry, the Base Commandant, and their respective staffs.

65. In my final report on the conclusion of the operations of the force, I shall have the honour to bring the services of the officers above briefly referred to more fully to the notice of His Excellency the Commander-in-Chief.

66. Major H.A. Deane, C.S.I., Political Agent, Dur, Chitral and Swat, was in separate and independent charge of the political arrangements connected with the operations I have described, as far as Nawagai. He accompanied my headquarters to Ghosam, where I left him on the 12th September, and rejoined me at Inayat

Kila on the 4th October. He gave much assistance in arranging for the collection of local supplies.

67. Mr. W.S. Davis was my political officer throughout the operations beyond Nawagai, and in the Mamund Valley prior to Major Deane's return to my headquarters on the 4th October. He carried out his duties to my complete satisfaction. His native assistant, Khan Bahadur Ibrahim Kham, also made himself very useful.

END OF TEXT

BIBLIOBAZAAR

The essential book market!

Did you know that you can get any of our titles in large print?

Did you know that we have an ever-growing collection of books in many languages?

Order online:
www.bibliobazaar.com

Find all of your favorite classic books!

Stay up to date with the latest government reports!

At BiblioBazaar, we aim to make knowledge more accessible by making thousands of titles available to you- *quickly and affordably*.

Contact us:
BiblioBazaar
PO Box 21206
Charleston, SC 29413

MR/4
β 50

9 781426 435096